G000252755

Twentieth-Century Embroidery in Great Britain 1940–1963

Constance Howard

B T BATSFORD LTD LONDON

Acknowledgment

So many people have given me help and advice that it is difficult to know where to begin. First of all I would like to thank everyone who has kindly contributed photographs or information or both to the book; as well as answering numerous queries.

Especially I would like to thank my daughter for her tolerance in deciphering my writing and in improving my English as well as correcting sundry other faults in the manuscript while typing the book; also Thelma M. Nye for being so patient in waiting for its final chapter, and the Embroiderers' Guild for their very generous help in finding appropriate works to be photographed and the time involved in doing this research.

Finally I would like to thank Nick Nicholson of Hawkley Studios for his excellent photographs which enhance the appearance of the book.

Chiswick 1983

CH

First published 1983

ISBN 0 7134 3944 0

Filmset in Monophoto Times New Roman by Servis Filmsetting Ltd, Manchester and printed in Great Britain by Butler & Tanner Ltd Frome, Somerset for the publishers B T Batsford Ltd 4 Fitzhardinge Street London W1H 0AH

Contents

Introduction

Education in the twentieth century has been of prime importance in the development of embroidery from a so-called 'hobby' to a pursuit that is recognised to be of value as an art and a craft. At its highest level it is equal to painting and sculpture of standards already accepted as art forms. Different types of education have catered for various abilities, with different aims and levels of achievement. The art examinations and those examinations devoted to embroidery, the curricula in the training colleges for teachers specialising in art and crafts and in home economics, and the school leaving certificate examinations, have all been revised several times during the century and have been instrumental in helping to raise standards. They have contributed to the change in outlook on embroidery as a so-called 'woman's subject' by their wider scope for students and teachers alike, emphasising embroidery and its potential as an art and a craft, as a means of expression, both by artists, students and by those school children working in textiles rather than in other media.

The employment of good, part-time specialist teachers in educational establishments, who pursue their particular subject during much of their time, has also played a part in enlivening embroidery. One-man and group shows in well-known galleries have helped to give embroidery prestige as an art form rather than as a craft only, and during the period since the Second World War, specialist teachers have been employed in schools to teach children from junior right up to 'A' level, and to teach students in training colleges and those on advanced courses in colleges of art. The part-time classes sponsored by the local education authorities are being taught by specialists in their own subjects in many instances; thus the enthusiasm and a growing interest has been created.

Another aspect is the therapeutic value of embroidery, recognised during the War and afterwards, for convalescents and those suffering from certain disabilities. Although the aims in teaching the subject are different and the results not to be confused with embroidery as an art, some surprising work has been achieved by both men and women, the young and the old, in quite different circumstances.

All these aspects are important and since the Second World War have contributed to the development of embroidery in Great Britain and have helped to give the country a reputation for its creative outlook.

1 1941 – Lilian Dring. *In the Heavens Above*. A shelter hanging $36\frac{3}{4}$ in. × $25\frac{1}{2}$ in. (93 cm × 65 cm). Cords, couched wools, buttons, beads, etc, on a background of tailor's canvas, joined horizontally in shades of one colour. The vertical rows suggest 'strata' from the high blue sky, through grey cloud, yellow fire, purple buildings, green earth, blue water, pale green craters, brown Anderson shelters, and red and black deep shelters.

Beads in silver represent British planes and black bugle beads, enemy planes. Openings of windows in bombed houses in leather, the colour of fire. Ambulances in net and black rexine, with grey button wheels. Silver bugle beads suggest pools of water or broken glass. Shelters have black rexine doorways. Bunks and sleeping people are represented in couched wool. *Bought by J and P Coats Ltd for the Needlework Development Scheme in 1946. Given to the Royal Scottish Museum in 1962*

The War years

The first volume in this history of twentieth-century embroidery, *Twentieth-Century Embroidery in Great Britain to 1939*, begins in 1851 when the Great Exhibition was held and ends in 1939, the year the Second World War began. As the War had a considerable effect upon our lives and many changes occurred between September 1939 and May 1945, these War years seem an appropriate time at which to begin Volume 2.

The occupations and ways of life of many people changed because of the War and with these, attitudes and ideas were affected, including those of the artist and the artist-craftsman. As in the First World War, women entered the Forces or took over men's jobs, and schools were evacuated from danger zones.

War Artists' Scheme

Some artists were killed during this time, but with the re-establishment of the official War Artists' Scheme which had been formed during the First World War, other artists were able to extend their talents, becoming well known for their official recordings of war-time incidents.

Paul Nash, a painter and designer of embroidery in the 1920s, was one of these artists and had already been an official war artist during the First World War. **Graham Sutherland**, **Henry Moore** and **John Piper** made drawings throughout the War, particularly of the Blitz. Another scheme, one which continued after the War, was the Council for the Encouragement of Music and the Arts (CEMA), now the Arts Council, which was inaugurated by Lord Keynes.

The Arts in War time

After the declaration of War, life remained normal for a time in Great Britain, but in 1940 the Blitz on London began which, after serious destruction of life and property, culminated in the Battle of Britain. France was occupied by the Germans in the summer of 1940, thus becoming isolated from other countries. However, it carried on activities underground. In Paris the *couture* houses continued to function, although their output was restricted by the Occupation. Film making was conducted in secret: one film, starring Jean Louis Barrault and Arletty, now considered a classic, was *Les Enfants du Paradis*, a long romantic epic containing many characters and full of incident. The cinema flourished in spite of the War; Orson Wells, Charles Chaplin and other American producers as well as some from Italy, were making works of considerable import. The theatre too was lively, with productions by playwrights such as Bertold Brecht, while New York was becoming a centre for the visual arts where Surrealism was developing as Abstract Expressionism.

The Arts and Crafts Exhibition Society

The last peace-time exhibition to be held by the Arts and Crafts Exhibition Society was in 1938 but it was decided to hold another one in spite of the War. This was in 1941, the '. . . first War-time exhibition held at Hertford House, by permission of the Trustees of the Wallace Collection, who by this gesture . . . are recognising the importance of British crafts . . . . For this support all craftsmen will be grateful'. Nikolaus Pevsner writes in the Foreword to the catalogue '. . . people would say . . . times are too serious to spend so much energy and also a certain amount of scarce materials on such an exhibition'. He disagreed, saying 'If craftsmen believe as sincerely in their function as they should do they will do all that is within their power to keep their crafts alive . . . because times are so serious they will sacrifice belongings and even coupons to obtain materials . . . and they will work in odd hours left over from war jobs'. **John Farleigh**, the President of the Society, said 'The exhibition is a small one, but we thought it better to hold a show, however small, rather than remain inactive as a Society until the end of the war. Restrictions on materials have prevented craftsmen from producing much work'. Among exhibitors were Lilian Dring, Valerie Bayford, Margaret Kaye, Doris Anwyl, Hebe Cox, Louisa Chart and Margaret Holden-Jones. Among the exhibits was a machine embroidered cushion worked by Mary Bryan.

In the November of 1940, delegates from 27 craft societies met and the Central Institute of Art and Design was formed. This body did a great deal for craftsmen working during the War.

Embroidery *magazine*

The magazine *Embroidery* was published in June 1940, double numbers in 1941 and 1942, then intermittently until the end of the decade.

A suggestion in the 1940 issue said 'War-time is a hard time on all our pockets and many of us have to occupy ourselves with . . . needlework which will not be expensive. Patchwork seems eminently suitable for these days. The materials for the patches should not cost anything, and the usefulness of the quilt or curtain, whichever you choose to make, is evident'. The Challenge Cup competitions continued during 1940 and 1941, both for schools and for members, Joan Drew winning the Members' Challenge Cup in 1941 with a Mothers' Union banner.

The editorial in *Embroidery* in June 1941 (Volume VIII, number 2) says that 'It is hard to see to-day, how, except indirectly, needlecraft can help the national effort . . . members are beginning to replace lost treasures of embroidery in the bombed churches and to redecorate ruined homes. Teachers are busy in schools, colleges and hospitals. Talks and lectures are being given up and down the country. . . . The provinces certainly have the advantage over London . . . the severe bombardment and early blackout worked havoc with our winter studies'.

After the War, one number of the magazine was published in December 1945 and others in the spring and autumn of 1946. In 1947, owing to a paper shortage, there were only three leaflets and one small edition, but in 1948 the normal size of magazine was again published.

The Red Rose Guild and magazine

The Red Rose Guild of Designer Craftsmen held its first exhibition at the Whitworth Art Gallery in 1937 to show a selection of the best work by Guild members. It held another show in 1938 at the Gallery but by 1940 the venture was abandoned. However, a small exhibition was held at the City Art Gallery, Manchester.

The Red Rose Guild produced a quarterly magazine, *Crafts*, in the spring of 1940, with Harry Norris the editor, a craftsman who had first exhibited in 1928. This continued until 1942, then became an annual publication between 1947 and 1950 but, losing money, was discontinued.

The effects of rationing on dress

During the last two years of the thirties, decoration on clothes was returning, with embroidered blouses, beaded and sequinned evening wear and accessories, and the waspie corset. There was an altogether more frivolous outlook than at the beginning of the decade and for about a year clothes and fabrics were unaffected by the War, but in October 1940 Purchase Tax was introduced for garments and in June 1941 rationing began. Limitations of both the styles and the amounts of materials allowed in the manufacture of utility garments were imposed but they were not subject to Purchase Tax. Until 1941 embroidery in metal threads, beads and sequins still decorated the more dressy, unrationed garments, but these gradually disappeared from the shops except for export collections.

Patchwork

Patchwork clothes became popular, made from any available scraps of fabrics which were joined together and embellished with a variety of stitches to hide the many seams. Threads, also in short supply, were obtained by unravelling old knitted garments and by using string or anything suitable that could be found. Narrow strips of rag cut on the bias were useful, too, as a substitute for threads. War-time clothes were devoid of decoration as were household articles, so embroidery became a means of breaking the monotony. The idea of making garments that were difficult to obtain, using old blankets or other discarded clothing and enlivening these renovations with embroidery, appealed to both men and women.

The art schools

In the schools of art, full-time students were mainly juniors from 13½ to 16 or 17 years of age or, if older, were students with disabilities that prevented active service. Part-time day classes and evening classes continued in a number of places and were well attended in spite of blackouts and other difficulties.

West Hartlepool College of Art

During this time, **Dorothy Allsopp** continued to take charge of women's subjects at West Hartlepool College of Art, where her part-time classes increased in numbers. The fact that materials were in short supply was a challenge to the imagination and the inventiveness of the students. Dorothy Allsopp in her account of these times says '. . . it was necessary for everyone to "make-do-and-mend". But this activity became really exciting . . . and somehow we all responded. . . . We all searched the town for interesting coupon-free materials. We had outings to nearby villages on market days . . . we looked at fabrics with a fresh eye and a new appreciation of texture, pattern and colour. Coupon-free tailor's canvas was bleached, pure silk parachute cords were unravelled and separated into individual strands and were highly prized for embroidery. As time went on more ingenuity led to the use of anything that could be dyed, bleached or unravelled'. (*Embroidery* Volume 30, number 1). Meanwhile, throughout her 14 years in West Hartlepool, teaching and developing women's crafts, the classes expanded into a department of which Dorothy Allsopp became Head. At the same time, despite war-time difficulties, she continued to design and carry out many of her own embroideries. See figures 2 and 17.

Bromley College of Art

Iris Hills continued her embroidery classes at Bromley College of Art in Kent, despite the increasing number of air raids. She has written a graphic account of her teaching during the War. I have quoted from this as it is important to know what was accomplished during such difficult times. She describes her experiences when, for the very first time, she assisted Elizabeth Grace Thomson on a course for many teachers. She says '. . . I remember all the teachers received telegrams recalling them to different parts of England. Before things began to happen the art school staff, with others, manned Number 8 London Group Control, stationed under the police headquarters in Bromley Town Hall. Day and night shifts operated. After six months the College was re-opened, with excellent air raid shelters.' Iris Hills lived fairly near the College, arriving at 8.30 am every morning; if an alert was sounded the students were sent to the shelters. They often stayed there all day, staff passing down food from the canteen. The craft school received a direct hit in the front garden and more bombs fell at the bottom of the road. Once a week she, with Elizabeth Grace Thomson, took a car loaded with paints, drawing materials and needlework equipment to the Chislehurst caves, which had been made into shelters. An evening class was held in the 'chapel', a very tall cave, so deep that gunfire could not be heard in it, but with the greater intensity of the Blitz the class was disbanded. Iris Hills continues '. . . Once we were holding a City and Guilds practical test at Bromley, for the teaching examination in dressmaking. We had to organise this in the shelters, where the examiner assessed the students' work. We took everything in our stride, as we did in obtaining fabrics. The difficulties seemed to bring out the most imaginative ideas from the students and staff and, in a way, embroidery thrived on being starved of the easy answers'. Iris Hills' team at the College gave dedicated service, Lilian Willey, a machine embroidery expert, being in charge of the trade and domestic machines, while Joan Whayman, a hand embroiderer, gave the technical instruction in hand embroidery. They both worked with her throughout the War, continuing as part of the embroidery team.

Bromley College of Art now had one of the outstanding schools of embroidery. **Elizabeth Grace Thomson** became Head of the College when the principal, Baylis Allen, died at the beginning of the War. She was also Head of the Craft School, the special junior department for students from 14 to 16 years of age, who came for a two- or three-year course. The curriculum consisted of three days of design and practical work in dress, embroidery and millinery, with two days general education. These students could become a part of the College of Art only if they had reached the age of 16, and had been out in industry for trade experience, or had passed the College entrance interviews and tests. After their training, they obtained good posts in workrooms. Later a number of them returned for further instruction, as they wished to teach in evening classes. With an added art school training plus the trade experience afterwards, this meant that some excellent teachers were produced. The scheme ended when the comprehensive system for schools was introduced.

Kingston-upon-Thames School of Art

I was in charge of the dress and millinery department at the Kingston-upon-Thames School of Art during the War years. The School remained open for full-time and part-time students. With the shortage of materials and rationing of most commodities, ingenuity was shown by both the staff and the students in conserving what stocks of materials we had and in using them with care. We could not cut into our few good pieces of cloth, so students took turns to drape fabrics on stands to explore ideas, after which they developed their designs on paper, adding imaginative features such as patterns of embroidery to their drawings. Salvaged materials were bought at very low prices, pure silk taffeta was as little as 1/6 per yard and linen 1/– per yard. Make-do-and-mend classes flourished, old garments were refurbished and decorated with embroidery.

The staff from schools of art and other establishments visited the wounded and those who were convalescing to give instructions in crafts. Canvas kits with stamped patterns, together with a selection of stranded cottons, were issued to those in the Forces when hospitalised to give them some occupation. At the Kingston-upon-Thames School of Art we welcomed members of the Forces who were encouraged to attend the full-time day classes, those from overseas on a week's leave coming regularly. Men attended the classes, particularly the Canadians, bringing the canvas kits with them; but on realising that they were free to make whatever they wished, these were discarded. The men mixed with the full-time, young students, making their own patterns and embroidering mittens, caps and bonnets, as well as making dolls, for their families at home.

For the War effort I, with a few from among the part-time adult students, embroidered large maps for the Air Force. This we did during the vacations, working on a very tough, waterproof fabric that gave us sore hands from the effort of pushing the needles through the close weave. We worked wooded areas in french knots, placed solidly together, in tapestry wools and others of a similar weight in several shades of green on an olive green background. Stitches were worked over one another to give a slightly raised effect to some of the hills, stem stitch separating the fields and roads. These maps were, apparently, more accurate than photographs in depicting relief because of the raised stitches.

Eastbourne College of Art

Throughout the War years **Beryl Dean** taught embroidery, dress design and allied subjects at Eastbourne College of Art. She was in the school all day but in the evening, assisted by some of her students, she designed and made ballet costumes for the Arts Theatre Ballet, stationed in the Winter Gardens. She also designed both décor and costumes for other ballet companies. Besides all of these activities Beryl Dean taught handicrafts to convalescents in hospital.

Dundee College of Art

In Scotland classes continued to capacity. **Angela Bradshaw** has supplied a vivid description of the textile department of the Dundee College of Art and its range of students during the War years. She says 'The classes were enormous and despite the blackout and the first air raids, useful articles and ecclesiastical embroideries were made. As in England, materials were in short supply and jute, one of Dundee's main exports, was tried out as a fabric on which to embroider. Results that were the outcome of the nature of the jute and its particular quality were produced, intricate ideas evolving from its weave. The estuary of the Tay with its navigation difficulties, a deterrent to submarines, meant a plethora of foreign boats. The Free French Navy, Norwegian, Dutch and Polish soldiers, sailors and airmen found their way to the College for repairs to their tattered banners, uniform decorations and other garments. The theraputic value of the crafts was recognised by the Education Officer in the area and recovery by some of the casualties was aided through their attendance at classes in the College, becoming absorbed in embroidery and other allied crafts. The Free French had a banner embroidered by a Dundee student, while the great homes of Scotland commissioned repairs to their tapestries and embroideries, thus opening up more fields than might have been possible in pre-war days, to be explored by the students.'

Trade schools

Trade schools continued to operate, an example being the Barrett Trade School, which evacuated its junior technical school to Berkshire, but the main building, as soon as the gymnasium had been made into an ARP shelter, was reopened. The school suffered major bomb damage, but temporary accommodation was found for it. Embroidery using the trade machines and hand embroidery were part of the syllabus.

Exhibitions

Cultural activities were by no means abandoned during the War and the 'Modern British Embroideries' exhibition was mounted in Sunderland Public Art Gallery, in the spring of 1941, organised by Emmy Anderson. Work from all over England was shown with contributions from well-known embroiderers, among these were Mildred Lockyer's *Wind Flowers* and Dorothy Allsopp's *Tropical Greenhouse* (2). A set of six samplers came from Rebecca Crompton, Kathleen Harris sent two pieces, one entitled *Summer Flowers*, while Rosamund Willis showed *Dawn*, a panel in blues and pinks, with a shimmer of sequins (*Embroidery*, June 1941). Students from Bromley College of Art also exhibited work.

A travelling exhibition of paintings organised and collected by CEMA for the British Institute of Adult Education was circulated in the country from 1943 to 1945. This created much interest as visual stimulation in the form of colour and pattern was rare at the time. Exhibitions were mounted from time to time, too, for charities and the Embroiderers' Guild sent parcels to prisoners of war. The crafts continued to flourish under these difficulties.

End of War

In August 1944 France was liberated and was able to resume communications with other countries, while in May 1945 the War ended in Great Britain, although materials were in even shorter supply for some time afterwards.

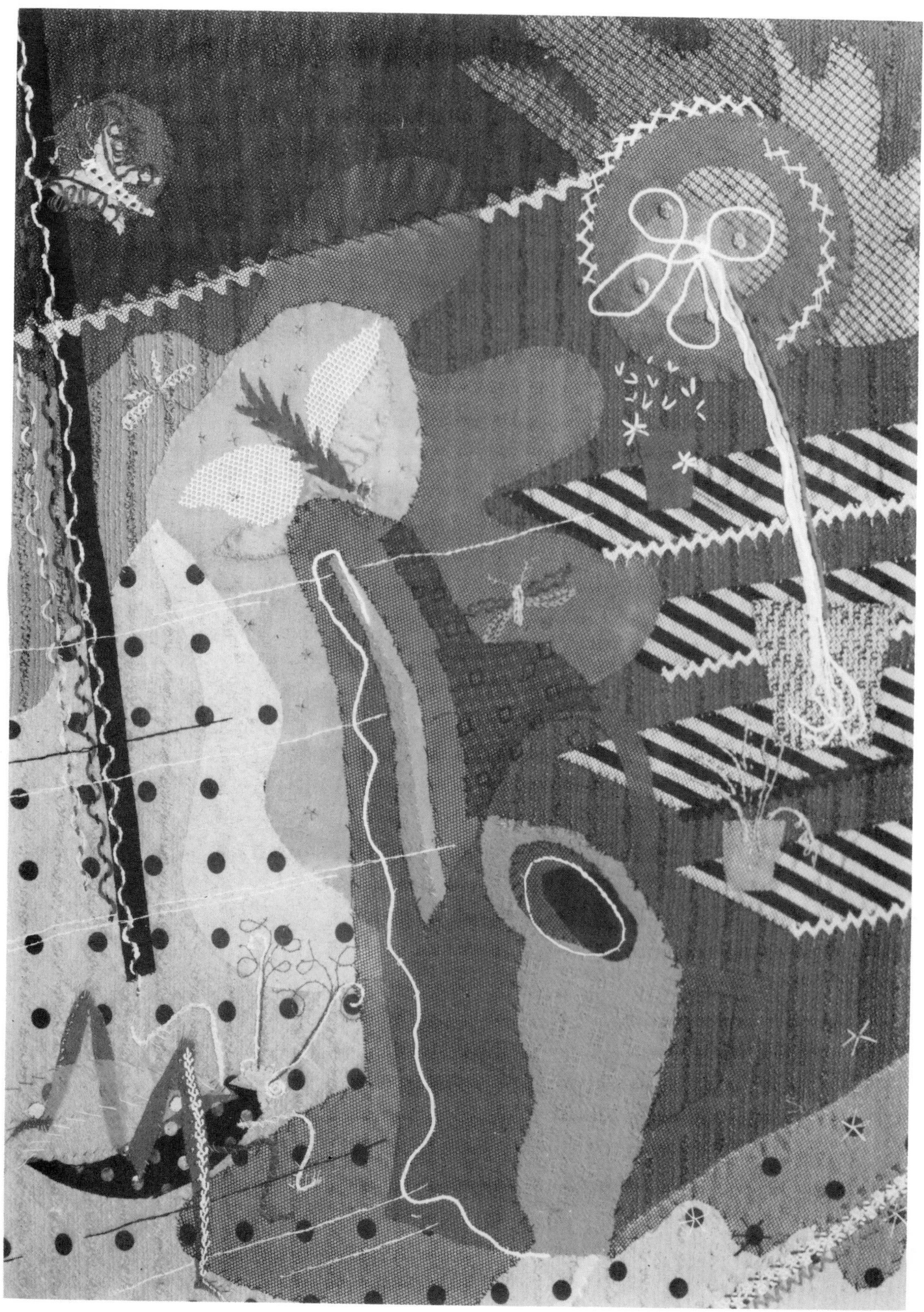

2 Left: Dorothy Allsopp, *Tropical Greenhouse*. A panel. *Exhibited in the 1941 Exhibition in Sunderland*

3 Right: 1944 – Wynn Phillipson. A panel, approximately 12½ in. × 6 in. (31 cm × 15 cm). She worked when a student under the tuition of Louisa Chart at Edinburgh College of Art. The design is drawn from nature and executed in wool and silk threads on cream linen, using a number of colours including dull greens, pinks, dark red, yellow and jade green. Stitches include french knots, stem and herringbone. *Photograph by Hawkley Studios*

4 Left: 1943 – Joyce Sturge. *Glastonbury Tor*. A Panel, 14 in. × 41 in. (35 cm × 102.5 cm), on oatmeal coloured furnishing fabric, with applied fabrics in grey and natural coloured Tyrian silks, shantung and tussore, lace, tarletan and hat muslins. The willow trees are in black stitching, with black or gold beads. The fields are textured with stitches or glass beads. *Owned by the Needlework Development Scheme*

5 Below: 1939–1940 – Rose Fielder. A panel worked at the Royal School of Needlework with applied, hand-dyed fabrics. Stitches include long and short, counted thread patterns and allied work. Stranded cottons in shaded colours, emerald green, pale green plum, pink and yellow are worked on a natural linen

6 Above: 1944 – Margaret Blow. A small quilted sachet, $7\frac{1}{2}$ in. × 7 in. (19 cm × 18 cm). Worked with Louisa Chart in Edinburgh College of Art. Chain and back stitches in yellow, pink, yellow-green and navy silk thread on green-blue silk. *Photograph by John Hunnex*

Grierson

7 Left: 1944 – Ronald Grierson. *Classical Jug*, designed and worked by the artist. Worked in two tones of brown, pale blue, yellow ochre and white silks on fawn linen. Darning, stem stitch and outline stitches. *Photograph: Commercial Studios of Ipswich*

8 Above: 1945 – Louisa Woollatt (née Judd Morris) taught for a time at Bradford College of Art after obtaining her associateship of the Royal College of Art in 1932. The panel *Susan Penelope* is worked on a coarse open-weave linen ground '. . . and controls and unifies both design and technique. This respect for the ground material, and its use as a determining factor in the design and working, is one of the secrets of a successful embroidery' (*Embroidery*, December 1945). Darning and patterns worked on the counted thread, all in strong colour, are a feature of the embroidery

9 Above: Detail from a bedspread started around 1938 and completed about 1945. Worked by Mrs Wallace for her daughter, Ursula, who was an invalid all her life. *Castle Howard Costume Galleries, Castle Howard, York. Photograph by Richard A Robson, Curator*

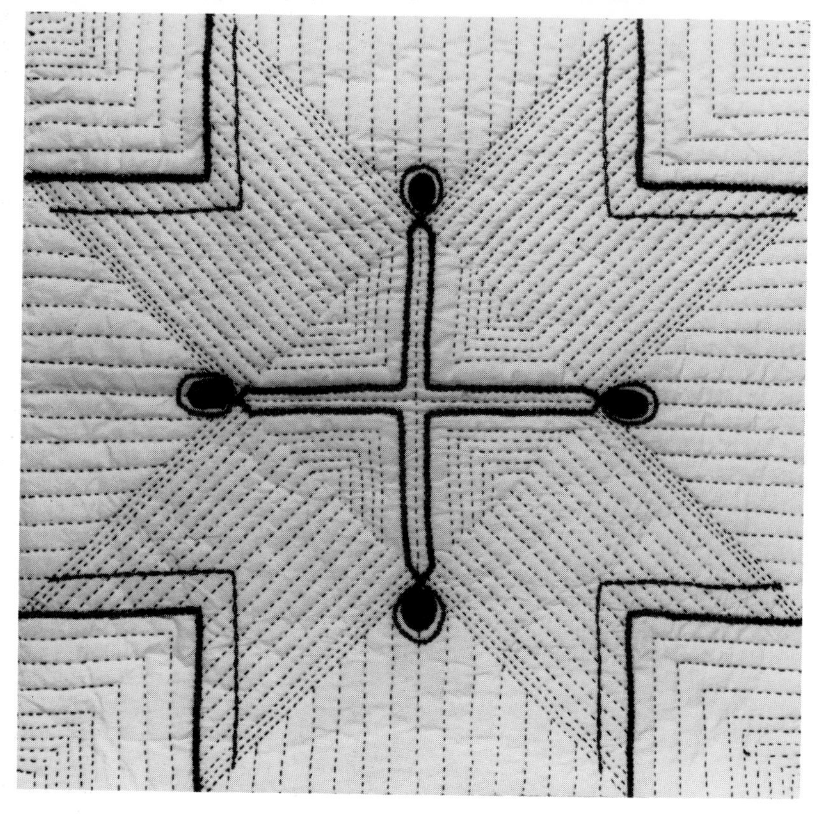

10 1945 – Valerie Bayford. A cushion cover, 15 in. (38 cm) square, in cream cotton, quilted in black running stitch. Formerly belonged to the NDS. *Loaned by the Embroiderers' Guild. Photograph by Nick Nicholson*

The Post-War years

The interest in crafts, especially in embroidery, did not cease at the end of the War; in fact the make-do-and-mend classes revived an interest in needlework and related subjects. Schools that had difficulties in obtaining fabrics improvised with scraps from anywhere that they could be found. The use of small pieces of fabric may well have fostered the revival of patchwork after the War, also of appliqué with embroidery. Mature students returning to the schools of art in order to finish interrupted training, or to start on new careers, helped to raise the standards of work to a more adult level as, during the War, most art schools contained mainly juniors on full-time courses.

Dundee

A plan in Dundee after the War to encourage the jute trade led to a pageant of the History of Dundee, organised by Angela Bradshaw and carried out by herself with the help of students. All the costumes were made from jute with quick but effective appliqué, with braiding and needleweaving introduced. This developed into instruction on stage design in the College and with students returning from the Forces to make up for lost time, a link was made with embroidery, fabric printing and costume design.

Courses for teachers

The Board of Education during the thirties held courses for teachers of 'women's crafts' Rebecca Crompton being one of their chief instructors, but these were discontinued during the War.

From 1946 onwards, the Ministry of Education held regular fortnightly summer courses for teachers in schools and colleges of art. These courses were in hand and machine embroidery and all dress subjects, and were organised at national level. For several years Bromley College of Art was chosen as the centre, as it was near London, had a staff trained to undertake the teaching of the subjects and possessed the specialist equipment necessary for these. Some vacation courses were held at the Central School of Art and Crafts in London and at the Royal College of Art, with Elizabeth Grace Thomson and the Bromley staff assisting, as well as others, myself among the visiting staff. This bringing together of specialist teachers from all over the country proved to be very successful and was a good meeting place for lively, creative staff, helping to develop a sense of unity and strength in these areas of study. The courses contributed to the influence that Bromley exerted nationally at this time. Later in the fifties the Ministry of Education, during vacations, conducted their courses in different parts of the country for crafts such as embroidery, dress and allied textile subjects. These were of value to teachers in stimulating their interests, in bringing them up to date as far as ideas and new methods were concerned, also in introducing them to subjects that they had not studied previously. During the fifties I taught embroidery on these courses for several years, with teachers coming from all types of schools. With the intermingling of students at different levels, ideas were exchanged between those from colleges of art, from evening institutes, from colleges of education, from grammar schools and so through to those teachers who had little experience of embroidery but who were keen to know more about the subject.

The trade

In 1945 among those working in the trade was Stanley W Lock, a designer of embroidery and beadwork before the War, who now acquired his own embroidery establishment buying the firm of Phipps for whom he had previously worked. He designed many of the embroideries for the *couture* houses, including such clients as Norman Hartnell and Hardie Amies.

Exhibitions

The Embroiderers' Guild

One of the first exhibitions to be held at the end of the War, in May 1945, was by the Embroiderers' Guild at the premises of the Royal Watercolour Society, where an example of a piece of work associated with the War was shown, designed and executed by Lilian Dring (1). This piece of embroidery caused considerable comment at the time, the review saying 'The sombre shelter hanging by Mrs L Dring was quite outstanding. . . . Actions performed "above the Earth, on the Earth and under the Earth", during the Blitz, were shown in appliqué and by various other speedy methods, such as the use of buttons to represent wheels . . . and ordinary bobbin cord for lettering. During the War embroiderers found themselves faced with difficult conditions, yet able to work freely under them. The limitations imposed by necessity have become the medium of new motives in design'.

It was mentioned in the review of the exhibition that 'the value of needlework in connection with occupational therapy, and the wonderful part this craft has played in hospitals during the War cannot be overstressed'. Through the 94th Red Cross Detachment helping to finish and mount a hanging carried out in Frilsham Auxiliary Hospital, this group became keen enough on embroidery to form the nucleus of a Berkshire branch of the Embroiderers' Guild (*Embroidery*, December 1945). See figure 35.

Heals at the end of 1946 sponsored an exhibition of needlework pictures and samplers, among these being a set of 'distinguished panels by Ronald Grierson, in sombre colours. Mary Bryan showed delicate handwork while Joyce Sturge presented a banner depicting St Francis and the birds.' Other shows followed during the next few years, embroidery for wall decoration becoming more popular than embroidery for the household or for dress. This pictorial embroidery was often built up with the scraps of fabric as collage and appliqué, materials still being in short supply. A greater freedom in the approach to design and techniques was noticeable, too, with edges left raw instead of being carefully covered with stitchery, with different kinds of fabrics put together and cotton, silk and wool threads used in one piece of work.

The Arts and Crafts Exhibition Society 1945

The Arts and Crafts Exhibition Society showed at Burlington House, where I exhibited embroidery for the first time. This was *Bird in a Cage*, an appliqué panel with stitchery. The criticism of this was that 'it was successful in both colour and design . . . and . . . some people may think that the finish or technique is lacking . . . a remark so often heard about modern embroidery . . . the general freedom employed throughout . . . makes it one of the most interesting in the exhibition'. Other comments were also expressed! Mary Bryan showed a machine piece entitled *Flowers in a Vase* (22) and Valerie Bayford a well executed stool top in fine tent stitch in subtle colour and of excellent design. Hebe Cox exhibited a bedspread, 'a well considered piece in design and colour'.

The Council of Industrial Design

As a reminder that design and colour were still alive, an exhibition was held at the Victoria and Albert Museum in September 1946 entitled 'Britain Can Make It', sponsored by the Council of Industrial Design. This was aimed also at proving to the world that the country could still produce goods of a sound standard of design and workmanship. The exhibition created great interest with its high content of pattern and colour.

'New Look'

In 1947 an exhibition was held in London of small-scale models, shown together with some full-scale examples, of Christian Dior's 'New Look' – the talk of everyone who saw the show. This 'New Look' was launched in Paris in 1947; Dior amazed us by the extravagance and exhuberance of his creations, particularly by the length of his skirts which came almost to the ankles and by their extreme fulness – both of these features being in such great contrast to the garments seen in Great Britain for some years. The colours of the garments, too, were brilliant in comparison with the drabness of many of the utility clothes with which we were so familiar. There was no embroidery in this show, for Dior's sumptuously decorated evening wear was yet to be launched.

Exhibition for schools

Pictures for Schools exhibition

In 1947, too, a scheme was devised by Nan Youngman, a painter; this became known as the Pictures for Schools exhibition. It was organised under the aegis of the Society of Education Through Art, as its members helped to organise the first exhibition. Embroidery and collage were accepted but the first show contained only one embroidery, this by Mary Dowse. In the second show embroidery was not mentioned but in the third one, in 1949 at the Whitechapel Art Gallery, six pieces were shown, two of which were mine. These exhibitions became increasingly popular and were one of the highlights of the year for those whose embroideries were exhibited; Eirian Short, Christine Risley, Esther Grainger, and later Audrey Walker and Richard Box were among the exhibitors. Their success led to the buying of works of art, including embroidery, by local education authorities; Leicestershire, under the directorship of Stewart Mason, acquired some of the best embroideries in the shows. Other local authorities followed, the London County Council buying a number of embroideries too. Such an outlet for marketing work was a great incentive for embroiderers to produce work of a high standard, each year more 'pictures' being submitted as the exhibition became known.

The National Exhibition of Children's Art

The National Exhibition of Children's Art was sponsored by the *Sunday Pictorial* in 1948 and became an annual event in London. It showed paintings, drawings, sculpture, embroidery and fabric printing. Many exhibits were received from all parts of the country, the show creating and stimulating interest in both teachers and children.

The Embroiderers' Guild Challenge Cup

The Embroiderers' Guild Challenge Cup competitions were re-started after the War. In 1935 a challenge cup had been given to the Guild by Mrs Lindsey Smith, for an annual competition by its members. In 1938 Mrs Newberry gave a silver challenge cup for annual competition by senior schools, while Mrs Tompkinson gave the Guild a junior challenge cup. In 1947 the lower standard of entries as compared with pre-war competitions for the Schools Challenge Cups was thought to be due to a shortage of materials, but the Vice-President said that 'more than once in the past a shortage of materials has fostered ingenuity and imagination'. The work submitted for the competitions was displayed at the Guild.

The Needlework Development Scheme

The Needlework Development Scheme was discontinued during the War, but in 1944 a request from the Glasgow School of Art asked that it should re-open. An advisory committee was set up in 1946 to ensure that the standard of embroideries chosen for the collection was sufficiently high. At the same time, a Director – Miss

E K Köhler, FRSA, ATD, STDC – an expert in embroidery, was appointed. She had a wide knowledge of foreign embroidery and had collected examples of these for many years.

Originally intended for the four Scottish art schools, the scheme was extended to include schools and colleges in England and Wales. By 1950, educational establishments of all types throughout Great Britain were able to borrow work from the collection which at the beginning of the War already contained about 900 embroideries, many from European countries as, when the scheme was started, embroiderers were commissioned to go abroad to buy suitable works. Dorothy Allsopp remarked that it was noticeable that the design of ecclesiastical embroidery, already in the collection, showed the beginning of a breaking away from tradition.

In 1946 Mary Kessel, a painter and War Artist, was asked to study embroideries in order to prepare experimental designs for hand and machine work. The Needlework Development Scheme had bought a large folio of her designs, mainly in chalk or cut paper, which they wished to be interpreted in embroidery. The thought leading to this commission was an attempt to enliven design and to provide a challenge to embroiderers in Great Britain. Iris Hills, who was instrumental in carrying out the final designs with her staff and students, said that the Needlework Development Scheme had not realised how ahead of their time the motifs were; as quite a number of art schools up and down the country attempted to use them, but failed. Eventually, Bromley College of Art was approached and Mary Kessel joined Joan Whayman's class in order to understand the limitations and techniques of hand embroidery, which she found very difficult (36 and 37, also colour plate 3). Both Joan Whayman and Lilian Willey experimented with ideas for themselves, while Iris Hills tried to prepare scaffold-like sketches from which the motifs could be developed. She has supplied the finer details on the whole scheme, saying that 'Joan was the first to captivate something of the quality required with the interpretation in counted thread, illustrated on page 20 of the NDS booklet on the experiment. Lilian Willey, however, found that machine embroidery was the most satisfactory and sensitive way for interpreting the project, so she expanded her ideas, even getting the girls from the Craft School to participate. Another of our ex-NDD students, Frances Beal, now employed by Messrs Singers, was given time off to work on the project. She worked full time on this, using both the Domestic and Irish machines. Marion Campbell, a teacher at Bromley Grammar School for Girls and a specialist in hand embroidery, was one of the successful interpreters of the motifs in a variety of hand embroidery methods. Meanwhile, Joan Whayman, Lilian Willey and I, continued to work on ideas and to organise a team of interested people to work on these experiments.'

By 1949 there was sufficient work for a public exhibition which was mounted in 1950 by the Arts Council. Marion Campbell carried out the hand embroidery and Frances Beal the machine embroidery, which predominated. I saw this exhibition which was one of the liveliest of the early post-war years, semi-pictorial and freely interpreted from the drawings, but keeping their original linear quality. Meanwhile, the post of Expert in Charge, held on a two-year basis, had changed, and in 1948 Ulla Kockum from Sweden, a designer of embroidery and weaving, was appointed. She introduced a number of Swedish embroideries into the collection.

Art examinations

The Board of Education, from 1944 re-named the Ministry of Education, reviewed its art examinations in 1946. The Drawing Examination became the Intermediate Examination and now included a craft as a part of its syllabus. Rosamund Willis was an assessor in 1947 and 1948 and Dorothy Allsopp a teacher assessor in 1948, both being specialist embroiderers, but also assessors of general art. Hand embroidery only was considered at this stage of the examination and those below 17 years of age were ineligible. In 1951 I was an assessor. The Industrial Design examination, with embroidery one of its crafts, became a section of the new National Diploma in Design, known as the NDD. Fine art, pictorial design, textiles, and three-dimensional design were all contained under this heading. Two lists, A and B, were provided, with no embroidery in section A but both hand and machine embroidery as separate subjects in section B, only one of which could be taken in one year. Original design, a supplementary test, with history and methods of production, comprised the examination and for part A students must be 19 years of age, but for part B the age limit was 18. Both full- and part-time students could enter for the examination and could obtain the NDD in one subject on list A or in two subjects on list B. Hand embroidery was not considered of sufficient content to be an approved subject on its own. Dorothy Benson had been an assessor of machine embroidery for some time and continued throughout the new examinations.

In 1952 a revised syllabus for printed and woven textiles was issued and schemes for other courses, which were not already covered, could be submitted to the Ministry of Education for consideration. By 1953 hand embroidery became a subject at Special Level on list A.

From comments by assessors on the examinations, standards fluctuated considerably. In 1948 Mrs McCredie, an NDD assessor for hand embroidery, along with a panel of examiners 'could not help feeling that embroidery may be regarded as an inferior craft, unworthy of the attention of the most talented students'. The report mentioned that there were 'good examples of useful embroidered articles which would . . . contribute to the effective decoration of a room or . . . a table laid for a meal'. Also that 'good candidates in the supplementary test . . . found means of solving difficulties caused by shortage of materials'.

It was necessary for a school of art to receive recognition in order to qualify to train students for the National Diploma in Design, a number of art schools obtaining this status in embroidery and in other craft areas.

Embroidery was omitted from the curricula of some colleges that before the War had included the subject, among these, on their return to London, were the Royal College of Art and the Central School of Art and Crafts, both of which had been evacuated during the early forties. However, other colleges introduced the subject for the first time; Goldsmiths' School of Art doing so in the late forties, where the art examinations of the Ministry of Education were taken. From 1947 a renewed interest was noticeable in embroidery in spite of some colleges discontinuing courses and in spite of an acute shortage of materials. Mrs Platt offered suggestions, saying 'The shortage of materials is so complete . . . we have now to seek in unlikely places for parachutes, architectural tracing canvas, old cambric shirts, sugar bags, army mattress covers, even sacking in which overseas parcels have been packed'. (*Embroidery*, December 1947.)

The Crafts Centre

The Central Institute of Art and Design, formed by the Red Rose Guild in 1940, began to show disinterest in the crafts after the War, so the craft societies, under the leadership of John Farleigh, President of the Arts and Crafts Exhibition Society, also a member of the Society of Wood Engravers, evolved a plan with a council composed of members of the craft societies, to establish a centre for the crafts, in London. An important event took place in 1947, the birth of the Crafts Centre. John Farleigh, after a long struggle, was able to put into practice the scheme for a permanent centre where artist-craftsmen could exhibit their work. From temporary premises the Centre moved by Hay Hill from where later it moved again and, after many vissicitudes, has now become The British Crafts Centre, in Earlham Street, London. The venture in Hay Hill was the beginning of recognition that the British craftsman was making an important contribution to society, but that premises were needed where the crafts could be displayed. Mixed exhibitions and one-man shows were held where the public could see what was being produced in the way of handmade artifacts of good quality. Hebe Cox and Margaret Holden-Jones were founder members of the Centre.

Articles on embroidery

Rosamund Willis wrote an article entitled 'Embroidery as a living Craft' in *The Studio* magazine, February 1947. This described the exhibition 'Needlework and

Embroidery', a travelling show collected by her for the British Institute of Adult Education and circulated by CEMA from February 1943 to January 1945. In the article she extolled the virtues of embroidery saying 'embroidery is changing, this is most heartening – and – there is a vigorous quality in this new approach and a new tradition is being formed'. She mentioned work by Mildred Lockyer (which is illustrated in Volume 1) and says – Mildred Lockyer shows the exotic quality of the *Cactus Flower* by tone and texture. The materials are all greys, blacks and whites, some are transparent and occasionally there is a gleam of silver and gold. The visible stitching is in fact the thin hard line of the sewing machine. She continues 'Constance Howard . . . experiments with stitches and textiles and shows that her outlook is very much in tune with modern painting'. This was with reference to *The Balcony*, (see colour plate 1), an embroidery that was shown in the exhibition reviewed by Rosamund Willis.

An article on Birmingham College of Art in *Embroidery* for June 1949 demonstrated the growing interest in the craft. It said 'Birmingham College of Art reflects the present-day revival of this lovely craft, with its creative and experimental approach. Hand embroidery continues to set the standard of design and treatment, continuous experiment takes place . . . limited by the present difficulty of obtaining a full range of materials. Much embroidery is produced on machines'.

Artists and embroiderers in the forties and fifties

Among artists practising embroidery and/or teaching the subject were those who had been students during the thirties, those whose careers had been interrupted by the War years and those who had been teaching in the thirties or earlier.

Frances Richards, an artist already known as an illustrator during the thirties, also a painter, was producing personal embroideries during the forties and fifties. She came from a background of artists for many years connected with the Potteries. At the age of 15, while at the Burslem School of Art, she painted flowers on pottery, earning a small wage. Later, she modelled pottery figures and worked at Longton as a designer. She gained the one national scholarship granted to the Royal College of Art for those who had worked in industry. While there she studied tempera and fresco painting and the graphic works of William Blake. Having a passion for poetry, she read Blake and Rimbaud whose writings influenced her art throughout her life. She obtained commissions while still a student, carrying out illustrations by copper engraving and lithography. During the forties and fifties she produced most of her embroideries, quite different from any work seen at the time and highly individual. Backgrounds were usually white with patches of coloured fabrics applied to them, over which stylized figures were embroidered by hand and machine in fine black outlines, the forms extending over the appliqué.

In the catalogue of an exhibition held in London in May 1980, showing her illustrations and engravings from 1926–1979, the introduction says that she was 'a visionary artist . . . as seen in the uniquely original embroideries of the early forties and fifties. . . . It is difficult to think of any work in this . . . medium of comparable modernity or artistic quality'. See figures 25, 53–56.

In 1950, **Esther Grainger** was appointed to the staff of a supplementary course in art and craft in Cardiff, in order to qualify primary school teachers, straight from college or serving in schools. She thought that embroidery was a suitable and useful craft to offer, so started to experiment, learning with the students. As embroideries were included in the Pictures for Schools exhibitions she began to show regularly in England and also in Wales where the exhibitions were also held from 1958 onwards. She felt that the whole idea was 'splendid and a typically English, voluntary effort in the field of education: and for two decades an extremely successful one'. She also felt that it was 'a seminal factor in the development and popular acceptance of embroidery and embroidered collage as an art form'. (Letter to the author). See figures 143 and 150.

Emmeline Thomson did a great deal to encourage embroidery and to raise the standard of design and craftsmanship in Scotland during the forties and fifties. She was assisted from 1950 by Margaret Boyd who has supplied the information on Emmeline Thomson's career. She was born in Scotland, trained at the

Manchester School of Art and returned to Scotland in 1943 as Art and Craft Adviser for the North East Committee for Recreational Activities. This appointment was for five years. Emmeline Thomson had a considerable influence on youth clubs, community centres and other organisations throughout north east Scotland. In 1948 she became Art and Craft Adviser for the Scottish Leadership Training Association for the whole of Scotland. The Association was dissolved in 1952 and she then took charge of the Scottish Women's Rural Institutes crafts van in which she toured throughout the more remote areas of Scotland, conducting classes and holding exhibitions, mainly of embroidery and weaving. At the same time, as Handicraft Supervisor for the Royal Highland and Agricultural Society of Scotland, from 1949 to 1963, she raised the standard of design, craftsmanship and display at the annual Highland shows to a very high level. With her enthusiasm and her ability to impart her own appreciation of design and colour in all its aspects she had a strong influence on all those with whom she came into contact, although she had little time for embroidery herself after her training.

Other embroiderers who had started their careers during the thirties and forties became prominent during the forties and fifties. Among these was **Evelyn Woodcock** who had started teaching during the late twenties, continuing her career throughout at Harrogate School of Art until her retirement. Little is known about her as a person, but she was an excellent designer according to her students Margaret Melliar-Smith and Gay Swift, who studied embroidery with her and knew her as a very retiring person who gave a sound training to her students. Her work shows her individual style of design (30 and 31). She put her enthusiasm into teaching and having taken a machine embroidery course with Dorothy Benson, became fascinated by the technique. During the fifties a number of her students took the National Diploma in Design in machine embroidery producing distinctive work. In an article in *Embroidery* (summer 1955) she said 'To divide design from workmanship is indeed to rob it of its *raison d'être* – that of expressing something in an individual way. . . . By the right choice of material, stitch and technique . . . and an experimental attitude, a work vital and individual may be produced. Machine embroidery . . . has its own peculiar character. Its delicate and rapid line work . . . is a medium in which to create lively impressions, textured surfaces. . . . There is much scope here for the designer of talent'.

Lilian Dring had a personal and original outlook and executed mainly machine embroidery, working on a 1912 hand-operated sewing machine. She was keen on using materials economically, producing clear-cut designs, often with symbols. She produced panels, commemorative cushions and domestic articles. More recently she was commissioned to make machine portraits of people's houses, has produced embroidered Christmas cards and executed a number of ecclesiastical embroideries. See figures 1, 35 and 40.

Valerie Bayford trained as a painter, after which she studied embroidery. Details of her work are given in Volume I as she commenced her teaching during the thirties. She continued to teach in the School of Art, Reading University, although in poor health much of the time and, until her death in 1958, was chief examiner of embroidery for the City and Guilds of London Institute. See figures 10 and 26.

In an interview for *Embroidery* magazine (Summer 1955), Valerie Bayford said that 'it is necessary to experiment continually and create new designs and new processes . . . never becoming static, as this is the beginning of the end'.

Margaret Nicholson studied embroidery and dress design. She taught in several colleges, including Sheffield where she had trained, and also worked in industry for seven years. Her work is often delicate in both choice of colour and fabric, with design semi-abstract or figurative, containing swirling lines carried out in fine hand and machine stitching on layers of transparent fabrics and similar to sensitive pen and ink illustration (113). She has carried out both ecclesiastical and secular projects, experimenting with design, where one idea is worked out many times in different materials and methods by her classes. When teaching at the London College of Fashion she became fascinated by beads, producing freely interpreted examples, using a variety of beads in an individual way.

Joyce Sturge attended an art school at an early age studying painting on a general course for a year, after which she changed to crafts where she was taught embroidery and weaving by Rosamund Willis in the Design School at Armstrong College, University of Durham. During her student days she executed a number of ecclesiastical embroideries and also did some part-time teaching in Tyneside and Cumberland. She continued later to work as an embroiderer and a painter, also teaching these subjects. See figures 4 and 20.

Pamela Pavitt was trained at Bromley College of Art, after which she taught in several colleges of art. When Iris Hills was appointed as Expert in Charge with the Needlework Development Scheme, commencing in January 1955, Pamela Pavitt (then Willard) took over the post at Bromley. She was a specialist in machine embroidery (18), writing a number of articles on the subject for *Embroidery* magazine (spring, summer, autumn and winter numbers, 1960).

Sylvia Green taught and also worked as a freelance artist. Girls from the Mary Boon School, which adjoined the Hammersmith College of Art and Building, attended her classes two days a week, studying embroidery for the Associated Examining Board, London. Their work became well known for its high standard of design and execution, winning awards in the Embroiderers' Guild Schools Challenge Cup competitions (99). Her own work is geometric in structure, with an architectural bias and she uses strongly contrasting tones and economy of line in her design, much of which is for ecclesiastical embroidery. All of her work is meticulous in execution, whatever methods she employs. Her first commission for ecclesiastical embroidery was in 1954. See also figure 138.

Dorothea Nield was assistant teacher in the Training School of the Royal School of Needlework in 1938 until the War and resumed her career in the School in 1945–46 when she was a freelance lecturer. In 1951 she became Head of the Training School at the Royal School of Needlework, taking the place of Marguerite Randall who retired from the School in 1950. The courses she supervised consisted of three years' training and one year teacher training for the Diploma of the School. There were also certificate courses of one or two years planned for mature students and those specialising in technical skills but ten students only were accepted each year for the course. Private lessons and part-time day classes were also held in the School. In 1960 the Training School was closed due to the general reorganisation of art education throughout the country.

Dorothea Nield's special interests were the study of embroidery techniques and effects found in period and foreign embroideries and interpreting these with present-day materials; also bobbin and needlemade laces, developing traditional methods into her own contemporary designs using various threads. Her personal preference is freehand stitchery (ie not counted). See also figure 15.

Since she had enjoyed her student days at Grays School of Art, Aberdeen, where she trained as an embroiderer, **Kathleen Whyte** continued to pursue embroidery and hoped to teach in a school of art. During the depression of the thirties she taught in several secondary schools, some with little or no equipment. During the War years she taught adult evening classes and also conducted classes in leatherwork for the Forces. She was fortunate in meeting Ethel Mairet, then a well-known weaver, who inspired her, encouraging her to spin her own threads for embroidery and to weave.

In 1947 Kathleen Whyte was appointed as Instructor in charge of embroidery and weaving at the Glasgow School of Art. According to Crissie White, a former student, she raised the standard of commissioned work for ecclesiastical and other purposes 'to a level not seen since the fourteenth century in Great Britain'. Kathleen Whyte has continued to execute her own work throughout her teaching career, exhibiting both embroidery and weaving. See also 23, 24 and 107.

Joan Nicholson studied as an embroiderer and taught at Farnham College of Art in Surrey and also at the Regent Street Polytechnic, London. Her interest in promoting enthusiasm for embroidery among the young and old, has led her to experiment with ways in which the craft could be simplified for these different age groups, in order to encourage them to make their own designs. She was keen also on community projects and village schemes in which crafts predominated, particularly embroidery. Her designs for canvas 'multiples', in which a choice could be made by the worker in assembling different patterns was an idea to promote the creation of individual schemes of pattern (75).

Iris Hills became Head of the Craft School at Bromley College of Art in 1942, as a part of her full-time post and in 1946 took over the whole of the embroidery department when Elizabeth Grace Thomson was appointed as His Majesty's Inspector of Women's Crafts, the first of such appointments. It was said of Iris Hills that 'There are few art schools in the country in which embroidery is taken at advanced level, that have not been stimulated by her, either at Bromley, or through special courses for teachers, run by the Ministry of Education', (Keith Coleburn, Head of Bromley College of Art, in an interview with Kathleen M Greenwood (*Embroidery*, summer 1955).

A number of students who trained under Iris Hills have become well-known artists and teachers. Among these are Alison Liley (née Erridge), Mary Bryan (now deceased) who taught embroidery at Brighton College of Art, Jennifer Gray, Moyra McNeill (née Somerville), and Joyce Conwy-Evans. Joy Clucas (née Dobbs), Elizabeth Geddes, and Nancy Kimmins (née White) were older students on war grants and Barbara Snook was a part-time student with Iris Hills.

In 1946 **Beryl Dean** left Eastbourne to take up a lectureship at King's College, Newcastle, but occasionally still made costumes. She left Newcastle in 1947 to start a workroom for theatrical costume. This became an *haute couture* workroom for evening gowns, continuing for five years. Her main interest, however, was in embroidery. She was keen on old techniques re-interpreted in non-traditional design. In the early fifties she met Dorothy Allsopp again, now with the Needlework Development Scheme, and was commissioned to work five pieces of ecclesiastical embroidery for the Scheme. Three of these pieces are now in the Victoria and Albert Museum, London.

Lilla Speir took a general art course, after which she taught in several colleges of art, where she developed an interest among her students in embroidery for dress, and a sensitivity to the qualities of materials with their appropriateness for embroidery. Her own work was versatile showing a wide interest in a variety of subjects, particularly landscape as a basis for design. During the period from 1940–50 she was concerned particularly with the human figure and experimented with and explored the possibilities of tie and dye methods of patternmaking. She also painted on linen for backgrounds for her hand embroideries as she did not start to machine embroider backgrounds until around 1958. During her early days in Manchester about 1960, she used ideas based on microscope slides of insects (106), and other natural objects. See figure 93.

Winsome Douglas was a part-time student with Dorothy Allsopp at West Hartlepool College of Art. She showed a facility in choosing and in using appropriate stitches expressive of the work in hand, together with a strong sense of decoration. She could also use beads and sequins with skill, embellishing boxes and embroidering toys to which she gave a jewel-like quality. For the Needlework Development Scheme she designed and worked articles such as cushion covers, table cloths (79, 80), beaded objects and embroidered hangings. Her books contain ideas suitable for both school children and adults.

Edith John trained and taught at Doncaster School of Art, later the College of Art, continuing to teach there from the mid-thirties until her retirement. Much of her earlier teaching was in the old West Riding Institute of Yorkshire. She exhibited her work in various places, carrying out embroidery on a chasuble for the British Artist Craftsmen exhibition in 1959 (110).

Lynette de Denne's training was interrupted by the Second World War, but in 1947 she continued with this again, after which she taught embroidery and needlework in several different schools and worked for a time at Messrs Foyles. She became a part-time embroidery consultant with the Embroiderers' Guild in the mid-fifties, working in the mornings and giving advice on design and techniques and occasionally a private lesson. At the end of the sixties she became a full-time member of the staff of the Guild, giving general advice on all aspects of embroidery, planning designs and projects. She organised many exhibitions and was a prime mover in obtaining new premises for the Guild. She became the secretary of the Guild in 1978.

Margaret Kaye, who taught printed textiles at Birmingham College of Art, from 1949 held regular exhibitions of her collages at Messrs Rowland Browse and Delbanco. Her work was highly individual even then, her ideas mainly derived from her interest in animals and birds (16 and 181), her collages being built up without preliminary drawing. At first the forms were flat but she began to use twisted up, small pieces of coloured rags, rather in the manner of tesserae or dabs of paint. She did not profess to be an embroiderer but used threads to make textures in stitchery, the stitches often being invented, to emphasise the design and the colours of the fabrics. Fighting cocks, owls, monkeys, bulls, lions and leopards, all closely observed, were among the subjects used; from a distance, the method of working producing movement, rather than hard-edged compositions of shapes with confining outlines (175). She was interested in textural and tonal variations and the effects of light, as seen in sculpture and *bas-relief*. This has been very important to her way of working.

Barbara Dawson had a wide training, with experience in teaching dressmaking, needlework and embroidery techniques. She was responsible for the history of embroidery at the Royal School of Needlework and is an expert in techniques, specialising in gold and metal thread embroidery (34, 42 and 167).

Barbara Snook was a prolific worker and everywhere that she travelled collected flowers, fruit and other natural forms which inspired her drawings for designs. She was a great traveller, visiting Peru before package holidays were developed. She produced many books for Batsford, her first, *Learning to Embroider* in 1960.

Joan Drew continued to design and carry out embroidery and, in 1940 and again in 1949, won the Members' Challenge Cup of the Embroiderers' Guild, the latter time with an altar frontal. (Information sent by her aunt.)

In 1949 **Dorothy Allsopp** was appointed to the post of 'expert in charge' of the Needlework Development Scheme, where she remained until 1954. During this time she visited many educational centres in order to ascertain what was being done in the way of embroidery. Through these visits she discovered what was needed as inspiration in order to help them. She found that she was able to offer many suggestions that could be put into practice, subject to approval by the Scheme and its advisory committee. Meanwhile, the collection grew and embroideries were lent, free of charge, to those who asked for them. During her five years in office, Dorothy Allsopp helped to publicise the Scheme which became well known and was instrumental in raising the standards of embroidery in all types of schools and institutions in Great Britain. Leaflets on aspects of embroidery and, later, on plain needlework, were published, all those establishments that asked for them being issued with free copies. Later, a small charge was made for these leaflets. Elizabeth Grace Thomson had been determined that no poor commercial embroidery leaflets should be sent round the schools, so she had encouraged Colin Martin of the Needlework Development Scheme to produce the firmly controlled series of booklets. A group of teachers was called together who were likely to be able to produce simple work, showing an imaginative use of basic embroidery stitches. The following booklets were produced all on different aspects of stitchery:

No 1 by Iris Hills and Joan Whayman
No 2 by Marion Campbell
No 3 by Iris Hills and Joan Whayman
No 4 by Dorothy Allsopp
No 5 by the Bromley Group

These were very popular in schools and training colleges, continuing for many years.

Lectures and courses were given at the Central Offices in Glasgow, where there was an excellent reference library with photographs and slides available. Examples of embroidery for the collection were bought from exhibitions and commissions were given to embroiderers and to students.

Doris Anwyl, who had been accustomed to teaching older students in colleges of art, was invited in 1949 to teach at Benenden School in Kent. She realised that the invitation was a challenge which she accepted and straight away she began a reorganisation of the embroidery classes, allowing many children to attend. A tradition commenced, with even the lowest forms taking part in a project which was given yearly to Dr Barnardo's Babies Castle in Kent. The ABC hanging (51) was one of the projects. The School took part in the Embroiderers' Guild Challenge Cup Competitions, winning on at least two occasions and for several years being awarded the Individual Cup for the best piece of work in the exhibition. Embroidery could be taken also at Ordinary Level in the School Certificate examination. Doris Anwyl continued with her own embroidery during her teaching at Benenden. See figures 52 and 58.

Artists working during the thirties and forties continued to carry out commissions, some producing weaving and embroidery, among these **Ronald Grierson** designed and carried out a large hanging in 1950 for the church of St Alban the Martyr, Oxford.

Trade school

In 1948, the Barrett Trade School became known as the Barrett Street Technical College and, eventually, with other branches, became the London College of Fashion. The embroidery course at the end of the decade trained girls from 16 years of age for two or three years in machine embroidery, hand embroidery and tambour work, after which 'many secure work in the design room or open their own businesses in fancy art needlework' (Prospectus of the School, 1949–50).

Summary 1939–1949

Prominent people

Dorothy Allsopp
Dorothy Angus
Valerie Bayford
Dorothy Benson
Louisa Chart
Averil Colby
Hebe Cox
Beryl Dean
Christian Dior
Lilian Dring
John Farleigh
Ronald Grierson
Kathleen Harris
Iris Hills
Constance Howard
Margaret Kaye
Mary Ozanne
Nikolaus Pevsner
Rachel Kay Shuttleworth
Ernest Thesiger
Mary Thomas
Elizabeth Grace Thomson
Kathleen Whyte
Rosamond Willis
Evelyn Woodcock

Societies, schools, exhibitions, events

Bromley College of Art prominent throughout the decade

The Royal College of Art and the Central School of Art and Crafts discontinued embroidery after the War

1939 The Second World War commenced
1940 The beginning of the Blitz
1940 The Arts and Crafts Exhibition Society held a small exhibition
1940 France was occupied by the Germans
1941 In June clothes rationing began in Great Britain
1943–45 Travelling exhibitions were sponsored by CEMA
1944 August – France was liberated from the Germans
1945 May – the War ended in Great Britain
1945 The Embroiderers' Guild held an exhibition
1945 The Arts and Crafts Exhibition Society exhibition at Burlington House

1946	Messrs Heal held an exhibition of embroidery
1946	'Britain Can Make It', exhibition at the Victoria and Albert Museum
1946	The renewal of the Needlework Development Scheme which was now extended to include England
1946	The Art examinations of the Ministry of Education were revised
1946	Bromley College of Art began a project with Mary Kessel for the Needlework Development Scheme
1947	The 'New Look' exhibition of clothes designed by Christian Dior was shown in London
1947	The 'Pictures for Schools' exhibition was launched by the Society for Education Through Art
1947	The Crafts Centre in Hay Hill opened
1948	The Royal College of Art Fashion School was opened
1948	The *Sunday Pictorial* National Exhibition of Children's Art was on show for the first time
1948	Dorothy Allsopp was appointed 'expert in charge' of the Needlework Development Scheme for five years

Main types of embroidery

Limitation of fabrics due to rationing
Make-do-and-mend
Renovations
Decoration with embroidery
Patchwork appliqué
Figurative
Post-war figurative work tending to illustration
Household articles in pulled work, appliqué, surface stitchery

Magazines and books

1941	*Adventures in Embroidery*, Ernest Thesiger
1945	*Fifteen Craftsmen and their Crafts*, Hebe Cox, contributor
1946	*Linen Embroideries*, Etta Campbell
1948	*Simple Embroidery*, Hebe Cox
1949	*Your Embroidery*, Helen Brooks

11 Right: 1946 – Constance Howard. Panel in appliqué, approximately 20 in. × 30 in. (51 cm × 76 cm). Various fabrics including black-and-white checked gingham, bright pink silk for the dress, with a cream textured fabric hat. Running, couching and herringbone among the stitches. ***Now in the USA***

12 1946 – Constance Howard. *Goldfish Bowl.* A panel approximately 20 in. × 25 in. (50 cm × 62.5 cm), on furnishing fabrics, with appliqué in woollen and cotton fabrics and gauze

13 Right: – Constance Howard. Panel, approximately 12 in. × 13½ in. (30.5 cm × 34 cm), in applied plain and patterned fabrics, and beads. A variety of stitches include herringbone, cretan and fly. *Exhibited at the Arts and Crafts Exhibition Society, Burlington House 1946*

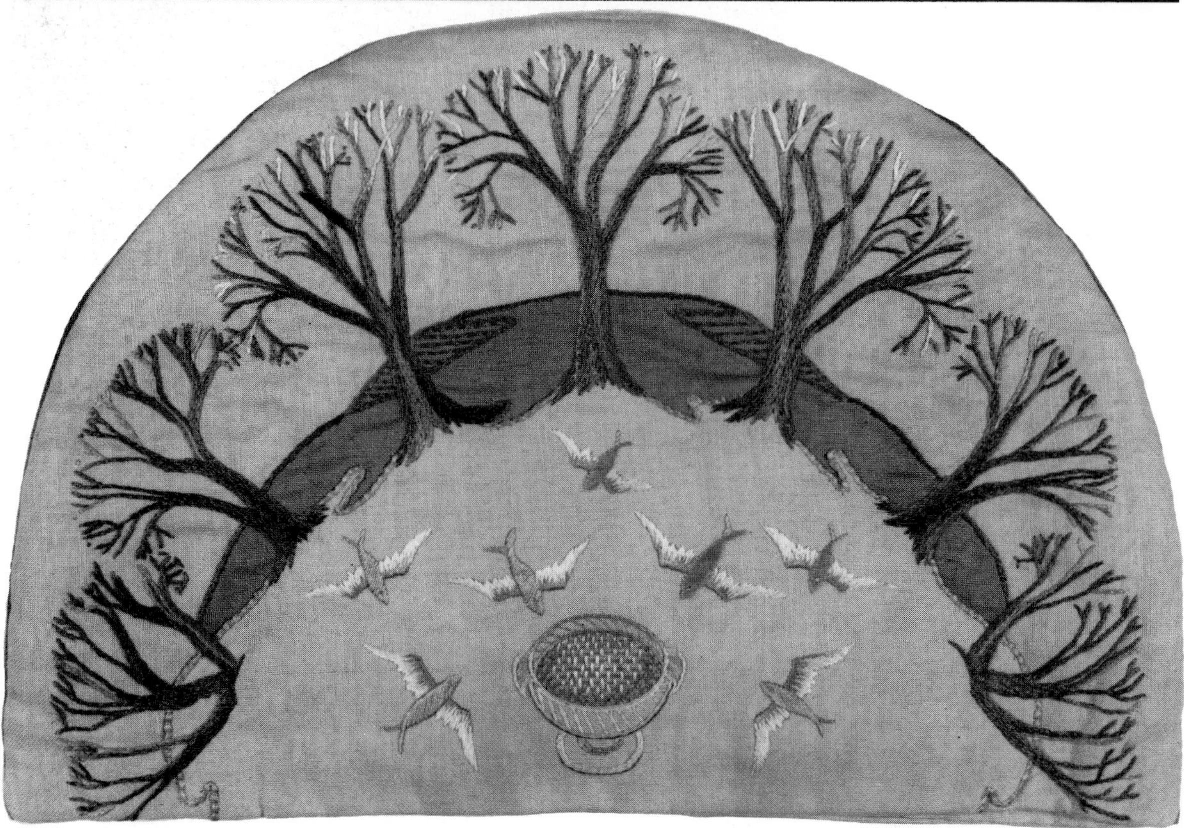

14 Left: 1946 – Dorothy Benson. Machine-embroidered tea cosy, width 12 in. (30.5 cm) in green thread on white organdie. *Loaned by the Embroiderers' Guild. Photograph by Nick Nicholson*

15 Below left: 1940s – Dorothea Nield. Tea cosy, width 15 in. (38 cm), in linen, blue for sky, green for ground. Trees in browns, greens and pale bronze, birds with grey bodies, cream and blue wings, all in long and short stitch. Bowl with centre in blue and grey burden stitch. *Loaned by the Embroiderers' Guild. Formerly belonged to the NDS. Photograph by Nick Nicholson*

16 Above: Mid-1940s – Margaret Kaye, *Lion.* A panel of applied fabrics and stitchery, on a dark natural background. The lion is in yellow felt, the trees in turquoise and black. Various stitches include running and french knots. *Victoria and Albert Museum Travelling Exhibition*

17 Left: 1948 – Dorothy Allsopp. *Madonna.* A panel with various materials applied – wool, cotton, silk gauze and metal ribbon. Dark red, dark pink, grey-blue and other colours on a navy ground. Various stitches are used including feather, herringbone and running, with sequins. *Victoria and Albert Museum, London*

9
10
17
11
18

18 Left: 1947 – Pamela Pavitt. *Time*. A panel worked on the Irish machine. Black and dark purple fabrics placed under white organdie, with pieces of net on the surface. The embroidery is worked in black, grey and white cottons, using whip stitch, running and satin stitch. *Photograph by Hawkley Studios*

19 Above: 1948 – Gladys Windsor Fry. Worked for *Embroidery and Needlework*, 5th edition. Organdie with white stitchery

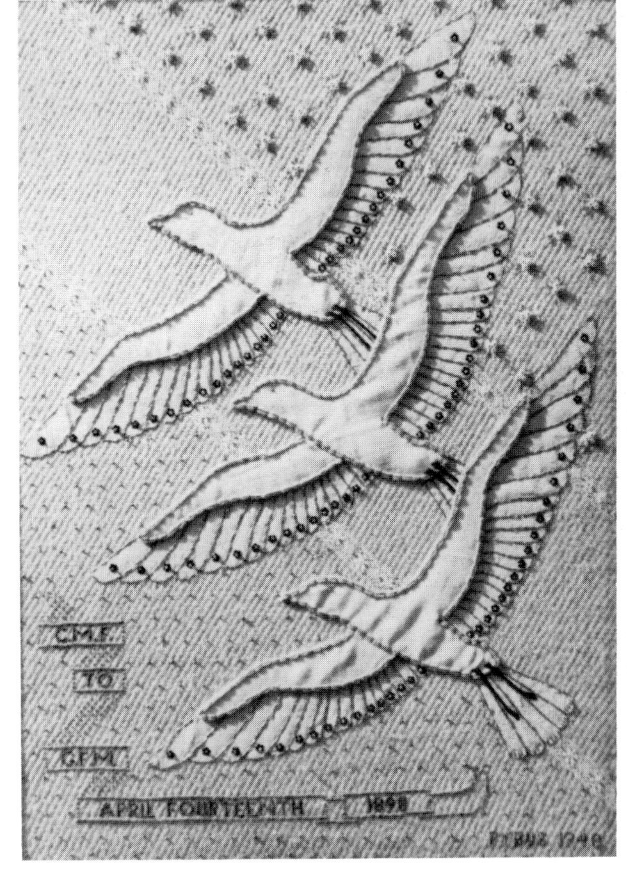

20 Right: 1948 – Joyce Sturge. A panel, 17 in. × 23 in. (43.5 cm × 57.5 cm), on cream twill furnishing fabric with applied white velvet and tarletan. Beads in black and various shades of turquoise, with stitchery in similar colours. *Owned by Mr and Mrs G F Mowatt*

21 1948 – Nancy Kimmins. Example of machine embroidery for the National Diploma in Design. An octagonal mat, 17½ in. (44.5 cm) across, in white organdie over a yellow cotton backing, with applied nets and a variety of colours of machine threads. *Loaned by the Embroiderers' Guild. Photograph by Nick Nicholson*

22 Right: 1948 – Mary Bryan. *Flowers in a Vase*. Machine embroidery in black stitching on white transparent fabric; appliqué of gingham and white ric-rack braid, black net and black sequins. *Victoria and Albert Museum*

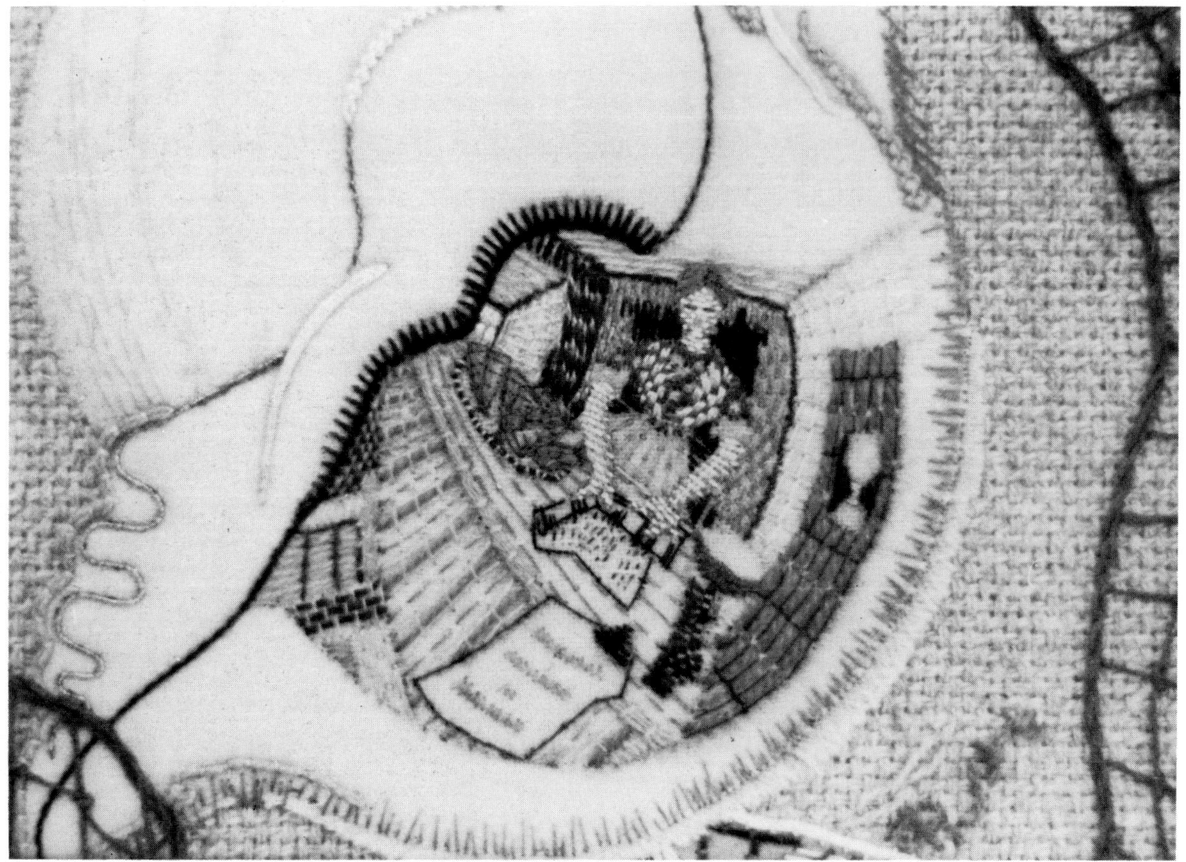

23 Left: 1948 – Kathleen Whyte. *Arbroath*. A panel, 26 in. × 15½ in. (26 cm × 39 cm), of three shells, padded and applied to linen, with figure details in surface darning

24 Below left: Kathleen Whyte. *Arbroath*. Detail of a figure in a shell. *Mary's Fish Shop*

25 Right: Late 1940s – Frances Richards. A panel, 6 ft × 4 ft (180 cm × 120 cm) for the P & O Line. The ship 'Orcades' commissioned the work for a private flat on board. *Photograph by Paul Laird*

26 Right: Late 40s – Valerie Bayford. Machine embroidery. *Victoria and Albert Museum, London*

27 1948 – Rose Fielder. A circle in dark red and black, couched in dark red and gold thread. Darning and blackwork patterns decorate the shapes. Worked at the Royal School of Needlework

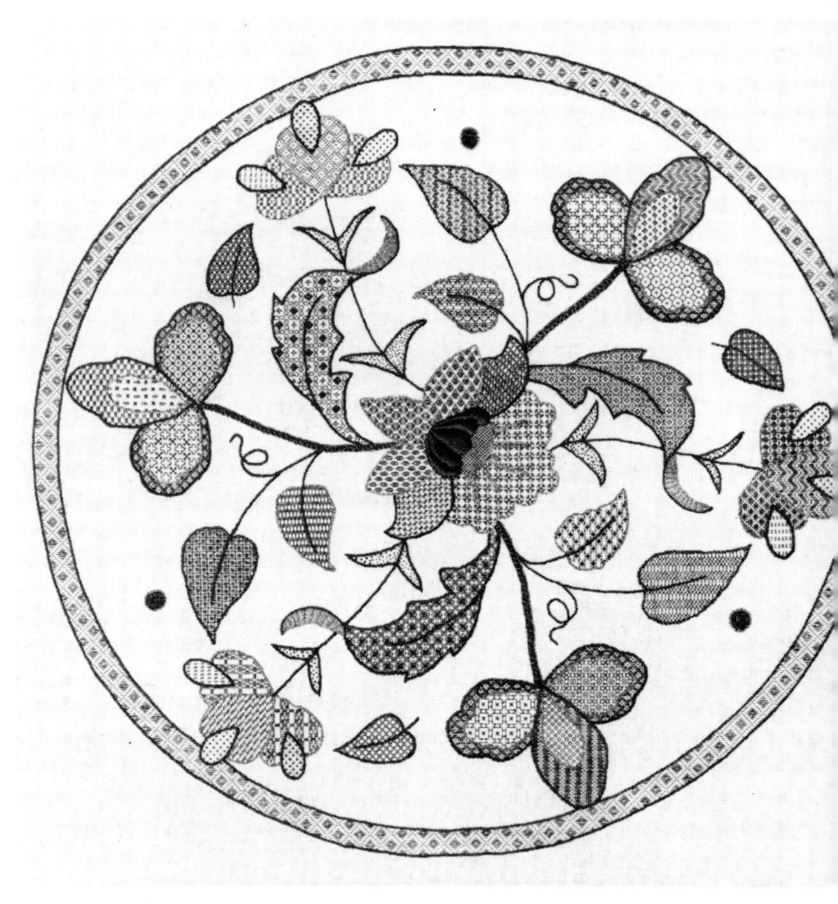

28 Below: 1949 – E Kay Norris. *Birds*. A panel in applied white linen on natural, with finely hand-stitched birds in delicate colours of greys, cream and pinkish brown. One red eye and red beaks provide points of colour

29 Right: 1948–51. One of 31 stall banners in Wells Cathedral to commemorate some of the 73 bishops who held the see since its foundation in 909. The main colours are red and blue for the scheme, mostly worked in cross stitch, some satin stitch and others. *Photograph by Hawkley Studios, by permission of the Lord Bishop of Bath and Wells*

1626
WILLIAM
LAUD
1628

30 Late 1940s–early 1950s – Evelyn Woodcock. ***Children Playing***. A panel 12 in. (30 cm) square. White cotton lawn is used for the background, with organdie on pale pink, pale blue, and yellow. The figures are in machine stitching in black, blue, rust yellow and white cottons. *Owned by Margaret Melliar-Smith. Photograph by Hawkley Studios*

31 Late 1940s–early 1950s – Evelyn Woodcock. *Cows.* Machine embroidery, 12 in. (30 cm) square. The background of cotton lawn is painted with dye in parts, on pale pink and ochre and some green blue: applied organdie and black net with some yellow silk, with stitching in brown and black thread complete the work. *Owned by Margaret Melliar-Smith. Photograph by Hawkley Studios*

32 1949 – Christine Risley. *Two ladies of 1827*. A panel, 14 in. × 18 in. (36 cm × 46 cm) in machine embroidery

33 Right: Late 1940s – Frances Richards. A panel in hand and machine stitching on linen. ***Owned by Mrs Hammond***

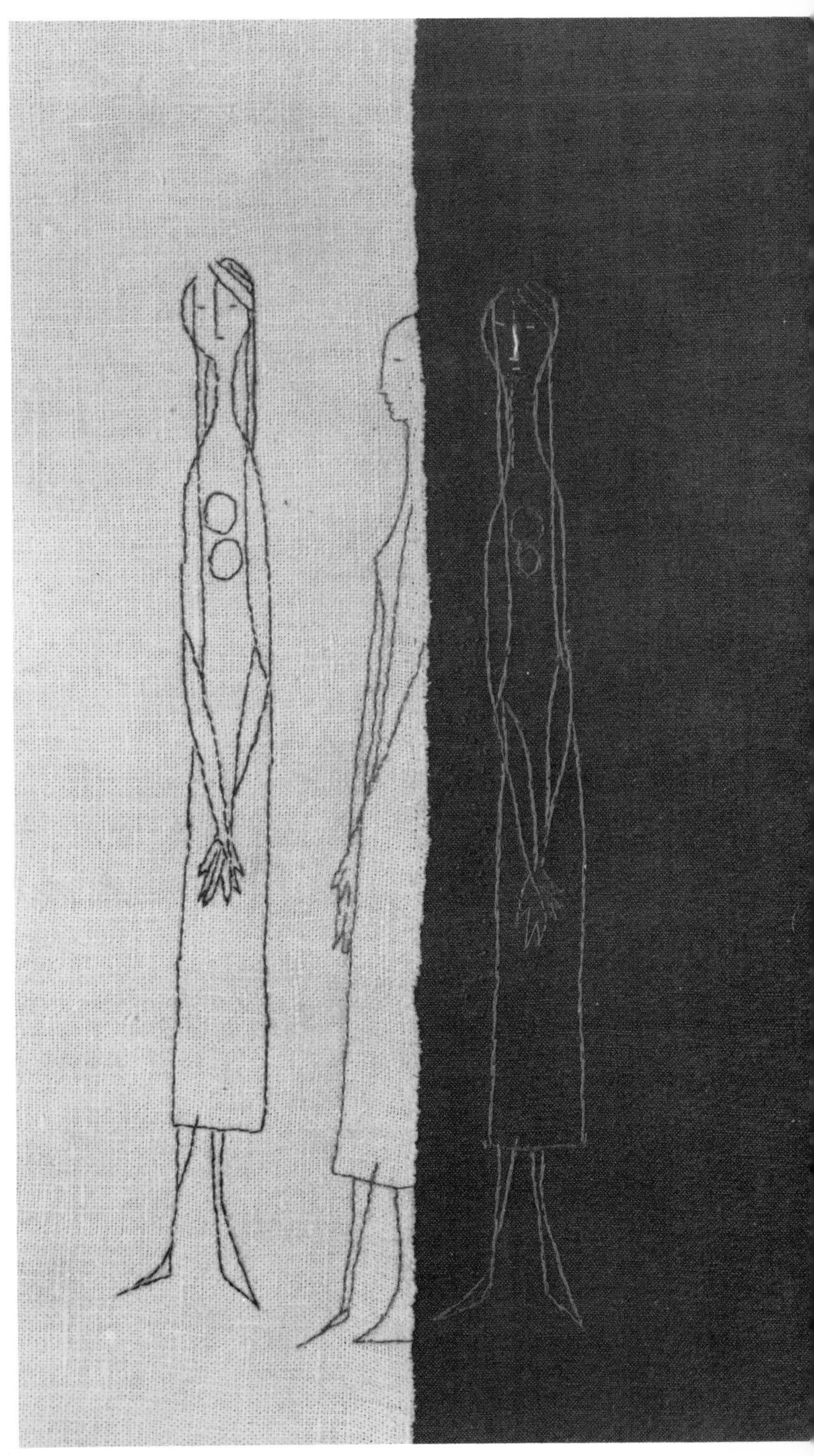

34 Below: 1949 – Barbara Dawson. Royal School of Needlework, detail from sampler of gold work techniques

The Fifties

The fifties was a period of increasing affluence, particularly among the young; the cult of youth was exploited, society becoming more permissive. During the decade television gained in popularity and in 1955 commercial television appeared as a result of the interest aroused by televising the Coronation in 1953. With the popularity of this entertainment the cinema declined, although the making of films continued.

The mass production of clothes increased considerably as well as the establishment of British *haute couture*, Hardie Amies becoming one of Princess Elizabeth's dressmakers. Mary Quant, after opening her shop 'Bazaar' in 1955, rose quickly to fame as a designer of clothes for the young with money to spend.

Materials

New fabrics entered the market, nylon taking the place of rayon while a variety of synthetics was developing such as polyesters, acrylics and mixtures of natural and man-made fibres. The first wholly synthetic fabrics lacked pliability, so when possible the natural ones were sought after for embroidery. As time went on, however, both the mixed fabrics and the synthetics improved in handling qualities, later vyeing with the purely natural ones, although some frayed badly while others tended to remain harsh. Threads of all kinds became available for embroidery, including metal threads and a variety of knitting and weaving yarns suitable for couching. By the end of the decade fabrics and threads were plentiful.

Magazines

In 1950 the Embroiderers' Guild's magazine *Embroidery* was on sale to the public for the first time. It stated that 'the Guild is the first corporate body whose sole object is to encourage and to assist the art of embroidery'. Kathleen Harris became its editor in 1951. In October 1950 *Vogue* magazine said that there was a renaissance of embroidery: '. . . the art of embroidery is once more widely practised'. In 1949 the magazine published their embroidery book Number 1 and in 1950 Number 2 appeared. These books contained designs for tapestry work, lingerie and children's clothes, followed by instructions on what *not* to do. Broderie anglaise, smocking, also fine shadow work were illustrated, the designs often of earlier styles.

The Festival of Britain

The 1951 exhibition, The Festival of Britain, on the derelict South Bank of the river Thames in London, was the highlight of the early post-war years. Gordon Russell, later Sir Gordon Russell, in his introduction to *Design in the Festival*, said '. . . an avowed aim in the Festival of Britain is to show a high standard of industrial design. . . . There is no logical reason why well designed things should not be available to all of us . . . the 1951 exhibition shows designs for machine production and also a small amount of our best work made by hand . . . after all, one can hardly expect to get a high standard of design unless there is a critical and appreciative public . . . design must be taken much more seriously in the future than it has been in the past'.

1 1946 – Constance Howard. *The Balcony.* A panel, approximately 10 in. x 14 in. (25 cm x 35 cm), in applied fabrics and hand stitchery. *Exhibited at the Arts and Crafts Exhibition Society*

2 Early 1950s – Margaret Treherne.
The Annunciation. Red woollen fabric, with heavy outlines in machine stitching. *Loaned by Dorothy Allsopp. Photograph by Hawkley Studios*

3 1950 – Joan Whayman and Mary Kesell. Panel 7 in. x 9 in. (18 cm x 23 cm) with surface stitchery on cream coloured flannel. See also canvas stool seat, figure 36

4 1950 – Drawing of the design from which the above and the canvas stool seat were worked

5 Late 1950s – Marjorie Kostenz. *Boy and Kid.* The background is of thick blue tweed and a flecked tweed. The kid is in two different tweeds and is outlined in yellow couched thread. The figure is outlined in black threads and has white skin with brown shadows
Loaned by John F Guilfoyle

6 1958 – Elspeth Crawford. *Boy with Loaves.* A panel using stitches to give strong texture. Couching and straight stitches worked freely add vitality to the composition

MH

8 1961 – Margaret Nicholson. *Angel.* A panel in fine hand stitching, in silk and metal threads, with sequins

7 1960 – Maureen Helsdon. *Pied Piper.* 21½ in. x 31 in. (55 cm x 79 cm). A machine-embroidered hanging with applied fabrics. *Loaned by the Embroiderers' Guild. Photograph by Nick Nicholson*

9 1961-62 - Pat Russell and Elizabeth Ford. Festival frontal for St Mark's Chapel, Alban-Neve Centre for the Deaf, Luton

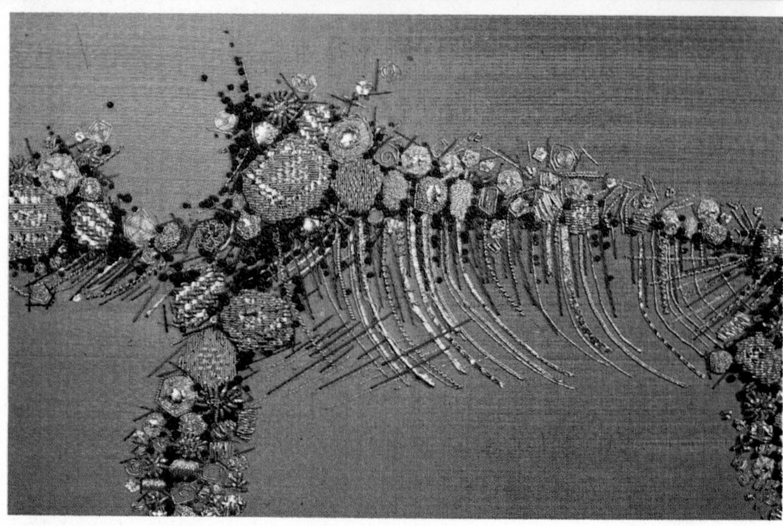

10 1963 - Pauline Watson, student, Goldsmiths' School of Art. A detail of a goldwork panel, based on drawings of a skeleton in the Natural History Museum. Gold kid and a variety of gold threads and silks on a greyish-green silk background

Artists were commissioned to design murals, fabric hangings, sculptures and fountains, among other things, for the exhibition. Both Margaret Kaye and I were given commissions for the Country Pavilion. Margaret Kaye constructed a three-dimensional collage depicting saddlery, while I was asked to design and carry out a fabric mural showing some of the crafts practised and some of the activities of the Women's Institutes (40). The mural was carried out as a large stumpwork, with padded figures five eights the size of an average person. These figures were in high relief on flat felt backings, and when sewn down appeared rounded. Everything else was designed to the same scale.

Experts in the various crafts contributed examples of embroidery, knitting, toy-making, gloving, lace and other crafts which were applied to the mural where appropriate. This was done on the site as the embroidery was too large to be seen in its entirety in my studio; also the doll's house, the hobby horse and the lace-making stool, all in wood, could not be assembled until the work was erected. I inspected the 'muriel', as it was called by many in all seriousness, almost every weekend because things 'disappeared' from it, particularly the fishes which were heavily embroidered. I replaced these three or four times, also the scissors, which were real and had to be renewed many times, until a rail was put in front of the work.

At the closure of the exhibition the embroidery was given to the headquarters of the Women's Institute at Denman College, Oxfordshire, where it remains. Once or twice I had occasion to repair stockings that had laddered and to renew stitching that had loosened on the panel. While doing this at Denman, various people used to come into the room, and not knowing me, made remarks such as 'Do you call that embroidery? I think it is terrible' and 'I don't know what embroidery is coming to'.

Joan Nicholson also designed work for the Festival, which was for embroidered wall hangings for HM the Queen's bedroom on the Royal Yacht Britannia. These were executed by the Royal School of Needlework.

The Needlework Development Scheme

The Needlework Development Scheme arranged an exhibition for the Festival of Britain, and further exhibitions in the fifties each with a different bias; these were shown in various parts of the country. The 1952 exhibition was at the South London Art Gallery and in 1953 at the Manchester Cotton Board. In the same year in Edinburgh, for the National Congress on Home Economics, a collection of embroideries was assembled, related to needlework in the primary schools. At the Tea Centre in London in 1954, an exhibition tracing the development of embroidery from the primary school to the school of art was shown. A small but similar collection of work was exhibited in Glasgow. At the Arts Council premises in London in 1955 another travelling show was mounted.

The Embroiderers' Guild

An exhibition arranged by the Embroiderers' Guild for the Festival of Britain showed work by well-known people as well as by those who were becoming known. Among these, Ernest Thesiger exhibited a rug, Madeleine Clifton a bedspread, Dorothea Nield a Noah's Ark play rug in felt appliqué, while Alison Liley showed a panel of birds, darned on net. A remark about the exhibition was that 'The rather self-consciously modern work, aiming at originality and excitement at all costs is less in evidence'. (*Embroidery*, autumn 1951.)

Community embroideries

The Friends of Wells Cathedral

A major undertaking to embroider hangings for Wells Cathedral was commenced at the end of the thirties but the War intervened and they were not fully completed until 1951. The work was undertaken by a group of embroiderers under the auspices of the Friends of Wells Cathedral, having started with a guild of needleworkers to make new covers for kneelers, cushions and runners for seats in the Presbytery. The Surveyor to the Fabric of the Cathedral, Sir Charles

Nicholson, suggested that embroideries with heraldic designs should be carried out for the backs of the canopied stalls (29). The Dowager Lady Hylton was the designer and secretary for the Needlework in the Quire. (*The Quire Embroideries 1962*, published by the Friends of Wells Cathedral).

Twickenham Women's Associations

Lilian Dring designed a hanging for the Festival, which was worked as a community project by a group of women. This was a patchwork depicting The Battle of Britain called *Patchwork of the Century* (40). She designed most of the squares which were worked by some 80 members of Twickenham Women's Associations for their Festival of Britain exhibition – Women of the Century 1815–1951, held at York House, Twickenham, in June 1951. Later it was displayed in the Shot Tower on the South Bank, remaining there until the end of the Festival. It was worked by people without particular training, some designing their own squares. Each year depicted some historic event or invention, showing buildings, people and places connected with these. A stipulation was that nothing should be bought specially for the work, so such things as old tablecloths, pieces of Air Force uniforms, and old black-out fabrics were utilised.

Other hangings

During the fifties a number of other communal hangings were executed in embroidery, one at the beginning of the decade was designed by a member of the Southampton College of Art Staff, a Mrs Christison, on the theme of D-Day which now hangs in the Civic Centre. Other community embroideries were being worked in different parts of the country. Another co-operative hanging, designed by Enid Marx, was worked in 1956 by 12 Bromley College of Art students; applied shapes in white worked with blue stitching enabling each student to work her piece separately. This was entitled 'In the beginning', with symbols of the Creation. Edith John designed a civic hanging, *Doncaster* (103), which was started in March 1957, the idea having been thought of by one of her students who wished to depict historic events in the city. A group of students worked on the hanging which was presented to the Doncaster Corporation in the following autumn.

Articles on contemporary work

Valerie Bayford writing at the beginning of the fifties about 'Contemporary Embroidery Design' said 'there is more scope for design in embroidered hangings than in any . . . other craft . . . one of the chief characteristics of contemporary embroidery is its spontaneity'. She also said 'I . . . wish readers . . . to appreciate fully the great embroidery of the past, but I would . . . like those who feel a certain antagonism to modern work, to appreciate our changing conditions of living. Embroidery must be correct in relation to the rest of living to-day, otherwise it will die altogether'. She mentioned, too, the fashion for quilted evening skirts using unusual materials such as velvets, fine woollens and metal fabrics, also the vogue for beads, sequins and semi-precious stones. (*Embroidery*, spring 1951.)

In the summer of that year another article, 'Embroidery Design To-day' by Emma Harvey Jones, stressed the importance of designing for the age in which we live. She said '. . . up till now a great amount of twentieth-century embroidery has been a frank imitation of historic work. Copies of period pieces have been sold at most embroidery shops. This passion for imitation . . . has not been shared by workers in the past. . . . There has also been a tendency to copy other arts, particularly painting. The best work has invariably been an expression of the age in which it has been produced. . . . A decided advantage of the recent post-War scarcity of materials has been the necessity of using available materials and designing accordingly'.

It was also remarked by Geoffrey Fields in another article on design in the same issue of *Embroidery* that 'Art is far more the product of hard thinking than of anything else'. All of these writers expressed valid reasons for their assumptions.

The Needlework Development Scheme

When Dorothy Allsopp completed her term of office with the Needlework Development Scheme in 1954, Iris Hills succeeded her. Owing to this appointment Pamela Willard was employed at the Bromley College of Art, taking over Iris Hills' post until 1957, when Enid Marx took over and then Freda Colebourne. With the influences and enthusiasms of both Dorothy Allsopp and Iris Hills the Scheme became well known and they were instrumental in introducing embroidery into many schools that had not previously studied the subject. The Scheme began to have an effect on secondary school work, with more interesting fabrics being provided in the schools for the children on which to build up patterns. Striped, spotted and checked fabrics were an incentive for much better approaches to design, becoming an easier way of making patterns than working on plain fabrics. Swedish embroideries on scarlet cloth stitched in black and white threads, which were loaned to the schools, created much interest but led to a preponderance of embroidery on red flannel also worked in black and white threads. However, the Scheme had far reaching effects in all types of schools, developing both appreciation and an awareness of the value of embroidery as an art and a skill.

Some personal comments on the Needlework Development Scheme exhibition at the Tea Centre in 1954 were written up in the summer number of *Embroidery*; Muriel Dale writing on the useful exhibits: 'This restoring of embroidery to its many natural domestic uses, will surely . . . increase its chances of flourishing even under the stress of modern conditions. Firstly . . . I note with some doubt the playing for safety with colours shown in the repetition of two colour schemes . . . red and white, black and white, which in the end produce a sense of monotony. Secondly there is still too great a leaning upon Swedish design as a source of inspiration . . . as for the influence of Swedish design which has been felt so strongly in furniture and interior decoration as well as in embroidery, surely its very excellence is due to the success with which Swedish designers have served contemporary needs while retaining the national character. Sometimes I . . . dream of an exhibition where contemporary embroidery will be wholly . . . British in inspiration as well as in execution and I hope that the great resources of the NDS will be increasingly used for . . . contemporary embroidery as distinctive in character and design as that of any other country'.

Alison Liley also commented on the exhibition, reminding us that 'the NDS catered for schools and adult education as well as for art colleges, its original intention. Red and black and white were dominant but a great variety of effects was obtained, although Scandinavian influence was obvious'. She asked the question 'Is it wise to educate young people in an alien tradition?' She said further 'There was work to inspire school girls and . . . work to interest advanced students, but they seemed unconnected'. She found Beryl Dean's 'St Peter', in contrast to much of the exhibition, subtle in tone, with its rich but subdued colour, and the dress embroidery showed restraint and a feeling for line.

Another comment was by Bettie McPhearson, who said 'The NDS is doing admirable work in encouraging the young to take up needlework and embroidery . . . one hears on all sides the complaint of the loss of craftsmen. Time is the factor that is missing for skilled handwork in this machine age. The . . . chance of good handwork surviving and increasing, is to stimulate the interest of the young folk at school and technical classes. Criticism that the designs are too influenced by the Swedish and by the touch of one or two embroideresses seems quite unimportant. The more one studies the embroideries of past ages, the more one sees the influences of different countries at certain times'. In conclusion, Bettie McPhearson said 'all successful ventures are indebted to one especially hardworking inspirationalist . . . Dorothy Allsopp is to be congratulated on her enthusiasm and in projecting it to others'.

Trends in design and technique

Certain tendencies and styles were noticeable during the mid fifties, as embroidered panels and hangings gained in popularity. One was the employment of layers of net which give a misty, naturalistic effect, rather imitative of watercolour painting; net was also used to indicate shadows, sometimes most effectively.

Another was the use of fine black outlines, often machine stitched, just slipped off the edges of applied fabric shapes. This fashion for the slipped outline was used in many two-dimensional patterns and was found on printed textiles and wallpapers as well as in embroidery, becoming a gimmick to give a liveliness to the design. The idea was first seen on printed textiles in the 1946 exhibition, Lucienne Day, using this fine slipped black outline on her textile and wallpaper designs, but as the fifties advanced, design became more abstract and this device gradually disappeared.

The prevalence of birds in design during the mid fifties was perhaps fostered by some of the Swedish embroideries collected by the Needlework Development Scheme, where birds were often a part of the embroideries, combined with plant forms; but the birds on the British work were often poorly drawn, almost caricatures, of all shapes and sizes and everyone became heartily sick of them, although we had all used them at one time or another in our embroideries. Birds in trees, birds in nests, birds by themselves, such as pigeons on the ground, were all popular for some considerable time. Margaret Kaye used birds successfully, her compositions of owls, fighting cocks, pigeons and others avoided the banality that crept into so many embroideries of these subjects (162 and 181). Various materials were employed until rationing ceased; the boxes of bits and pieces were still a valuable source of supply. Pulled work on the counted thread was popular throughout the fifties, often repetitive in pattern. Much of the embroidery until the end of the decade was pictorial, possibly due to the fact that several of us teaching at that time had trained as illustrators. Figurative subjects particularly portraits, buildings and natural forms were popular, with hand or machine stitching or a combination of both techniques. Some decoration of household articles and embroidery on dress continued. When rationing ended in 1954, both the choice in the now more numerous fabrics on the market and their availability, together with the technical freedom that could be employed in embroidering wall hangings, appealed to the young full-time students; the painstaking, fine hand embroidery tended to give way to coarser work in wools and heavier threads as the decade advanced.

Some subjects were universal and proliferated across the country, and a description of Doris Taylor's voluntary class by one of her students, Isobel Watson, at the Manchester College of Art, gives an idea of the interest in embroidery and some of the subjects chosen during the decade. She says: 'I was a student of Doris Taylor in the fifties. She was Head of Dress Design but taught embroidery too. Officially I was in the Printed Textiles department, but the design school was very closely integrated and I became so excited at what was being done by the embroideresses, that I joined a voluntary class.

'We were given our heads as to subject matter and designs ranged from underwater scenes, stylised plants and birds, fungi, cats on roof tops, Persian flower and foliage inspired patterns, to deer, trees and cacti. Techniques were taught in a most unobtrusive way so that without realising it, one "chose" the right technique for the embroidery in hand, such as shadow work in pink and white threads of varying thicknesses on nylon organza or organdie. I remember a curtain and a panel worked in this way.

'One of the dress designers embroidered very freely by machine, an evening dress of white tulle in black thread with appliqué in black velvet. Another embroidery was of a fire screen, depicting a vase of stylized plant forms carried out in felt appliqué with large jet beads and crewel work.

'We were encouraged to experiment, we dyed our own materials to obtain the colours we wanted and I can still remember the thrill of using beads and sequins (obtained by the ounce at a nearby theatrical costumiers) for the first time. Provided the end result justified our use of them, we could combine any materials we wished.

'We were fortunate at the time to have the Cotton Board in Manchester, to whose exhibitions we were sent. One was staged by the Needlework Development Scheme and I can see now the fabulous and glittering three-dimensional creatures and mobiles of Winsome Douglas.

'Doris Taylor with John Willock, Head of the design department and Ralph Downing (Head of Printed Textiles) worked very closely together. There were no rivalries there – each department had something to give to the other. Doris Taylor was a truly inspired teacher, she never imposed her will on ours, so that every student's work was dissimilar.' See also figure 60.

Joan Archer, a student contemporary with Isobel Watson said that through Doris Taylor's enthusiasm and sound advice, she has had a lasting interest in embroidery, teaching the subject wherever and whenever possible. After her training in Manchester she started to teach, her first post in the Friends School, Saffron Walden, where she obtained excellent work from her pupils. She teaches adults now, training students for the City and Guilds of London Institute in embroidery, also continuing with her own work. See figure 50.

Exhibitions

Exhibitions became part of the fifties scene. An important show of domestic crafts by the Women's Institute was held at the Victoria and Albert Museum in 1952. One of the highlights was a panel designed by Sybil Blunt; it was worked in canvas stitches as a communal project under the guidance of a Mrs Littler. A number of banners was exhibited too, also quilted pieces, among which was one by Averil Colby entitled 'High Summer'. Schools of art and other educational establishments during the fifties held annual shows to which the public flocked. Galleries, too, held craft exhibitions in which embroidery was included. One in 1952 at the Crafts Centre in Hay Hill, of embroidery and other crafts, was criticised for its stark simplicity 'which looked as if there had been a lack of time in producing any but the most simple articles . . . on the other hand, the work showed a contemporary approach and a great improvement in colour'.

Pictures for Schools

The annual exhibition of Pictures for Schools now attracted more embroiderers who submitted work of a generally high standard. Imaginative and lively ideas were forthcoming. The number of education authorities who bought embroideries was increasing, thereby spreading interest in the schools during the decade.

The Red Rose Guild

The Red Rose Guild of Craftsmen continued to hold exhibitions during the late forties and in the fifties, the 1950 exhibition being planned 'to present the craftsman to the public as a creative artist'. The Guild had no permanent home, but in the early sixties, the Crane Gallery in Manchester was acquired as a permanent exhibition centre.

The Arts and Crafts Exhibition Society

At the exhibition at the Tea Centre in November 1952 held by the Arts and Crafts Exhibition Society, embroiderers, now well known, showed work. Eugene Alexander's *Queen Elizabeth* was exhibited, while Christine Risley showed three pieces, Margaret Treherne, Margaret Kaye, Lilian Dring and myself one each, while Ronald Grierson showed rugs. The Commissioner of the Tea Bureau, Don Forrest, suggested that the general theme should be 'The Craftsman and the Tea Table', also saying that 'the taste for fine and beautiful hand-made things is fighting a not unnecessary battle against the mechanistic tendencies of recent years'.

Bromley College of Art exhibition

An exhibition was put on by 12 students from Bromley College of Art in September 1953 at Artists' House, London because, according to press reports, they were dissatisfied with 'contemporary standards'. They paid for this show themselves and formed a group 'to hold an exhibition to stimulate the interest of the general public in the design of contemporary embroidery for interior decoration'. By all accounts the show was a great success, containing both hand and machine examples of work by students, some of whom are now well known. Among these was Jennifer Gray, one of the organisers, along with Alison Liley, Joyce Conwy-Evans, Elizabeth Geddes, the Rooke twins and Moyra Somerville.

The Embroiderers' Guild Challenge Cup

During the fifties the Embroiderers' Guild Challenge Cup competitions for schools continued to foster interest. Through these, much good work was produced, helping to create an awareness of the craft of embroidery and what could be achieved by young people with a needle and thread. Certain schools appeared prominent in obtaining prizes, among these being Shoreditch College for the Garment Trade, Benenden, and Purley County Grammar School. Valerie Bayford remarked on the 1952 exhibition of work from the competitions, shown at the Embroiderers' Guild, that 'it would be a good thing if there was more liaison between the art and needlework classes, although this one did show more of the feeling of the child than the teacher . . . a criticism levelled at some work in the past'. The finish of the work and the technical standard were good.

Art schools

Bromley College of Art remained one of the most outstanding centres of embroidery in England during the early and mid-fifties; all aspects of the craft were taught there. The College was noted for machine embroidery, producing wall hangings and household articles as well as decoration for dress. Hand and machine embroidery were combined in small, framed, finely worked panels; table linen was popular; plant forms and geometric shapes being favourite subjects of design. Quilting, counted thread techniques and appliqué by hand, as well as fine line stitching by machine were seen.

Goldsmiths' School of Art

I was teaching history of costume and wood engraving part time at Goldsmiths' School of Art, London, in 1948 and was asked by the staff in charge of needlework in the Teachers' Training Department of Goldsmiths' College if I would take some students for embroidery. I had not taught the subject although I showed work in exhibitions and this request led to embroidery being taught in the School of Art. Students from the Training College increased in numbers, part-time students from outside the College appeared and part-time day and evening classes were established in the early fifties. Students from the Art Teachers' Certificate course attended for one day a week. These classes were the nucleus of what became a department in the School of Art at the end of the fifties.

Goldsmiths' School of Art received recognition as a centre for hand embroidery at Special Level for the National Diploma in Design in the early fifties. It also became a centre for the City and Guilds of London Institute examinations in embroidery, both full- and part-time students enrolling for courses for these examinations. For the National Diploma in Design students were mainly full time, having obtained the certificate for the Intermediate Examination in Art of the Ministry of Education. After passing this examination they were eligible to study for the NDD, which was a two-year course. The Diploma examination could be taken at Special Level or at Main and Additional Levels, where machine embroidery was considered as a separate subject. Work produced during the two years of study was submitted; a formal examination in designing on paper was taken, the design being carried out as practical work during the two ensuing weeks. There was a group of specialists examiners for this area of textiles among whom Dorothy Benson was the examiner for machine embroidery and I was the examiner for hand embroidery. The City and Guilds examinations consisted of two parts: the first part was the Ordinary Level, and the second part the Advanced Level. Sound technique was important in this examination with a written and a practical test at each level, developed from the design paper. Examples of work carried out during training were submitted at both levels.

Having obtained their National Diploma in Design at Special Level, or at Main and Additional, where two subjects were studied, a number of art students continued their training on the Art Teachers' Certificate course, or the Art Teachers' Diploma course, the name varying with the area of the country. Students on the ATC course (as it was known) at Goldsmiths' College, both men and women, attended the classes in embroidery. The students on the teaching course, with their uninhibited and fresh approach to embroidery, together with their previous training, were instrumental in raising the standard of design to a high level. They were eager to experiment and became adept at selecting appropriate materials from the rag-bags, which were still the main source of fabric supply. Through these students, whose work was often exciting but unorthodox, a gradual change in outlook took place, with freer technique, and stitching often invented to express what they had in mind.

This less conventional approach led to the realisation that the careful, traditional methods of working were one aspect only of embroidery and that this individual interpretation of ideas by painters, sculptors and others, with no technical training in the craft, but with previous art training, possessed a breadth of vision seldom seen earlier among more conventional, trained embroiderers who seldom drew but possessed excellent technical ability.

It was possible for students who had obtained diplomas in other art subjects to attend part-time classes for two years in order to gain the NDD in embroidery at Special Level. A number of students now teaching in part-time or full employment, returned to the evening classes in order to obtain a second qualification; after which several obtained posts where they developed embroidery departments.

Embroidery was now becoming a feature of a number of the needlework classes and also of some of the art classes in both junior and senior schools. It was offered for examination at Ordinary and Advanced Levels, although not recognised for university entrance.

Associated Examining Board

A new schools examination board was established in 1953, the Associated Examining Board, the ninth in England. It offered the Ordinary and Advanced Levels of the General Certificate of Education examinations. One of the reasons for its inception was to 'offer examinations to enable creative and practically-biased students and to encourage a recognised place in the curriculum for subjects such as Embroidery. A knowledge of history and of practical techniques and skills is required and course work, completed during a two-year period, is submitted for the examination, which includes both written and practical papers.' (Leaflet, Exhibition, Foyles Art Gallery, London, 1979).

Ecclesiastical conservation and embroidery

After the War, with numerous churches bombed, both in London and in the provinces, much renovation and repair of vestments and church furnishings was necessary. In Cardiff, the South Wales branch of the Embroiderers' Guild re-applied on to new fabric a set of motifs from a frontal and also repaired the vestments for Llandaff Cathedral. Rachel K Shuttleworth made a plea for the conservation of nineteenth-century works for the church, saying that there were far too few skilled workers capable of this undertaking and that more embroiderers should be trained to do this work by those already skilled.

At the same time, new embroideries were being worked for ecclesiastical establishments, such as in Edinburgh, where the Second World War commemorative chapel in St Giles Cathedral was presented with an altar cloth, designed by Jean Gracie and worked by her sisters. Other cathedrals and churches were receiving gifts, too, and embroideries were beginning to be replaced. Chelsea Old Church, in London, was destroyed by enemy action in April 1941 but was later restored. The kneelers for this new church were designed to commemorate the well-known persons whose plaques had lined the walls before the church was destroyed, and also in remembrance of the people who had lived in the vicinity and were killed in the raids. The overall design of each kneeler consisted of a panel with the name and date with four Maltese crosses, one in each corner, which left the embroiderer free to add other motifs expressive of the person concerned. Colours selected for the scheme were added as the embroiderer wished. The work was voluntary; among those carrying out the embroidery Ernest Thesiger completed two kneelers.

Community projects were being organised now in many church schemes, and in cathedrals such as Liverpool, Guildford and Worcester, where volunteers repaired vestments and furnishings as well as working on new ventures. Among repairs were those to altar frontals designed by G F Bodley for Liverpool Cathedral at the beginning of the twentieth century. In Guildford, the working of kneelers for the Cathedral was curtailed during the War and they were recommenced in 1953. The designs of the kneelers were by Sir Edward and Lady Maufe (61 and 62), with a diagonal line bisecting each pattern, one half representing Stag Hill on which the Cathedral is built, with a blue ground and a grey sky, on which various symbols together with the worker's initials and the date were incorporated. A variety of stitches was employed. In Worcester Cathedral the kneelers were designed locally, with central medallions on different grounds. Stitches were the choice of the worker; colours to blend in with the sandstone of the Cathedral were pre-selected, including rose pink with contrasting greens and greys. The cushions and seats for the choir stalls were designed with animals as a theme, to go with the stalls which were carved with animals.

Bromley Parish Church in Kent was being rebuilt after the War and in 1953 a group of students under the supervision of Iris Hills was asked to design and carry out a set of altar frontals. Pamela and Patricia Rooke, students, made scale drawings for the green and white frontals (69, 70 and 71), Patricia Breasley designed those for the purple and red ones. Elizabeth Geddes was in charge of the practical work which was carried out in a studio in Chislehurst, as the College was unable to accommodate the work. The white frontal became the prototype with a bold but simple treatment using heavy Japanese gold and a variety of threads for the embroidery.

Conservation was beginning to be a consideration in the preservation of textiles in museums and where there were private collections. An important part was played by **Karen Finch**, trained at Kunsthaandvaerker-Skolen, Copenhagen, a college of decorative arts. She worked in the Victoria and Albert Museum and at the Royal School of Needlework. In 1959 she left the Museum in order to study textiles and techniques further and she started conservation in her own home.

Articles on embroidery

In the early fifties various articles were written on the future of embroidery, or in retrospect, on its past achievements. One in 1952 in *Embroidery* magazine on the last fifty years, said that the changed outlook since the War had encouraged students to use their environment for design. It said also that by accepting the limitations of the craft, they could produce work that was 'embroidery' and not 'painting with the needle'.

An article in *House and Garden* in December 1953 on 'Needle Works as Art' gives a good idea of the interest that was developing in embroidery as a craft worthy of notice. It says 'embroidery pictures have come into their own again as an art form; needlework, patchwork and appliqué are no longer confined to the bedspread, cushion, chair seat and tablecloth. They bear an affinity to stained glass, to mosaic and collage as well as to painting; yet they are individual. More and more people are working pictures in this medium, and these new needlework designs may well be to this time what samplers were to the eighteenth century and patchwork was to the nineteenth century; for the use of contrasting textures, bold colours and fine lines of stitching are particularly suited to the contemporary idiom. Many interesting designs, both sophisticated and simple, are now shown at art galleries, but there is endless pleasure in doing pictures oneself. . . and the best effects are often got by the simplest means. . . for instance, many designers use the sewing machine. There is now almost a bewildering variety of fabrics for texture, colour and pattern.'

Machine embroidery

This was beginning to be a means of sewing down applied fabrics and straight stitching for fine outlines was used alone or massed together to make more solid areas of texture. Small pieces of embroidery were framed in card mounts, with wooden frames, in the manner of prints or water-colours. Elaborate frames in gilt, with fabric mounts in silk or velvet surrounded some of the more richly worked pieces. This fashion continued for some time.

Embroidery on the domestic sewing machine was practised during the decade in the schools of art, in colleges of education and in the secondary schools. With the introduction of the swing needle, which could be adjusted for satin stitch, the possibilities for experiment were widened considerably. Previously the running stitch (sometimes called straight stitch) was used rather as a pen line, although Dorothy Benson in the thirties had produced lacy, openwork effects, as had the Bromley College of Art in the forties. The many possibilities of embroidery on the domestic sewing machine were being re-discovered in the late forties and the early fifties. Richer textures using cable stitch with a heavier thread, mossing and whipping, were obtained by a change of tension. A great deal of experiment was taking place, all these techniques now being exploited.

Colleges of art and trade schools where embroidery was taught possessed trade machines, among these the Irish and the Cornely. At this time two colleges, Birmingham and Nottingham, possessed Schiffli machines which were able to work a number of patterns at one time, repeated by the pantograph method. Articles appeared frequently on machine embroidery in *Embroidery* magazine although many stitchers still thought that hand techniques were the main criteria of embroidery and were horrified by the idea of the machine taking over, or of using machines at all. It was, in its early experimental stage, perhaps too soon for the non-professional hand embroiderer to understand that work produced on the machine, whether using the domestic or trade models, should be entirely different from that produced by hand. At first the aim was to try to imitate hand work, or to use the machine needle to draw what looked like fine pen lines. Conflicting ideas were rife but by working experimental samples those interested in machine embroidery realised that the domestic and the trade machine could do a great deal in the way of developing techniques peculiar to their capabilities, if used with an open mind and without trying to ape hand embroidery. Bromley College of Art which had been one of the pioneers of machine embroidery in the thirties continued to carry out excellent work on the domestic and trade machines under the guidance of Lilian Willey. In Harrogate, where a number of students sat for the National Diploma in Design examination, a distinctive style of machine embroidery was developing for the decoration of wall hangings and other articles already mentioned. These students were taught by Evelyn Woodcock. Throughout the work at Harrogate there was a general vitality with the use of bright colours such as pinks, reds and oranges, in felt and other fabrics; black and white bed ticking was also a favourite. The fine black machine lines slipped off the main areas of colour, or heavier couching in black wool or cotton, were noticeable features of much of the work. See figure 65.

Beaded evening wear

Wall decoration proliferated during the fifties; household embroidery and the embellishment of dress was less popular although, in the trade, there was a market for the beaded evening gown for formal occasions. Norman Hartnell was asked to design the dresses for the Coronation in 1953 (67). For this important event he re-introduced the richly beaded and jewelled garments not seen during the War in England although, in France, embroidered and beaded clothes were made even during the German Occupation. Christian Dior was noted for fabulously embroidered and jewelled garments in the fifties. He died in 1957 but the tradition was carried on for some years. Balmain and the Spanish designer Balenciaga were also designing beautiful garments at this time, using jet, beads and sequins with embroidery. In England the trade produced these elaborate clothes for evening wear, but embroidery on dress was not fashionable otherwise.

In his workroom **Stanley W Lock** designed embroidery and carried out a great deal of beading on evening gowns; he also did work for the stage and films during the fifties. This was executed by both workroom assistants and outworkers, using tambour hooks with which to attach the beads to the fabrics. See figures 57 and 58.

Embroiderers in the fifties

A number of embroiderers started to teach during the fifties and the names of new embroiderers appeared in exhibition catalogues. Among these was **Christine Risley** who had become a part-time lecturer at the end of the forties and, although she had trained as a painter, her interest in embroidery had been stimulated by attending my part-time classes in hand embroidery. She taught basic design at St Martin's School of Art. She became an expert, too, in the use of the domestic sewing machine for embroidery and also in the use of the Irish and Cornely trade machines. Her work was pictorial, often figurative in concept, with appliqué of nets and transparent fabrics, overlaid to give depth of tone and colour changes (32). Sometimes she used machine outlines only, with very little appliqué. She has designed for textiles and wallpapers and produced some embroidery for advertising. In 1955 she became a part-time lecturer in machine embroidery at Goldsmiths' School of Art. See figure 77.

Guy Barton had no formal art training but taught art as a career. He started to design for embroidery in the early fifties while at Marlborough School. This beginning was due to his being asked to consider designing stall cushions and kneelers for the chapel, so he visited a number of churches well known for their canvas embroideries. Among these were the Winchester embroideries carried out by Louisa Pesel, and the canvas hangings and cushions in Wells Cathedral. From this study he developed his own approach to design. His first commission, at his own suggestion, was for Lancaster Priory. He put up cartoons *in situ* which were approved so work was started on the embroidered panels in 1961 (150). Cushions and seat backs were designed, too. Twelve women worked the panels, taught by Guy Barton's wife who carried out preliminary samples. The hangings proved so successful that Guy Barton was commissioned by many churches in Lancashire and Yorkshire to design embroideries for them; again his wife taught the women involved in carrying out the work. He also designed altar rail kneelers in Winchester Cathedral, another successful undertaking. (Information by Stuart Watson, BA, and Keith Lawson, BA.)

Eugenie Alexander's career as an illustrator was interrupted by the War but she recommenced her studies in 1946. She started to make fabric collages in 1950, having tried a number of crafts with which to express her ideas. She found fabric, threads and beads most satisfactory as a means of achieving a number of different effects within the limitations of the medium. Her subjects were varied, including the human figure, animals, fruit and flowers, parks and jungles (68 and 123). She worked with applied fabrics on a variety of backgrounds, embellishing these with stitchery and beads, often leaving parts of the fabrics detached as she found that laces, braids, ribbons and richly textured fabrics are suitable for her ideas. Her scale of work ranges between 5 in. (12 cm) and 10 ft (3 m) in size. She wrote two books during the decade: *Art for Young People* in 1958, and in 1959 *Fabric Pictures*, both published by Mills and Boon.

Margaret Treherne studied stained glass and textiles and has a particular interest in colour and light. She is a versatile artist and during the fifties executed many embroideries, each with a distinctive style. She applied patches of brilliantly coloured fabrics to different coloured backgrounds, surrounding these with many lines of machine stitching in black thread, closely worked, to obtain a jewel-like quality. Her design was mainly figurative, with an individual stylisation; her subjects often based on Biblical literature (79 and 80). Occasionally she worked entirely in line in close tones of pale colours. She designed ecclesiastical vestments during this time (109) and carried out commissions for stained glass, more abstract in concept than the embroideries, which also were commissioned. She taught machine embroidery in several colleges and schools of art.

Marjorie Dyer, although trained as a painter, later became interested in textiles and attended evening classes in design and embroidery during her time at the Slade School of Fine Art. She taught for a couple of years before moving to the Far East. When she returned to England she resumed her interest in embroidery, with experiments in colour and tonal values, working sometimes in black and white, at other times in primary colours, mingling threads, materials and stitches. Her embroidery has a geometric bias (185).

June Tiley studied lithography and dress design but taught both embroidery and weaving, among other subjects. She returned to Cardiff to teach art and design, including dress, in the College of Art. She has taught embroidery at the Barry Summer School for a considerable time. Her interest lies primarily in the structure of artifacts, the construction of fabrics and the use of threads as art forms, rather than in the application of surface decoration. She has carried out both embroidered and woven hangings. See also figures 122 and 152.

Maureen Helsdon trained as an illustrator, using engraving and screen printing, among other techniques. She discovered that the potential of machine embroidery offered many possibilities compatible with her training, and always includes appliqué and machine embroidery in her work (139 and 171). This was based earlier on natural forms but the human figure is a favourite subject which she regards as the ultimate challenge. Her earlier work was illustrative, stylised, sometimes with almost geometric figures in appliqué, with pattern worked over them in machine stitching. She thought that the use of hand and machine embroidery together gave greater richness of pattern and texture than in using each technique alone. Her work showed imagination with rich colour obtained by applying bright fabrics to dark grounds, emphasising shapes with contrasting outlines. Her variety in sizes of work show techniques suitable to these, from fine machine stitched lines, to bold shapes cut in felt.

Constance Howard. During the decade the human figure was a popular source of ideas for design by embroiderers and I executed a number of panels, all containing figures, mainly based on drawings from life, often of children (11, 12, 13, 39, 88, 89 and colour plate 1). Appliqué and hand stitching with the fine lines of machine stitching in black slipped over the edges, were my chief means of working out my ideas in the early fifties. Fabrics were plain, colours strong and contrasting in many of my embroideries; some were in black machine stitching only, on white fabric. All of these were framed. I also carried out a number of ecclesiastical commissions at the end of the decade (117, 134 and 148); the designs for these, except for banners, were non-figurative although I found that the figure interested me more than any other subject. However, the abstract concepts led to a widening of experimental work and a change of style. See figures 120 and 138.

Alison Liley began teaching in 1953 as a part-time lecturer. In her teaching of adults she felt that her main talent was in convincing students that they could learn and that this was worthwhile. As a designer she said that she was an adequate academic draughtsman, but being left-handed her aim was to obtain regularity of stitch. She produced fine machine embroidery as well as hand stitching, often based on plant forms, for household articles. Some of her work was bold, incorporating human figures which she included in banners and hangings on woollen fabrics; other pieces were on organdie or sheer fabrics with delicately drawn patterns worked in machine stitching (83 and 163).

Marjorie Kostenz studied as a painter during the early twenties and started to embroider during the early fifties at Goldsmiths' School of Art. She found that in this medium she was able to express her ideas more successfully than in any other way and began to exhibit at a number of galleries. In the introduction to the catalogue of a retrospective exhibition of her work, there is an evocative description of her style. It says that 'her work was bold in design, rich in colour and entirely original. Provence was . . . her chief source of inspiration . . . the stone villages perched on hills . . . details of houses, trees and rocks. Her designs were often very elaborate . . . depicting group activities such as religious festivals'. Other such scenes included grape harvests and occupations in Provence (136). She often outlined shapes with heavy black threads couched down with brilliant colours, she also used many beads, all of these contributing to an individual style which developed during the fifties. See colour plate 7.

Diana Jones taught in Stroud School of Art and other places during the fifties. Her work was bold, often containing mixed media, with an experimental outlook (65). She felt a strong reaction in the early fifties to the commonplace embroidery worked from unimaginative transfers. These formed her early schooling in embroidery, household linens with lazy daisy and long and short stitch putting her off these stitches. She learnt a great deal about design and stitchery from looking at Elizabethan embroideries, particularly the floral patterns. To her there were two levels of embroidery, the practical and experimental, but the protection of panels with glass seemed a barrier in conflict with the character of textiles. During the mid and late fifties Diana Jones was not attracted by patchwork or canvas work: she found the design possibilities restrictive.

Margaret Forbes after training at the Royal School of Needlework, was with a firm of commercial embroiderers for a short time. She returned to assist in the workroom of the Royal School of Needlework, then taught from 1953 at a school of domestic science for several years and the Hampton School of Embroidery, Twickenham, for a year. She then had a period at Bromley and Ravensbourne Colleges of Art. During this time she carried out the embroidery for a set of six chasubles for Chichester Cathedral, designed by the painter Ceri Richards (183 and 184). She said that she did not do a great deal of her own designing.

Eirian Short trained as a sculptor but embroidery fascinated her and she did not return to her original subject. She taught part time in several schools and also carried out her own ideas. She has a facility for using stitches expressively, whether for dress or wall decorations; she also feels that when she has chosen a subject she is compelled to design and execute the idea several times, until she has exhausted its possibilities as far as different approaches are concerned. Early examples of her work show her interest in fabrics and colour, with patchworks merging from dark to light, with the juxtaposition of tones that simulated transparency or relief. Her subjects include 'Night and Day', houses, figures, animals and insects. In an article in *Embroidery* she has given an interesting description of her thoughts on the fifties scene at Goldsmiths' School of Art, which is illuminating. She says: 'In the early fifties, when I first worked in textiles, there were certain unwritten, but widely accepted "rules". Embroidery was recognised as the embellishment of a flat surface of cloth, and anything which destroyed that two-dimensional quality was considered wrong. A feeling of distance was tolerated if it was suggested by overlapping shapes or by variation in size, but using vanishing point perspective was taboo. The modelling of form by the use of shading was also frowned upon: the decorative, flat pattern was the accepted convention for embroiderers.

'Subject matter, in the fifties, was never treated naturalistically – there was a prescribed sequence of stages through which it must pass to make it suitable for embroidering. First, a study, or studies, must be made, in the form of black and white or wash drawings. The drawing was then "formalised", ie abstracted and simplified. The formalised version was presented, more often than not, as a self contained motif, a decorative vignette. To allow the subject to appear to continue beyond the edge of the fabric, or to be cut off by the frame was considered "painterly" which was a perjorative term.' (*Embroidery*, Summer 1980.)

At the end of the fifties Eirian Short was interested in the richness obtained by making jewelled pincushions with pins, beads, silks, velvets and satins, and gold kid (165 and 166).

Elizabeth Geddes intended to become an illustrator, but decided finally that she wished to embroider. She therefore studied hand and machine embroidery, having previously obtained the National Diploma in Design in typographical design. She taught part time in a number of schools and colleges of art and assisted on courses for teachers. She worked as a freelance artist, designer and embroiderer, assisting Iris Hills while she was with the Needlework Development Scheme, when she made samples and designed and worked a number of embroidries for the Scheme. Her technical expertise led her to interpret the designs of other artists, among these being Margaret Treherne and Joyce Conwy-Evans. She continues also to design and carry out her own work, which is meticulous in execution (69, 70, 71, 95, 96 and 97).

Nancy Kimmins, who studied embroidery, has been much concerned with the care of historical embroideries and through this interest, developed a deep feeling for textile conservation. In 1950 she took over most of the responsibility for the Embroiderers' Guild collection of historic embroideries and lace. Nancy Kimmins' own work is experimental in outlook, often bold and sometimes three dimensional in structure. She uses subtle colour combinations and finds that textures are important in her work, these being created in very thick wools in raised stitches (21). To this end she spins and dyes her own threads, having become fascinated by the qualities obtained with yarns of various weights and their effects on textile structures.

Elizabeth Ford studied hand and machine embroidery and taught in Nottingham College of Art (now a part of Trent Polytechnic). She became an expert in machine embroidery and during the fifties worked with Gerald Holtom and David Holt, both of whom were carrying out large commissions executed in machine embroidery. Her own work was finely drawn and carried out on net and other delicate fabrics in machine stitching (44). She taught part time at the Oxford School of Art towards the end of the decade. During the early sixties she assisted Pat Russell on some of her ecclesiastical commissions (155 and colour plate 9).

Joy Clucas trained as an embroiderer after which she had several jobs. In 1956 she lived in Nigeria where she designed textiles and worked in a commercial studio. On her return she carried out freelance work. She designs almost entirely for machine embroidery, mainly using straight stitching. Her subjects are diverse, with ideas developed from geometric pattern, floral pattern and the elements, among others. Sometimes she uses appliqué incorporated with machine stitching but much of her work is entirely in line, very finely drawn and stitched (47, 141, 160 and 168).

Betty Myerscough was trained as an embroiderer and weaver. She worked in industry with Messrs J & P Coats after obtaining her Diploma and in 1959 became a full-time lecturer at Grays School of Art, Aberdeen. Her work is vigorous with strong textural qualities; her subjects wide, including buildings (127), animals and the human figure.

Sister Kathleen joined the Society of St Margaret at St Saviour's Priory in 1932. She was asked by the Reverend Mother to make vestments, but had no training in embroidery so took brief instructions in gold work at the Community in East Grinstead. She continued on her own until she joined Beryl Dean's class at the Hammersmith College of Art and Building in 1955, where she learnt design and techniques. She assisted Beryl Dean on projects and carried out embroidery designed by others, becoming well known for her technical excellence, later carrying out some of her own designs. See figures 114 and 164.

Moyra McNeill trained as an embroiderer in both hand and machine embroidery, after which she taught part-time in a number of schools. In 1963 she exhibited at the Crafts Centre in a two-man show with Olivia Fryd. She designed and worked household articles as well as wall decorations and had a particular interest in the techniques of embroidery and their interpretation in a modern way. Her own work is meticulous in execution although she experiments freely with different approaches in carrying out ideas, often wittily.

Susan Riley had a distinctive style, mainly illustrative and developed during the fifties when she was a student with Beryl Dean. Her subjects were figurative, sometimes carried out in appliqué over which she stitched many fine curving lines in black machine thread, or in stitchery alone, using lines close together to give solidity; the curves adding movement, the lines reminiscent of fine pen drawing. Her work was sometimes large in scale, but whatever size, was filled with detail. She designed a number of ecclesiastical vestments worked by other embroiderers, among these the cope and mitre, for St Paul's Cathedral, an idea originally conceived by Beryl Dean as a communal project for her class at Hammersmith College of Art and Building. See figure 176.

Rosalind Floyd trained as a printed-textile and embroidery designer. She continued with embroidery in evening classes, working on figurative subjects, using appliqué with manipulated and padded fabrics to obtain relief. As she progressed the figures became abstracted as simple forms (100). Later, she developed an interest in geometric and near geometric design, working on a larger scale than for her first examples.

Designers who had been embroidering before the War continued to produce work and to exhibit during the fifties and after, among whom Joan Nicholson was now working for commercial firms including William Briggs. She wrote in her introduction to *Contemporary Embroidery Design*, published in 1954, 'Perhaps the most important quality needed in a competent embroideress is an inquiring mind, an awareness of things. She should be capable of realising the limitations as well as seeing the possibilities of the craft'. When this book was published, the wrapper said 'her book is quite exceptionally valuable and original. . . . The desire to enrich an article . . . by means of embroidery, may be fulfilled without resort to second-rate machine transfers'. It was suggested that by carrying out 'her own embroidered work in its entirety . . . each person's individuality can be expressed and asserted'.

Hebe Cox helped to arrange a show by the Suffolk Embroiderers' Guild, to aid the Expansion Fund for the Guild Headquarters. She lent a number of her embroideries to this show which was held at Tunstall Hall in June 1959, the home of Captain and Mrs Bunbury. See figure 179.

Having taught embroidery since her appointment in 1920, Dorothy Angus retired from Grays School of Art, Aberdeen, in 1955, but continued with her own work.

The Arts and Crafts Exhibition Society

At the 24th exhibition of the Arts and Crafts Exhibition Society at the New Burlington Galleries in London, in 1954, work was shown by embroiderers who were already well known and by those who since then have become known. Lilian Dring showed embroidered birthday and Christmas cards in hand and machine stitching, also a cushion, while Hebe Cox entered two pieces of work – a canvas stool seat and a hanging. Evelyn Woodcock showed a hanging for a girl's room in hand embroidery. Among the less known at the time were Eugene Alexander with ten pieces, five of which were floral panels, Margaret Treherne with a panel *The Miraculous Draught of Fishes* and two cushions, while Christine Risley showed one piece and Eirian Short two pieces of work. Moyra Somerville exhibited a nursery panel and Maureen Helsdon machine embroidered cards and panels. Luncheon mats, Madeleine Clifton's bedspread, cushions and stool tops were among the useful articles shown; embroidered hangings and panels, often machine stitched, predominated. Other techniques included patchwork, pulled work and canvas work as well as appliqué and collage. Altogether 63 pieces of embroidery were shown in the exhibition, with a wide range of subjects.

New approach to embroidery

It was noticeable during the mid fifties that a lively element was infiltrating into the craft, due to artists trained in other subjects exploiting fabrics and threads in order to express ideas. As they possessed slight or no knowledge of the behaviour of these and little or no technical skill, they were breaking away from the traditional methods. By using the medium unconventionally and entirely to express what they wished to say, in any ways that they could devise, the results were varied and individual. However, they showed up the differences in approach by the artist and the embroiderer who appeared to be interested only in perfect stitching rather than in good design. The disparity was noticeable between someone who could draw and was aware of its importance in design in comparison with someone who was concerned only with technique. There were still articles in magazines on the technical perfection of some embroiderers with a lack of design and vice versa but embroidery was now firmly established as a subject of interest both to the artist and to the amateur stitcher.

Exhibition at the Medici Gallery

In the spring of 1955 an exhibition of embroidered pictures was held at the Medici Gallery in London, where it was suggested that the influence of modern painting was noticeable. Several now well-known embroiderers exhibited work. Among these, according to the catalogue, were Eirian Short who exhibited an appliqué picture of a *Bowl of Fruit* showing a strong influence of Braque, while Christine Risley showed two delicate embroideries in appliqué with fine stitched lines, one a hand holding a rose, the other a hand holding a daisy. Materials were frayed out purposely, nets and gauzes were overlaid to give illusions of depth; hand and machine embroidery were employed sometimes in one piece of work. Ideas were lively although pictorial in style. Dora Billington, a prominent potter, inspired by the exhibition, wrote an article on embroidery for *The Studio* magazine. This was entitled 'Contemporary Needlework Pictures'. She stressed the fact that although some people felt that embroidery should be applied to practical articles, these present-day embroidered pictures were quite different in concept from those of the past. Now the aim was in trying to ascertain how an idea could be expressed most successfully in fabric and thread. She felt that colour and texture and the stitched line had distinctive qualities which gave validity to the use of embroidery for pictures. (*The Studio*, September 1955).

Mary Quant

Mary Quant opened her first shop, 'Bazaar', in the King's Road, Chelsea, London, in 1955. This opening was a fantastic affair which I attended. Sausages were cooked on braziers on the pavement outside the shop and drink flowed freely. The whole venture was the beginning of an approach to clothes for the young which had an appeal of immediacy. The shop was small and she had made practically everything herself, clothes and hats, with some jewellery and accessories made by friends.

Glasgow Embroidery Group

In 1956 Kathleen Whyte promoted an exhibition group composed of former embroidery and weaving students of the Glasgow School of Art. From this time onwards, exhibitions of work were shown every two years in Glasgow and other places, including Manchester and London as well as in Scotland. New members joined the group after they had completed their training successfully.

The exhibition was to demonstrate the fact that embroidered wall decorations were suitable for present-day homes. It was realised that framing was important so some students obtained the frames first of all and designed embroideries to suit them. A sense of humour was a feature of a number of the embroideries, such as 'Man Eating Macaroni'. A variety of fabrics was employed in these embroideries and colour was often excellent, according to the description by Kathleen Whyte who was in charge of the embroidery department.

Judging embroidery

Notes on Craft Judging – a booklet for the National Union of Townswomen's Guilds and the National Institute of Adult Education – was written by Lucile Spalding in 1956 the aim being to get a level of craft judging comparable for all subjects. About the judging of embroidery she said: 'In teaching embroidery it is all too easy to adapt stereotyped styles of so-called original design, which have lost their freshness. There are the not-very-original leaf patterns, taught in the same class as fish with bubbles or again, the contemporary "cockyolly bird" style, which is rapidly becoming as over familiar as the crinoline lady in her day'. In 1959 in another booklet she wrote a complete article on 'The Crinoline Lady and the Bluebell Wood'.

Magazine articles by embroiderers

Well-known artists contributed articles to magazines and journals as the interest in embroidery grew. Margaret Kaye, who was already teaching in the late thirties, wrote an article on her approach to her work in *Far and Wide* published by Guest, Keen and Nettlefold in the winter number 1957–58. In this she explained her aims and views. She said '. . . as a medium for producing works with great richness and depth, I found possibilities in appliqué equal to those of mosaic, tapestry or even painting . . . I never draw a line on paper . . . a line drawn with pencil or brush on paper is very different from one cut with scissors from material. '. . . My criticism of a good deal of machine embroidery is that it looks like a coloured drawing on paper. . . . Recently there has been a slow but steady improvement in the standard of design for embroidery in the art schools. This has extended from hand to machine work . . . the fault with most embroidery to-day is not bad technique, but a tired and stale approach to the design'. She claimed that she was not an embroiderer but that she used stitches to emphasise particular parts of her design.

Eleanor Scarfe, who was teaching embroidery at the Regent Street Polytechnic, made some pertinent remarks on embroidery during the mid-twentieth century, saying that 'It has a style of its own, quite free from "Victorianism" or any previous styles. It is against this background – optimistic and exciting – that the present movement of embroidery design must be seen. . . . There has been a great deal of confused thought about the "usefulness" of embroidery in the last 50 years

. . . it cannot at any time be called strictly utilitarian . . . its value is as a luxury – it is an art of decoration. There are two spheres in which embroidery might be called utilitarian – in its application to dressmaking and in ecclesiastical work. . . . To-day there is once more the desire for individual ornamentation of dress, for day wear with tapes, braids and simple embroidery, for evening with spangled ornaments, metallic threads, pearls and beads . . . ecclesiastical embroidery is another matter . . . it is very much at a standstill artistically . . . there is very little work done comparable with the stained glass, the tapestry, the sculpture and other decorations of our new Cathedral at Coventry. . . . Here we need a new enlightenment on the part of those who commission'. (*Embroidery*, winter 1956–57.)

The Needlework Development Scheme exhibition 1957

The most enterprising exhibition so far staged by the Needlework Development Scheme was shown at the Tea Centre in London in 1957, it was entitled 'Contemporary Needlework Design'. This was planned by the Nicholson brothers and arranged by Iris Hills. The subject was 'How and where to find inspiration for embroidery design'. The exhibition was divided into sections, each showing one source, but with ideas from these developed in several ways. The sections were under the headings of: (1) designing with fabrics, (2) with textures, (3) with cut paper, (4) with plant forms, and (5) design from traditional embroidery, such as quilting, patchwork and canvas. The aim of the exhibition was to inspire the embroiderer so that ideas were 'sparked off' but not copied. Well-known embroiderers contributed. Among these were Elizabeth Geddes whose dark green bedspread with sprays of roses was, according to the review 'most effective' (95 and 96). The whole exhibition was another step forward in helping people to become aware of design and what could be done with needle and thread and fabric, as well as ways in which to obtain ideas. Section five showed contemporary embroideries based on traditional examples. Through the exhibition it was hoped that design could be seen as developing from stitchery '. . . with an appreciation of fabric texture, colour and arrangement'. Some of the embroideries based on plant forms showed Swedish influence, with an almost geometric stylisation of flowers and leaves in clearly defined shapes; black and white stitchery was prevalent, too.

Ecclesiastical embroidery

Beryl Dean, after a period of travelling and some teaching, obtained a post at the Hammersmith College of Art and Building where, in 1955, Dorothy Allsopp had now become Head of Embroidery and allied subjects. Through her, Beryl Dean was able to start an ecclesiastical embroidery class in 1958, devoted entirely to church work and the first of its kind in the country. She realised that help and encouragement were required by students who wished to design embroidery for the Church; also, that the clergy would need persuasion to give commissions to embroiderers for contemporary vestments and furnishings. However, this pioneer class was the beginning of the revival of church embroidery and a gradual acceptance of more adventurous design by both embroiderers and those in positions of authority in ecclesiastical establishments.

Beryl Dean's book *Ecclesiastical Embroidery* was accompanied in May to June 1958 by an exhibition of her work, held at the headquarters of the British Colour Council in London. She showed very fine white embroidery and her *Madonna* in metal threads (illustrated in Volume 1) among other examples. A review of her exhibition said that her technique was superb and that her range of work was wide. Her keen interest in the ballet was noticeable in some of her examples and her ideas appeared to evolve from combinations of unusual fabrics and colours which influenced her design and technique. The conclusion was that 'she is one of the foremost embroiderers of ecclesiastical work to-day'. See Figure 157.

The St Paul's cope and mitre (see also page 135) were worked in hand and machine embroidery but were not completed until the mid sixties. See figures 155, 157, 158 and 159.

Rosamund Willis with the help of a Finnish girl, Marita Björkholm, designed and executed four panels $16\frac{1}{2}$ ft × 4 ft (5 m × 1.22 m) for St Ninian's Episcopal

Church in Aberdeen. These were in memory of an American girl who had died while a student at Aberdeen University. Rosamund Willis commenced to work these early in 1958, completing them in 40 days. They are simple in design, the four almost geometric angels filling over half the height of each panel which alternate in colour of background in misty pink and grey-blue. Lurex thread in silver and copper add sparkle but are used with restraint.

Church Needlework Guilds

A number of Church Needlework Guilds were formed at the end of the fifties and in the early sixties, making their own vestments and furnishings. As these guilds often found the designing difficult, outside artists were sometimes employed to do this for them. Among these guilds the Gloucester Cathedral Needlework Guild was formed in 1957, their aim being to do what they could themselves, with the best materials and design that they could find. Beryl Clutterbuck, a professional embroiderer, with eight workers carried out repairs and worked designs often provided by others.

The growth of machine embroidery

In the colleges of art, experimental machine embroidery was now given considerable impetus. Christine Risley taught part time at Goldsmiths' School of Art and at St Martin's School of Art, as did Margaret Treherne, who also taught some machine embroidery at the Hammersmith College of Art and Building. Eirian Short taught part time at Hornsey College of Art, carrying out embroidery for dress, while Doris Taylor had introduced machine embroidery to Manchester College of Art. At Birmingham College of Art, students were using fine machine embroidery on dress, gaining a reputation for this work and producing some excellent results with sound design and technical ability. The Head of the department was Loveday Hedley who was known for her high standards and strict discipline.

Embroidery at the end of the fifties

Towards the end of the decade, embroidered wall decorations tended to become larger, with the fabric stretched over plain wooden frames, or on canvas stretchers. Some works hung freely. Design showed a leaning towards abstraction and sometimes to geometric forms, while the illustrative style prevalent throughout much of the decade diminished. Colour and texture of fabric became more important with the tendency to abstraction and some hand-dyed fabrics were incorporated with the commercially dyed ones. Hand and machine techniques were mingled and mixed media became a feature of some embroideries, such extraneous articles as tin lids, buttons and fur, appearing in students' work. Glasgow School of Art students were carrying out wall decorations among other articles, using hand embroidery in a variety of ways, under the instruction of Kathleen Whyte.

Early in 1958 an exhibition of work by both past and present students of Glasgow School of Art was held in the Fine Arts Gallery, Glasgow. Figurative subjects, buildings and a variety of other subjects were chosen in design with a wide use of fabrics and threads.

Exhibitions at the end of the decade

A collection of embroideries as part of a craft exhibition by selected artists and entitled 'British Artist Craftsmen', was sent to the USA in 1959, where it was exhibited at the Smithsonian Institute in Washington DC, and in other centres during the following two years. A number of well-known embroiderers contributed work to this section. Margaret Kaye showed five pieces of embroidery; John Piper, a cope worked by Winsome Douglas, while Frances Richards exhibited an altar frontal on which she worked the figures while Anne Roscal carried out the remainder of the design. Other artists who showed work were Margaret Treherne who designed a cope worked by Elizabeth Geddes (109); a design by Anne Bruce was embroidered by Edith John and Maria Sim (110), while Eirian Short carried out, and freely interpreted, a torah cover designed by William Gear (111).

The Arts and Crafts Exhibition Society held its 26th exhibition in December 1959 at Goldsmiths' Hall, the embroidery section according to the review, making up in quality what it lacked in quantity. It said that 'many of the leading embroiderers of the day are represented. . . . Now we are confronted with work of a different age . . . where design, colour and treatment are all important . . . works which breathe life and freshness into a craft that was fast becoming a "technique", instead of a craft, taking its part among the foremost arts of the day.' Embroiderers who showed work at the exhibition included Beryl Dean, Christine Risley, Hebe Cox, Eirian Short, and myself. Sir Gordon Russell in a Foreword to a booklet issued in conjunction with the exhibition said that the Goldsmiths' Company by giving hospitality to the exhibition was 'once more showing its belief in the value of hand-work of fine quality. . . . Such an exhibition is not only of value by enabling the public, that is the patrons, to see what is being done: it is equally important that the craftsman should assess his own contribution.The highest skill in workmanship is not always allied to the most imaginative design and it . . . is easy to become complacent. New, red blood is needed all the time. Hand-work is not valuable just because it is hand-work. It is valuable . . . when it enables something to be done in any other way. Any hand-worker worth his salt will have a proper respect for the beauty of precision which the machine can give when directed imaginatively'.

Schemes for churches

A scheme to embroider kneelers for the restored church of St Clement Danes was discussed in 1959. One of the restoration architects, S Lloyd, produced three designs with final colour scheme of blues for the majority of these. Red and gold, two of the original colours, were used in the crypt. Nancy Kimmins organised the complete scheme, an appeal for workers bringing in replies from people throughout the country.

Another scheme for kneelers and cushions for Eton College Chapel was begun in 1959, designed by myself and others, some kneelers by Lady Younger. The substall seat cushions, with the emblems of the four evangelists, and kneelers, with ideas based on the cross, were designed by Elizabeth Andrews, MSIA (135). Dark blue backgrounds with a variety of colours for the emblems and coats of arms, supplied unity to the scheme.

Publications

Many more books were published during the fifties, among which were *Contemporary Embroidery Design* in 1954 by Joan Nicholson, *Design for Embroidery from Traditional English Sources* in 1956 by Constance Howard, *The Colour Manual of Needlework*, in 1958, all published by Messrs Batsford. The fifth edition of *Embroidery and Needlework*, 1959, by Gladys Windsor Fry was published by Pitman and *Fabric Pictures*, 1959, by Eugenie Alexander, also *Canvas Embroidery*, 1959, by Hebe Cox were published by Mills and Boon. Barbara Snook and Winsome Douglas also had books published during this time.

Summary 1950–1959

Prominent people

Eugenie Alexander
Balmain
Balenciaga
Joy Clucas
Elizabeth Geddes
Esther Grainger
Jennifer Gray
Sylvia Green
Norman Hartnell
Maureen Helsdon
Edith John
Nancy Kimmins
Alison Liley
Joan Nicholson
Margaret Nicholson
Dorothea Nield
Pamela Pavitt
Mary Quant
Frances Richards
Christine Risley
Gordon Russell
Eiran Short
June Tiley
Margaret Treherne

Societies, schools, exhibitions, events

Exhibitions by the Arts and Crafts Exhibition Society continued throughout the decade, bi-annually. The Schools Challenge Cup and the Members Challenge Cup competitions were held annually by the Embroiderers' Guild with exhibitions of work

1950 *Embroidery* magazine was on sale to the public for the first time

1951 The Festival of Britain on the South Bank

1952–55 Travelling exhibitions arranged by the Needlework Development Scheme

1952 An exhibition by members of the Women's Institutes at the Victoria and Albert Museum

1953 The Ministry of Education allowed Hand Embroidery as a special subject in the examination for the National Diploma in Design

1953 Goldsmiths' School of Art started classes for full-time embroiderers wishing to take the examination for the National Diploma in Design

1953 The Coronation of Elizabeth II, with embroidered garments by Norman Hartnell. Beads of all kinds very fashionable

1954 The end of rationing

1954 Chanel in Paris returns to the fashion scene

1955 Iris Hills was appointed 'expert in charge' of the Needlework Development Scheme, at the end of Dorothy Allsopp's term of office

1955 The Medici Gallery mounted an exhibition of embroidery

1955 Commercial television began

1955 Mary Quant opened 'Bazaar' in the King's Road, Chelsea

1956 The Glasgow Embroidery Group was founded

1957 The Needlework Development Scheme showed its most important exhibition at the Tea Centre, London

1958 Beryl Dean started embroidery classes exclusively for ecclesiastical work, at Hammersmith College of Art and Building

1959 Marked the anniversary of the 26th exhibition of the Arts and Crafts Exhibition Society

1959 British Artist Craftsmen – travelling exhibition sent to the USA

Main types of embroidery

Interest in wall decorations rather than useful articles
Figurative design
Birds 'in' in design
Illustrative style during first half of decade, pulled work
Household articles such as tea cosies, tablecloths, cushion covers
Larger hangings, sometimes unframed
Small, elaborately framed pictures
Abstraction as decade advances
Mixed media appearing at the end of the decade
Machine embroidery growing in popularity
Embroidery on dress – mainly machine
Geometric style at the end of the decade
Appliqué throughout the decade

Magazines and books

1954 *Embroidery Technique and Design*, Hebe Cox

1954 *Traditional Quilting*, Mavis Fitz-Randolph

1954 *Contemporary Embroidery Design*, Joan Nicholson

1955 *The Flowerers*, Margaret Swain

1955 *Working Drawings for Embroidery*, Gladys Windsor Fry

1955 *Designing Embroidery*, Winsome Douglas

1956 *Historical Designs for Embroidery*, Louisa Pesel (published posthumously)

1956 *Design for Embroidery from Traditional English Sources*, Constance Howard

1957 *Dorset Feather Stitch*, Olivia Pass

1958 *Patchwork*, Averil Colby

1958 *The Anchor Manual of Needlework*, J & P Coats Ltd

1958 *Ecclesiastical Embroidery*, Beryl Dean

1958 *Art for Young People*, Eugenie Alexander

1958 *Your Machine Embroidery*, Dorothy Benson

1959 *Fabric Pictures*, Eugenie Alexander

1959 *Embroidery and Needlework*, 5th edition, Gladys Windsor Fry

35 1950 – Lilian Dring. Poster in appliqué, receiving the fourth prize in the ERP Poster Competition, United Kingdom section (European Recovery Plan) 'M Aid' Europe. *Upper Panel* – countries in national coloured small patterned fabrics, white net over blue paint ground. Coarse black net covers Iron Curtain countries. Strands of national colours radiate from 'R' of ERP, to appropriate M Aid countries. Letters in stiffened white linen, labels with machine stitching also in linen. *Lower Panel* – 'War-torn Europe' in tattered grey flannel on dingy brown scrim ground. White machine stitching 'lightens' western coasts; black darkens eastern coasts. National coloured strands rise from the countries

Weave the threads together
through
ERP
For a new pattern of life in Europe

36 Left: 1950 – Joan Whayman with Mary Kessel, designer, for the Needlework Development Scheme. Canvas stool seat, $15\frac{1}{2}$ in. × $12\frac{1}{2}$ in. (39 cm × 32 cm), in a variety of stitches. *Exhibited in 1951 at the Arts Council's premises in London.* See also colour plate 3. Formerly belonged to the NDS. *Loaned by the Embroiderers' Guild. Photograph by Nick Nicholson*

37 Below left: Early 1950s – Angela Bradshaw. A sampler using frayed hessian (jute) applied to a background of furnishing fabric

38 1951 – Mary Kessell. A bag designed by her for the Needlework Development Scheme experiment. Worked by Bromley College of Art in machine stitching. *Victoria and Albert Museum, London*

39 Left: 1951 – Constance Howard. *The Country Wife*. A mural, 18 ft × 13 ft (324 cm × 234 cm) approximately, in fabrics, commissioned for the Festival of Britain Exhibition, on the South Bank. A large 'stumpwork' with padded figures to a scale of five eighths the size of a human being. The small, 'real' crafts are to the same scale. The panel depicts some of the activities of the Women's Institutes, in flat and relief appliqué, using a variety of plain and patterned fabrics on a woollen furnishing fabric in mid green. The figures wear real nylon stockings. Cane and balsa wood are used for the furniture and toys. *In the possession of Denman College, Oxfordshire, Headquarters of the Women's Institutes. Photograph by Hawkley Studios*

40 Above: 1951 – Community project. *Patchwork of the Century*, carried out by Lilian Dring and a group of women. A hanging 10 ft square (300 cm square) with one hundred pieces, one for each year, from 1851–1951. The hanging was designed by Lilian Dring with much research by N Jordan. Almost 80 women participated, members of the Twickenham women's organisations, for their Festival of Britain exhibition 'Women of the Century 1851–1951' in June 1951. This exhibit was carried out by the Teddington and Hampton Women Citizens Association at York House, Twickenham. The panel was later hung on the South Bank in the Shot Tower. The panel was worked by women with little or no training in needlework, in just over two months. After the Festival of Britain it was shown in a number of different places. Each panel depicts an important happening, invention or well known person, for each year from 1851–1951, making an historic record of the century

41 Left: 1951 – Winsome Douglas. Cot cover, 28½ in. × 21 in. (73 cm × 53 cm), in red flannel with cream woollen cloth appliqué stitched in red, black and cream. Formerly belonged to the NDS. *Loaned by the Embroiderers' Guild. Photograph by Nick Nicholson*

42 Above: 1951 – Enid Mason. A small curtain, machine embroidered on transparent fabric. Formerly belonging to the NDS. *Loaned by the Embroiderers' Guild. Photograph by Hawkley Studios*

43 Left: 1951 – Barbara Dawson. Bromley School of Art short course. Machine embroidered panel of a masked head, worked on the Irish and Cornely machines. On a grey and gold background, puce fabric is applied, with black and white stitchery

44 Left: 1951 – Elizabeth Ford. The skirt of a christening robe, embroidered by machine on net. *Photograph by Hawkley Studios*

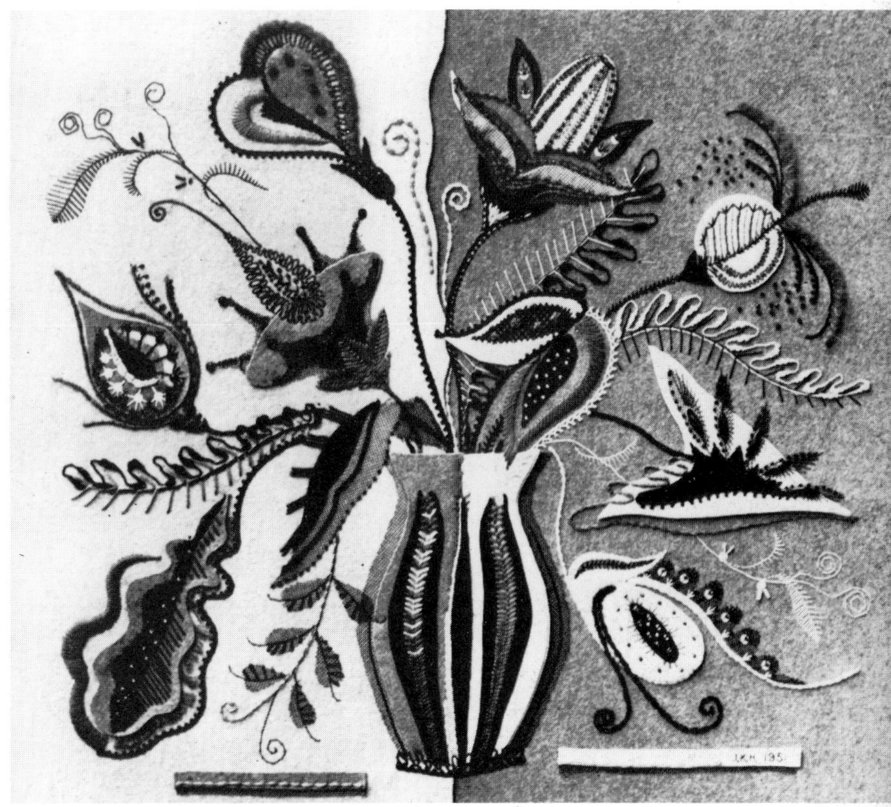

45 Right: 1951 – Joan Archer. *Vase of Flowers*. The background is in soft yellow ochre and white felt. The vase and plants are in terra cotta, black and white. Felts, net, beads and a variety of threads are used

46 Early 1950 – part-time student at Bromley College of Art. Tea cosy in black work on linen. *Photograph by Burwoods*

47 Above: Early 1950s – Joy Clucas. *Cat among the Flower Pots.* A panel in a variety of fine fabrics, appliqué in reds, purples, orange, black, white, grey and browns

48 Early 1950s – Valerie Bayford. *Mermaid.* The panel, $10\frac{1}{2}$ in. × 12 in. (27 cm × 30.5 cm), is executed in silks, mainly inlaid work and long and short stitch. The padded figure is in silvery-cream long and short stitching in silk. Blues and greens are intermingled in the pattern. The tails are inlaid work, padded. Dark couched lines emphasise the rhythms of the design

49 Above: 1952 – Joan Archer. *The Fair.* A panel in appliqué and stitching, including net darning in the background. A variety of fabrics and threads is used. *Manchester Education Committee Collection of Pictures for Schools*

50 1954 – Christine Risley. *A Bird on a Hand.* A small panel in black machine stitching, with some appliqué, on white fabric. *Shown at the Hanover Gallery, December 1954*

51 1952 – Benenden School, Kent. *Alphabet Hanging* made by girls of Benenden School for Doctor Barnardo's Babies' Castle, Kent

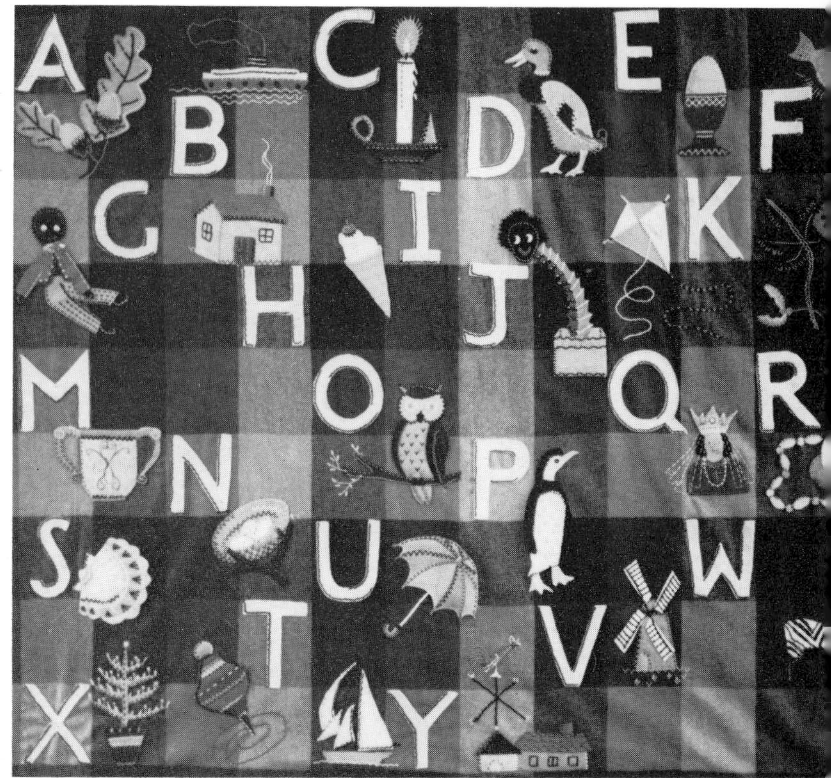

52 Below: 1953 – An exhibition of children's work arranged at Benenden School for the coronation

53 Far right: 1950s – Frances Richards. A panel in hand and machine stitching and applied fabrics. *Private Collection*

FR

54 1950s – Frances Richards. A panel in hand and machine stitching. The idea is based on Rimbaud's poems. The embroidery contains applied fabrics, straight stitches and running. ***In the collection of Douglas Glass***

55 Right: 1950s – Frances Richards. A panel in hand and machine stitching and applied fabric – piqué – on linen. The centre panel is textured with running stitches. ***Leicester City Art Gallery***

56 1950s – Frances Richards. A panel in hand and machine stitching with some appliqué.
In the collection of Mrs Colin Patterson

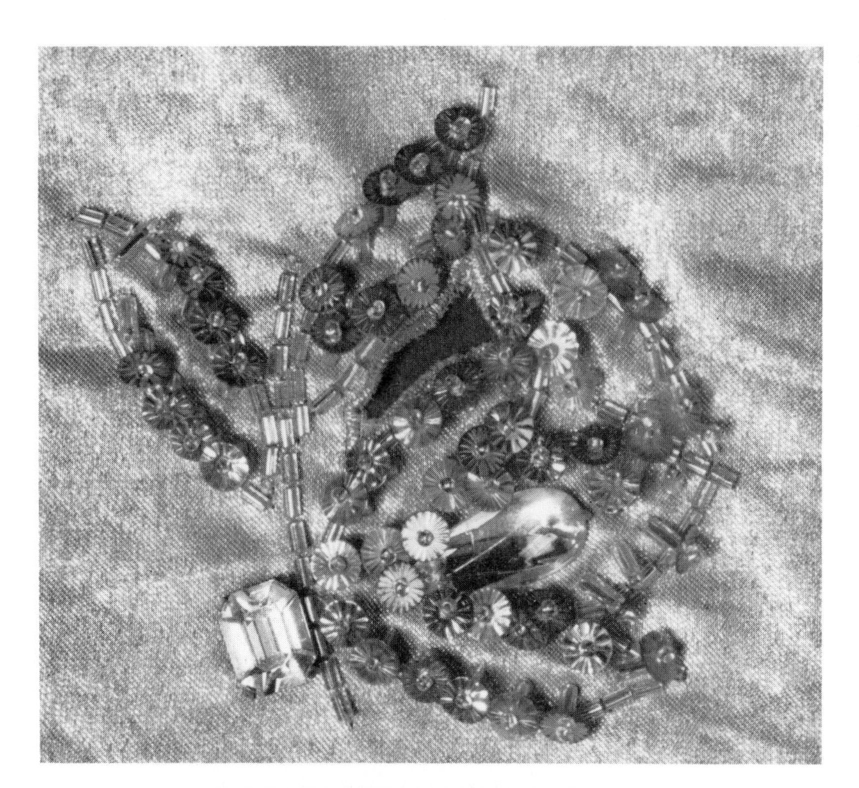

57 1950s – Stanley W Lock. Beadwork sampler using a variety of beads, fancy shapes, bugles and jewels. *Photograph by Hawkley Studios*

58 1950s – Doris Anwyl. *Sea Holly*. A panel, 8 in. × 10 in. (20 cm × 25 cm), in appliqué and embroidery

59 1950s – Stanley W Lock. Beadwork with metal threads, sequins and jewels for the decoration of a neckline. *Photograph by Hawkley Studios*

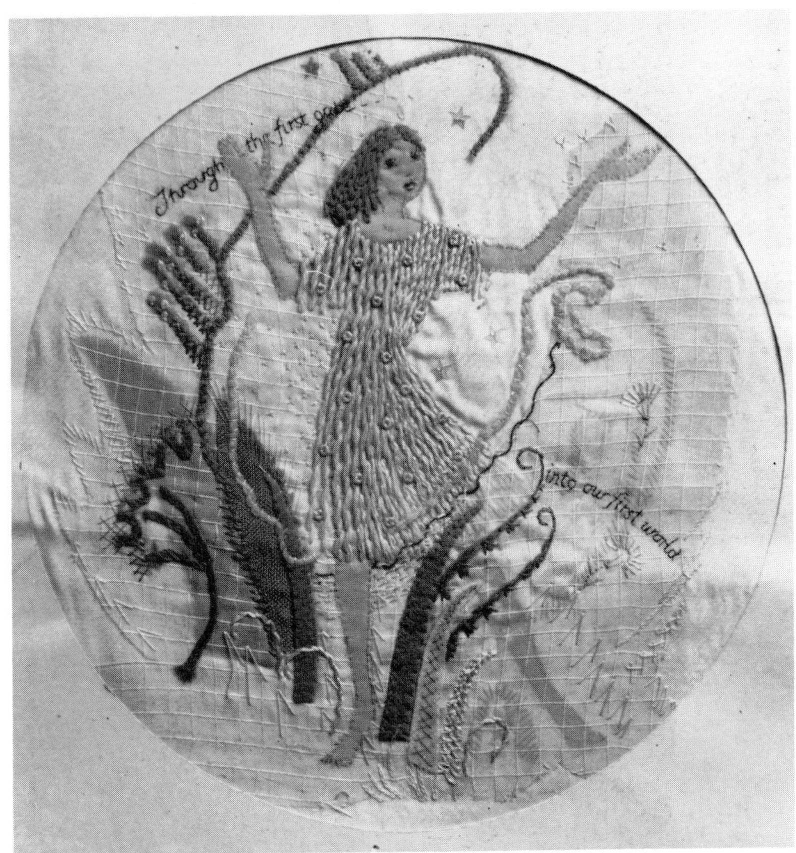

60 Early 1950s – Doris Taylor. Roundel, $7\frac{1}{2}$ in. (17 cm) in diameter, on fine fabric with applied fabrics of linen, muslin and cotton. Worked in several colours of stranded cottons. *Loaned by Margaret Wimpenny. Photograph by John Hunnex*

GUILDFORD

61 Left: Early 1950s – Lady Maufe, designer. One of the kneelers for Guildford Cathedral. Canvas stitches, including long-armed cross stitch. The diagonal line bisecting the design represents Stag Hill, the site of the Cathedral. The ground is blue, the sky grey. Various symbols are incorporated

62 Below left: Another kneeler for Guildford, incorporating 'Guildford' as a motto. *Victoria and Albert Museum, London*

63 Below: 1950s – Student, Bromely College of Art. A tea cosy in organdie embroidered in shadow work. *Photograph by Burwoods*

64 1953 – Pamela Rooke. A panel in machine embroidery and appliqué, executed for the NDD examination, List B, machine embroidery. Various fabrics, plain and patterned, are employed

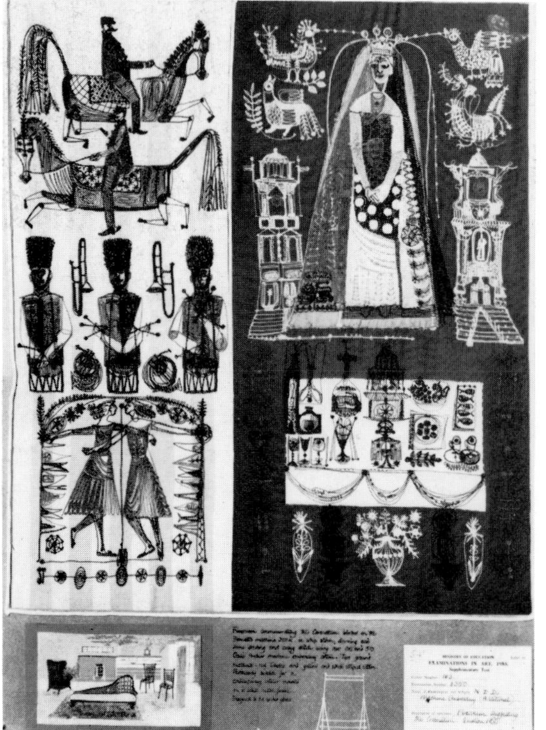

65 Above: 1953 – Diana Jones. A panel in appliqué for Coronation Year

66 Left: 1953 – Shirley Thompson. *Coronation.* A fire screen worked for the additional level examination, the National Diploma in Design, by a student at Harrogate School of Art. Machine embroidery on the 301K domestic machine, incorporating whipstitch, darning, some seeding and crazy stitch. The ground is red cotton and yellow and white striped cotton. *Travelling collection of 'English Embroidered Pictures'. Victoria and Albert Museum, London*

67 Above: 1953 – Norman Hartnell. Dress worn by HRH Princess Margaret, Countess of Snowdon, at the Coronation of HM Queen Elizabeth II. The dress is of heavy white satin, embroidered in a flower and festoon pattern, with pearls, rhinestones, spangles and silver thread. *The Museum of London*

68 1954 – Eugenie Alexander. *Queen Elizabeth.* A panel with applied fabrics from Victorian and Edwardian dresses, beads, pearls, sequins and metal threads

69 Above: 1953–54 – Pamela Rooke. Altar frontal designed by her and worked by Elizabeth Geddes. The frontal is in green damask with a cross applied in gold satin, the centre of which is in raised gold. *Bromley Parish Church*

70 1953–54 – Elizabeth Geddes and Pamela Rooke. The centre panel of the green altar frontal, adapted from the design by Pamela Rooke and worked by Elizabeth Geddes. Applied gold satin with Jap gold, laid and padded work. The centre is in raised gold and jewelled. *Bromley Parish Church*

71 1953–54 – Elizabeth Geddes and Patricia Rooke. The centre panel of the white altar frontal, worked on 'french cream' brocade. Ivory silk. Solid couched gold, gold basket filling, silk and satin appliqué, raised satin laid work. Couched hand-made cord outlines. Designed by Patricia Rooke, worked by Elizabeth Geddes. Actual area of embroidery shown is 2 ft 6 in. (75 cm) square

72 1950s – Jennifer Gray. ***Bull and Cow***. **Hanging of striped Welsh flannel with applied panels of canvas embroidery in various stitches.** ***The Needlework Development Scheme. Photography by Studio Swain***

73 1950s – Jennifer Gray. ***Fisher Girl***. **A panel in canvas embroidery using a variety of stitches**

74 1950s – Eirian Short. A cushion cover in light brown felt with machine embroidery in black and white

75 1950s – Joan Nicholson. A chair seat in canvas embroidery, designed by Joan Nicholson. *The Needlework Development Scheme. Photograph by Studio Swain*

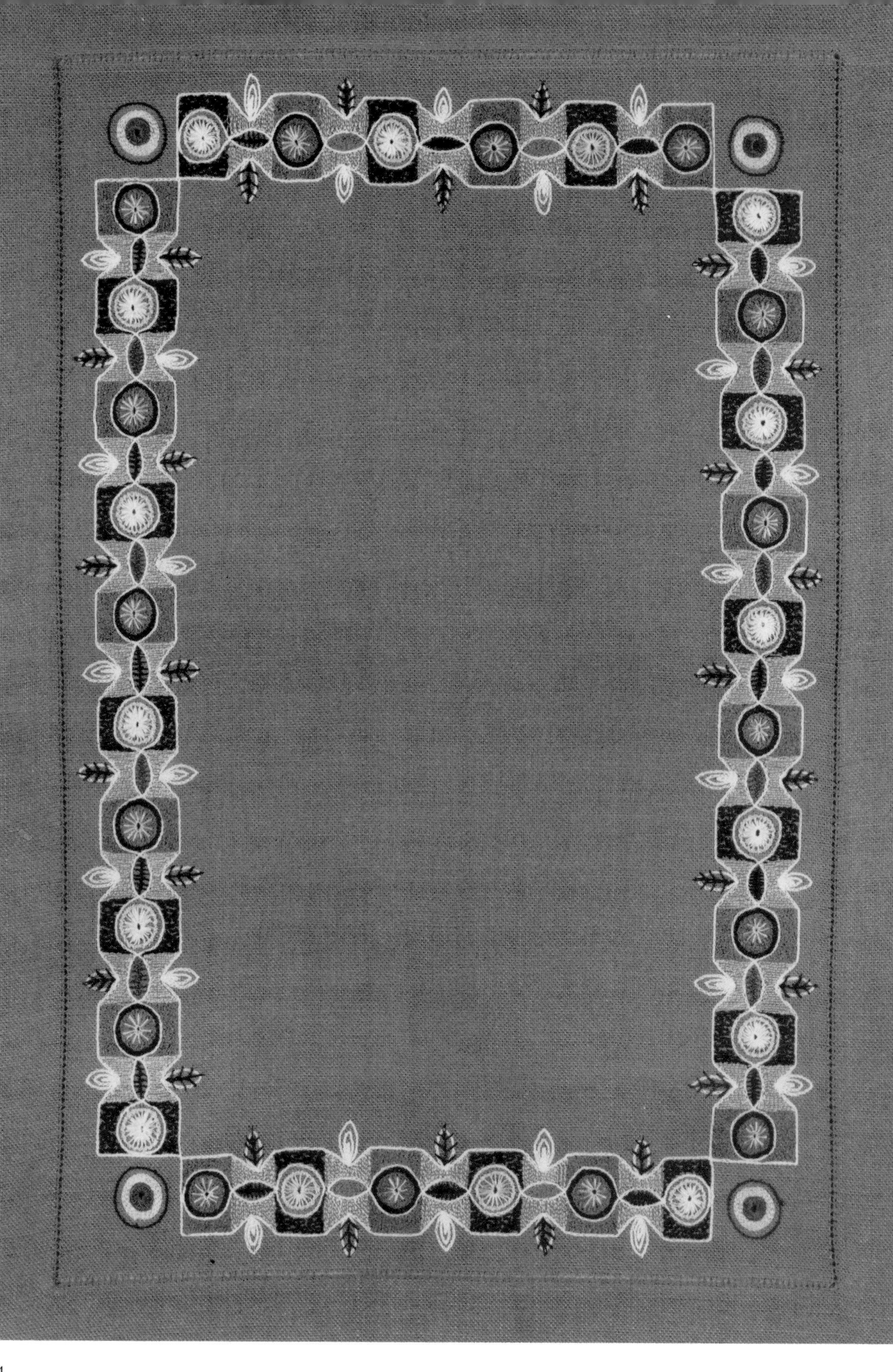

76 Left: 1950s – Lilian Willey. Tambour-embroidered tray cloth, approximately 12 in. × 16 in. (30.5 cm × 41 cm), in dark green linen, with stitching in grey, white, black, maroon and light olive greens. *Formerly belonged to the NDS. Loaned by the Embroiderers' Guild. Photograph by Nick Nicholson*

77 Right: Mid-1950s – Winsome Douglas. Part of a table cloth worked for the Needlework Development Scheme. Black, white and grey with green and some yellow stitching on a dark natural ground. *Victoria and Albert Museum, London*

78 Below: A detail of the cloth by Winsome Douglas

79 Below: 1950s – Margaret Treherne. A panel in appliqué, in reds, pinks, blues and turquoise on a rough textured ground. Lines of black machine stitching emphasise the forms

80 Above: 1950s – Margaret Treherne. *Virgin and Child.* A panel in grey-greens, black and grey. All machine stitched lines. *Victoria and Albert Museum, London*

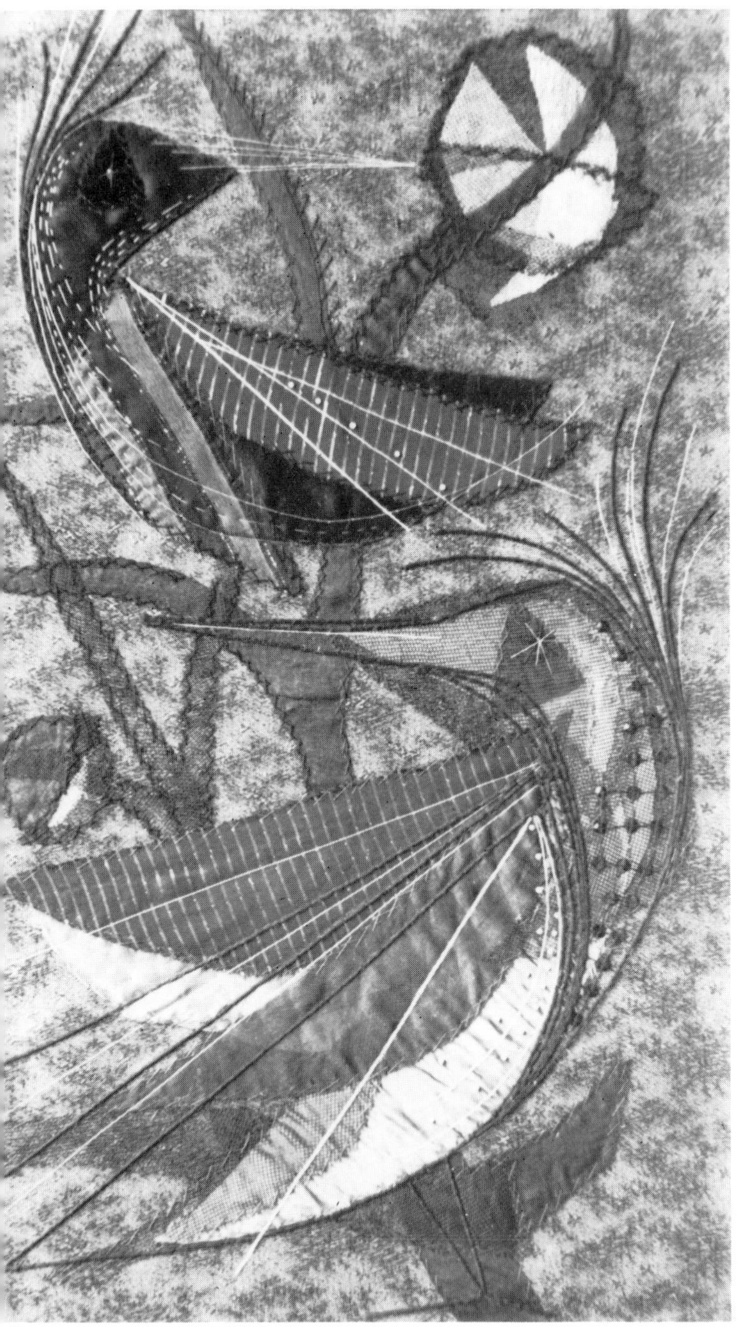

81 Mid 1950s. A student at Goldsmiths' School of Art, London. Appliqué of various fabrics on a textured background. *Goldsmiths' School of Art*

82 Right: 1955. A tea cosy in a shell pattern made of glazed cotton in two shades of grey, lime yellow, pale yellow, bright yellow, dark sage green and lime green. *Needlework Development Scheme. Photograph by Studio Swain*

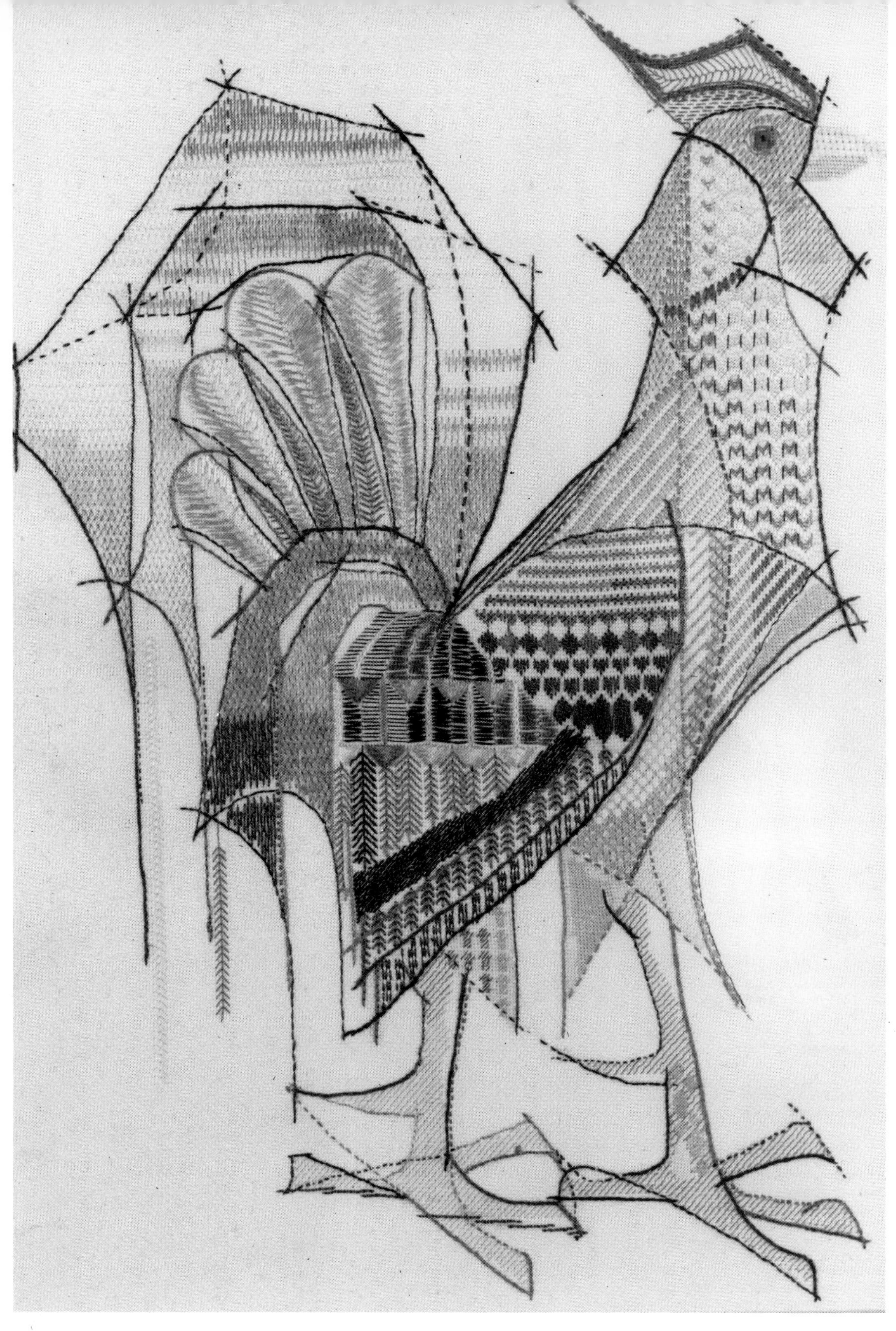

83 Left: Mid-1950s – Alison Liley. *Bird.* A panel $11\frac{1}{2}$ in. × 16 in. (29 cm × 40 cm), white evenweave fabric with darning patterns in a number of colours. Some *petit point* in bright yellow, outlines in brown. *Loaned by the Embroiderers' Guild. Photograph by Nick Nicholson*

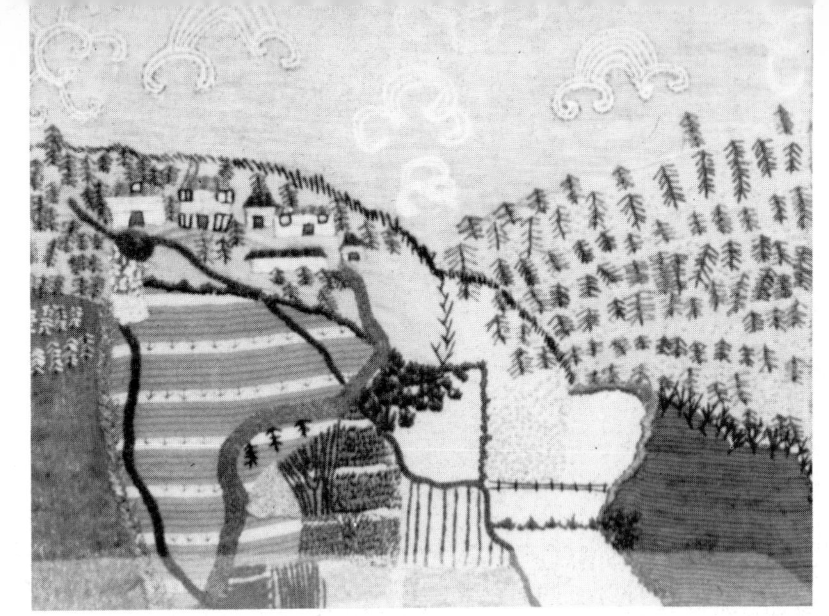

84 Above right: 1955 – Jean Osborn. *Landscape.* An embroidery 10 in. × 8 in. (25 cm × 20 cm), based on a linear drawing. In mixed fabrics including organdie for the sky, striped silk, cottons and organza, with stem stitch, french knots, whipped running and other stitches. Age between 11 and 12 years old, a pupil at Friends' School, Saffron Walden, Essex. Taught by Joan Archer

85 Right: 1955 – Susan Jones. *Swan.* A panel 11 in. × 9 in. (27.5 cm × 22.5 cm), in which the swan was worked separately and the background worked afterwards. The swan is in white silk and fine velvet with grey and white stitching on a background of grey organdie over white fabric. Various colours are used for the stitching. Age 14 years: a pupil at Friends' School, Saffron Walden, Essex

86 1955 – Bridget Moss. Party table cloth, 50 in. × 50 in. (125 cm × 125 cm). On green furnishing moygashel, embroidered in cream and red stranded cotton. The legend reads 'this table cloth belongs to Maria-Christoffel-Mathis who lives at the Geisstafel Conters, in Prätigau, Graubünden, Switzerland with her husband Christian and her children Leni, Hitsch, Dorli, Regina and Johannes. It was worked by her English friend Bridget Moss in the year 1955'. *Photograph by Reto Reinhardt-Chur*

87 Detail of party table cloth

88 Below: Mid-1950s – Constance Howard. A panel, 20 in. × 16 in. (51 cm × 41 cm), on a red woollen ground. The shapes of the garments are applied in pink, yellow, purple and cream woollen fabrics. Black hand-couched outlines in stranded cotton. Skipping rope in blue and white. *Leicestershire Education Authorities*

89 Left: Mid-1950s – Constance Howard. *The Beach.* Applied cotton fabrics on a woollen background. Dark tan, white, pale pink, with subtle pinks, greys and other colours for the stones and background hand stitching. Black and white machine stitching for outlines

90 Mid-1950s – Diana Lumb (nee Thompson), a student on the ATC course at Goldsmiths' School of Art. She already had the NDD in painting but returned in the evenings to work for the NDD in embroidery. Two small canvas panels, each approximately $6\frac{1}{2}$ in. (16.5 cm) square. The *Portrait*, a white figure with a pink face, is on a dark ground of canvas stitches. The *Mexican* has a light background with a dark blue-grey horse, with the ground in red and yellow

91 Below: 1957 – Jeanne Mount. *Henry's Book.* A rag book on natural linen in fine hand stitching in many colours. The front of the book is embroidered with birds, the back with insects. It folds or stands up

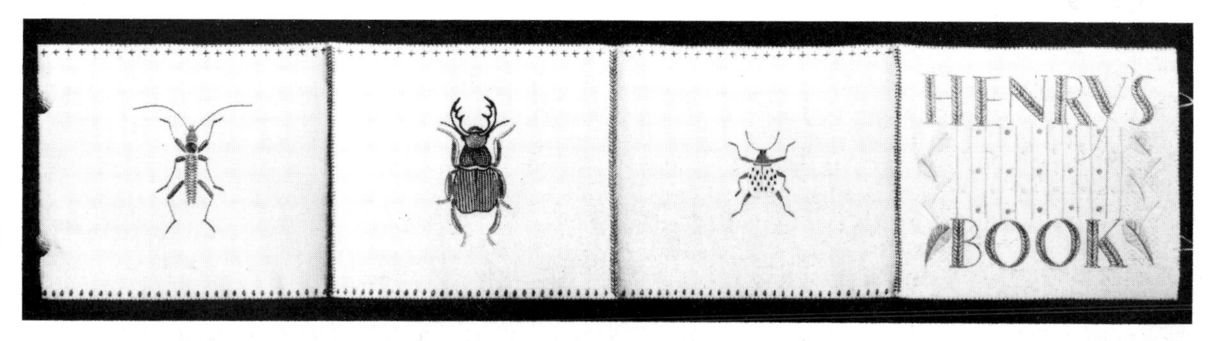

92 Mid-1950s. A cushion cover, machine stitching with pompons. Black on black-and-white bed ticking. *Needlework Development Scheme*

93 Mid-1950s – Lilia Speir. *Bird Woman*, on a background of dull pinks and bronze. The figure contains white satin, lace, muslin, organdie and net with shadows in black organdie. Pink and white feathers with white stitching

94 Right: 1957 – Norman Hartnell. State evening dress in ivory satin, embroidered in pearls, beads and gold thread. Flowers of the field of France and bees of Napoleon are in the design. The dress was worn by HM Queen Elizabeth II on her State Visit to Paris in 1957. *Victoria and Albert Museum, London*

95 1957 – Elizabeth Geddes' green bedspread with a design of roses in pink is based on a drawing by Robert Addington. The ground is dark almond green ribbed rayon, with bands of dull turquoise satin. ***Made for the Needlework Development Scheme and exhibited at the Tea Centre in 1957***

96 1957 – Elizabeth Geddes. A detail of the rose bedspread, exhibited at the NDS exhibition in 1957. Surface stitchery, appliqué on silk fabric. ***Made for the Needlework Development Scheme. Photograph by Studio Swain***

97 1957 *Left:* a drawing by Helen Stravens in inks. *Below left:* an embroidered adaptation by Elizabeth Geddes for the Needlework Development Scheme, in surface stitchery, including chain, backstitch, split stitch and french knots

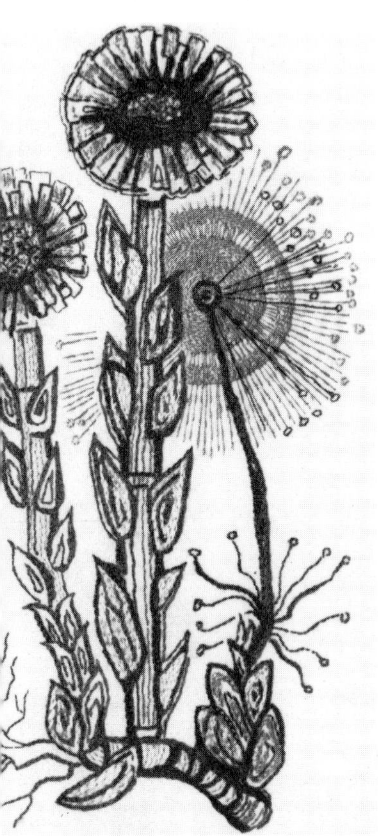

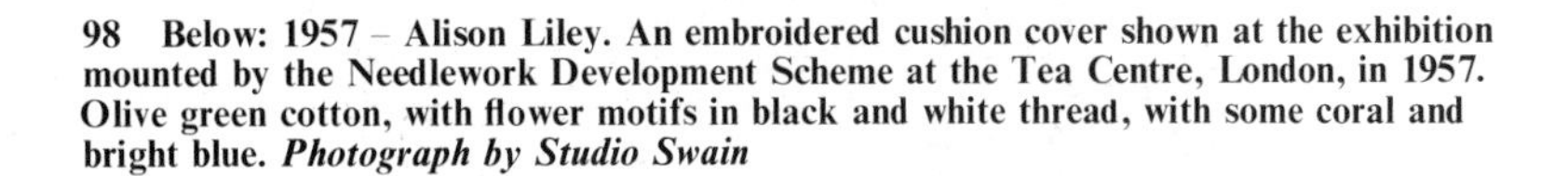

98 Below: 1957 – Alison Liley. An embroidered cushion cover shown at the exhibition mounted by the Needlework Development Scheme at the Tea Centre, London, in 1957. Olive green cotton, with flower motifs in black and white thread, with some coral and bright blue. *Photograph by Studio Swain*

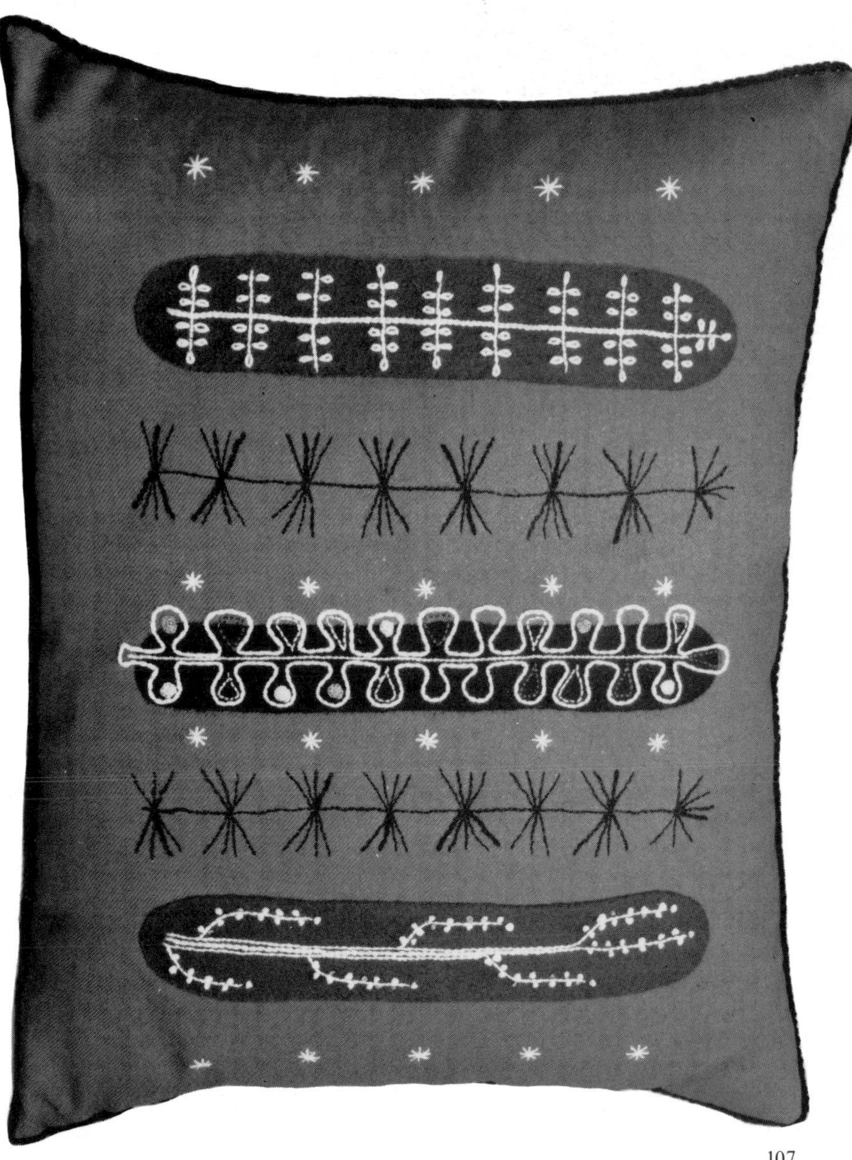

99 1958. A panel worked at the Mary Boon Secondary School by Leslie Sillitoe, one of the prize-winning entries in the Embroiders' Guild's Senior Schools Challenge Cup of 1959. The panel is worked on grey felt in appliqué. Grey, turquoise, white, black and gold are the main colours. Applied darned net, felt and satin, gold thread and stitching give a good balance of colour and design. The piece won a book token, this being the prize for colour and design

100 1958 – Rosalind Floyd. *Head of a Girl.* A panel, approximately 12 in. (30 cm) square, in appliqué and hand stitching on a mauvish brown ground. The arms are embroidered, the roses in relief in swathed white organdie. The dress is black, stitched in white

101 Above right: 1957–58. Kneeler in St Clement Danes Church. Designed by Sampson Lloyd and worked by Mrs Christopher Green. The background fabric is a blue-green woollen serge. The white central cross encloses a 'star' cross in gold, the whole surrounded by a crimson Crown of Thorns. Scrolling forms in gold, lime, grey and white, spread on either side of the central motif. At each end medallion-like forms contain emblems connected with the church. One of the three kneelers for the altar rails, 25 ft × 13 in. (7.6 m × 33 cm), and slightly curved

102 Right: 1957 – Beryl Dean. *Showboat.* A panel on mauve reversible satin, the central oval worked on the reverse side of the fabric. The idea is an interpretation of stump work as the design is slightly raised from the background. The panel is in black and white. Other fabrics used are felt, black net, ciré ribbon and American cloth

103 Mid 1950s – Edith John designed the hanging *Doncaster* and worked the rectangle containing the church. A student evolved the idea while at Doncaster School of Art, the design was worked out in 1956, the embroidery commencing in 1957. Scenes represent events and places in the history of Doncaster, starting with pre-Roman times, ending in 1953 with the mines. The working of the hanging was a communal effort by a number of students, the design based on Mrs Mason Humble's idea. Mrs John said that the hanging was an early attempt to experiment with stitches. The background is a natural linen twill with white linen borders. Colours are red, white, black, grey, green, blue and a little dull purple, with cotton threads and cotton snarl. *Photograph by Peter Byrne*

104 Right: Latter half 1950s – Laye Andrew, a student on the embroidery course at Goldsmiths' School of Art. A panel submitted for the NDD in a variety of hand-dyed fabrics, mainly organdie with some velvet, in pinks, reds, dull purples with dark green leaves

105 Late 1950s – Penny Mann. A base for a child's tray, to go under glass. Designed and worked by a student taking the Intermediate examination of the Ministry of Education, Goldsmiths' School of Art. Appliqué of satins, chiffon, beads, sequins and hand embroidery in a variety of colours. ***Photograph by Hawkley Studios***

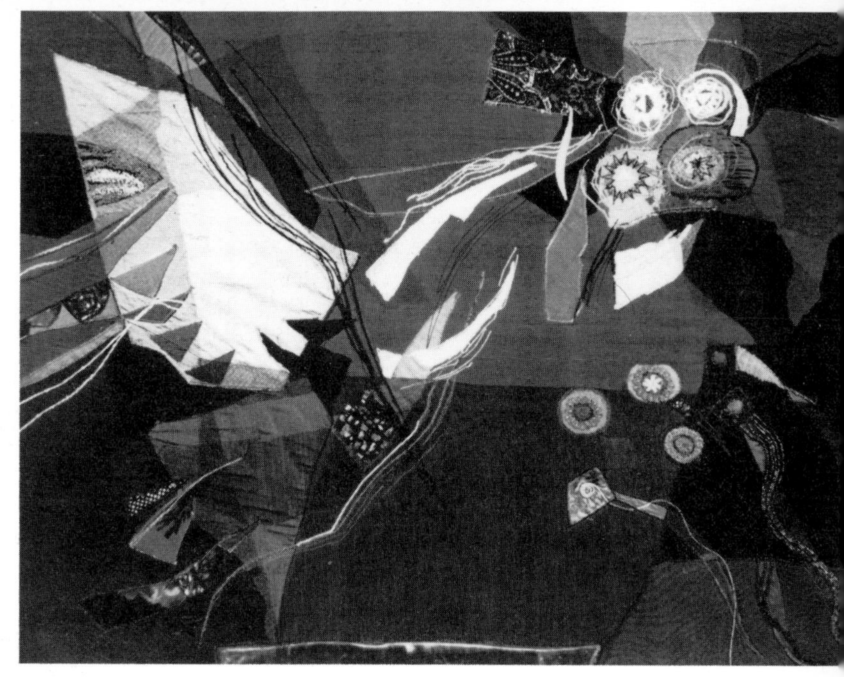

106 Right: 1958 – Lilla Speir. ***Bee's Knees.*** **A panel designed and executed from looking at slides of microscopic images. Appliqué and stitchery in various fabrics and colours**

107 Above right: 1958 – Kathleen Whyte. *Olive Grove*. A panel, $12\frac{1}{2}$ in. × $17\frac{1}{2}$ in. (31.75 cm × 44 cm), in wild silks, rayons and felt on a background of white, handspun cotton, in varying shades of grey-greens, puce, black and grey

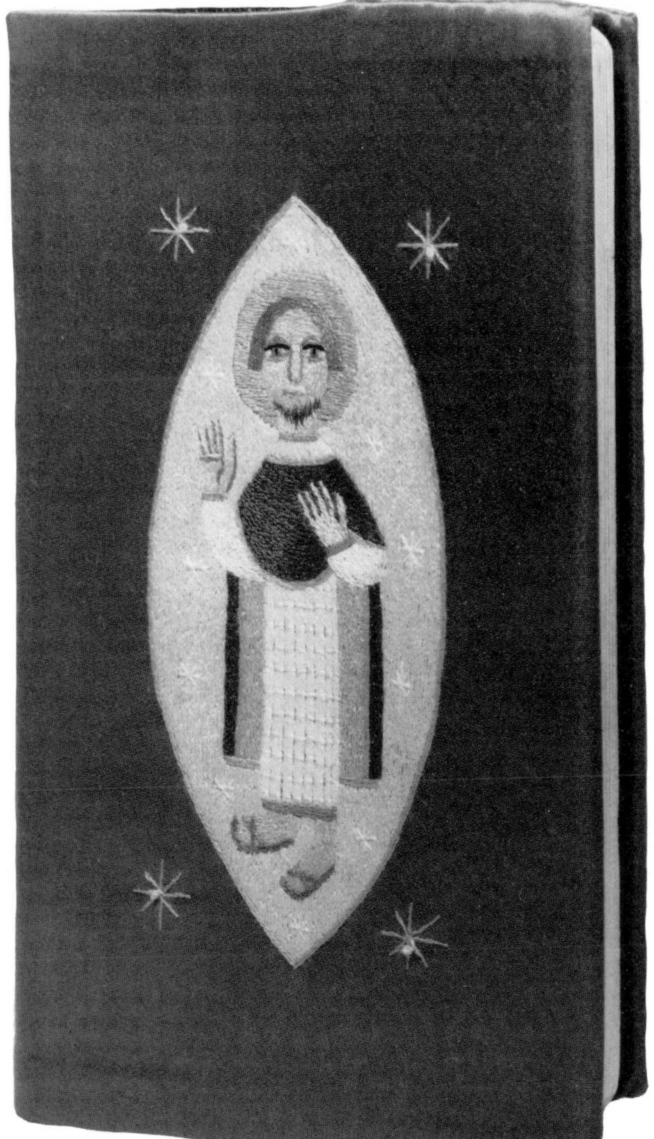

108 Right: 1958 – Joan Nicholson. A book cover, $3\frac{1}{2}$ in. × $6\frac{1}{2}$ in. (9 cm × 16.5 cm), designed by her and worked by A Roscoe. It is in dull pinkish-red satin with the oval in blue. The gown is in cream, the cloak dark turquoise and halo yellow. Solid fine long and short stitching. *Formerly belonged to the NDS. Loaned by the Embroiderers' Guild. Photograph by Nick Nicholson*

109 Right: 1958 – Margaret Treherne. A cope designed and worked by Elizabeth Geddes. It is a Passiontide cope for 'Artists Serve the Chruch' exhibition, later touring the USA in a show entitled 'British Artist Craftsmen' in 1959. The background of the cope is mulberry face cloth, with grey flannel and lurex fabric panels, the grey flannel applied shapes embroidered over with gold lurex material and various woollen threads. Greys, black, white and off-white are the main colours employed. ***Victoria and Albert Museum, London***

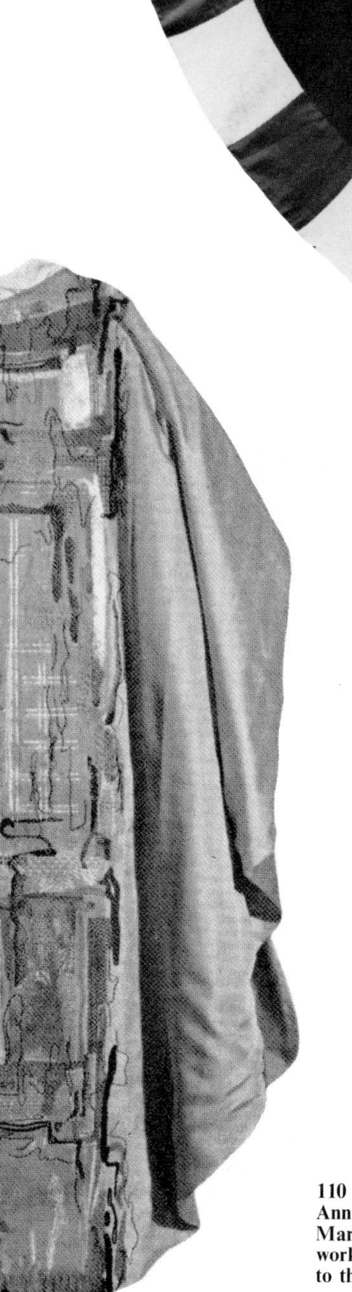

110 Left: 1958–59. A cope designed by Ann Bruce, worked by Edith John and Maria Sim. This was in the collection of work by 'British Artist Craftsmen' sent to the USA in 1959

111 Late 1950s – William Gear and Eirian Short. Torah cover designed by William Gear and freely interpreted by Eirian Short in applied Hebrew letters with hand stitching between. Oranges, pinks and reds with gold and black. *Commissioned for the 'British Artist Craftsmen' exhibition*

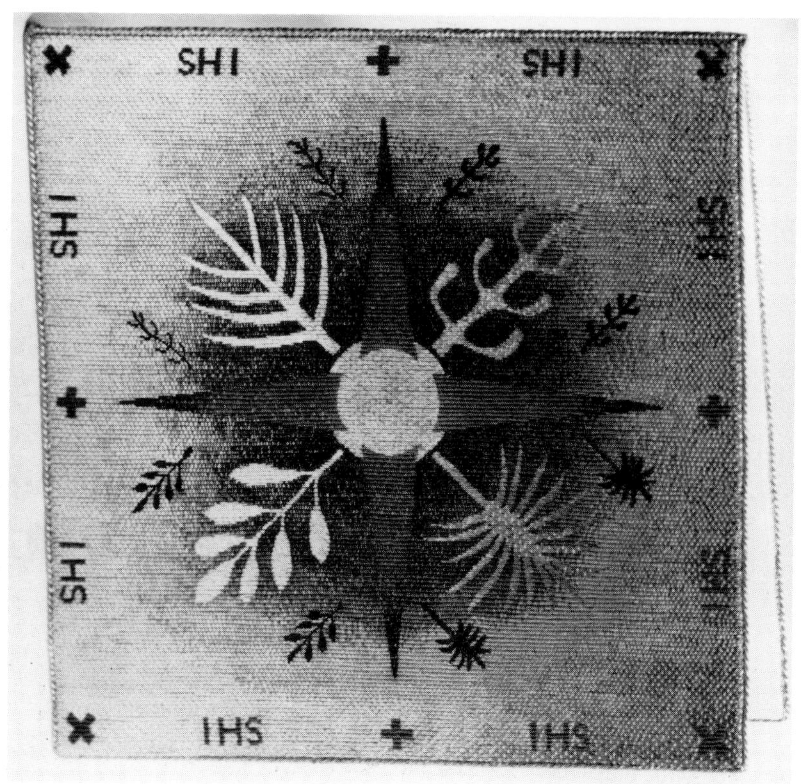

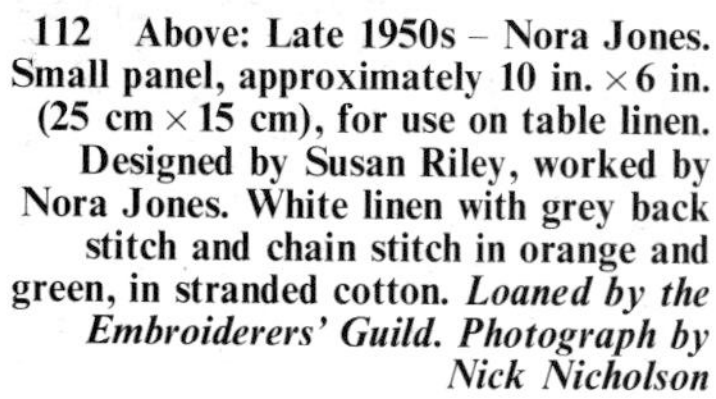
112 Above: Late 1950s – Nora Jones. Small panel, approximately 10 in. × 6 in. (25 cm × 15 cm), for use on table linen. Designed by Susan Riley, worked by Nora Jones. White linen with grey back stitch and chain stitch in orange and green, in stranded cotton. *Loaned by the Embroiderers' Guild. Photograph by Nick Nicholson*

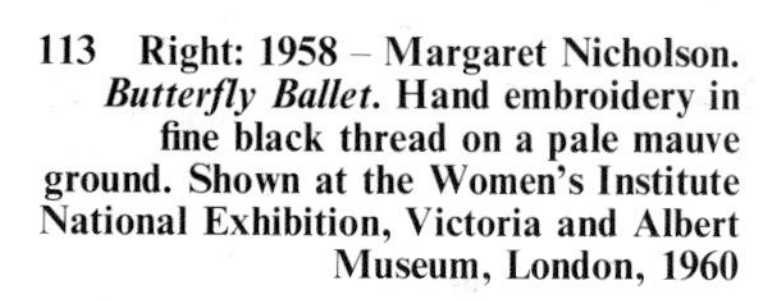
113 Right: 1958 – Margaret Nicholson. *Butterfly Ballet.* Hand embroidery in fine black thread on a pale mauve ground. Shown at the Women's Institute National Exhibition, Victoria and Albert Museum, London, 1960

114 1958 – Sister Kathleen (Snelus). A burse in the *or nué* technique, with a gold thread ground and pattern worked in coloured silks. In the 1958 International Handicrafts Exhibition this work won the first prize of £100

115 Below: 1958 – Robert Stewart. Kneeler designed by him and worked by M Pollock. It is in tent stitch using crewel wools and illustrates a passage from the 23rd Psalm.
Victoria and Albert Museum, London

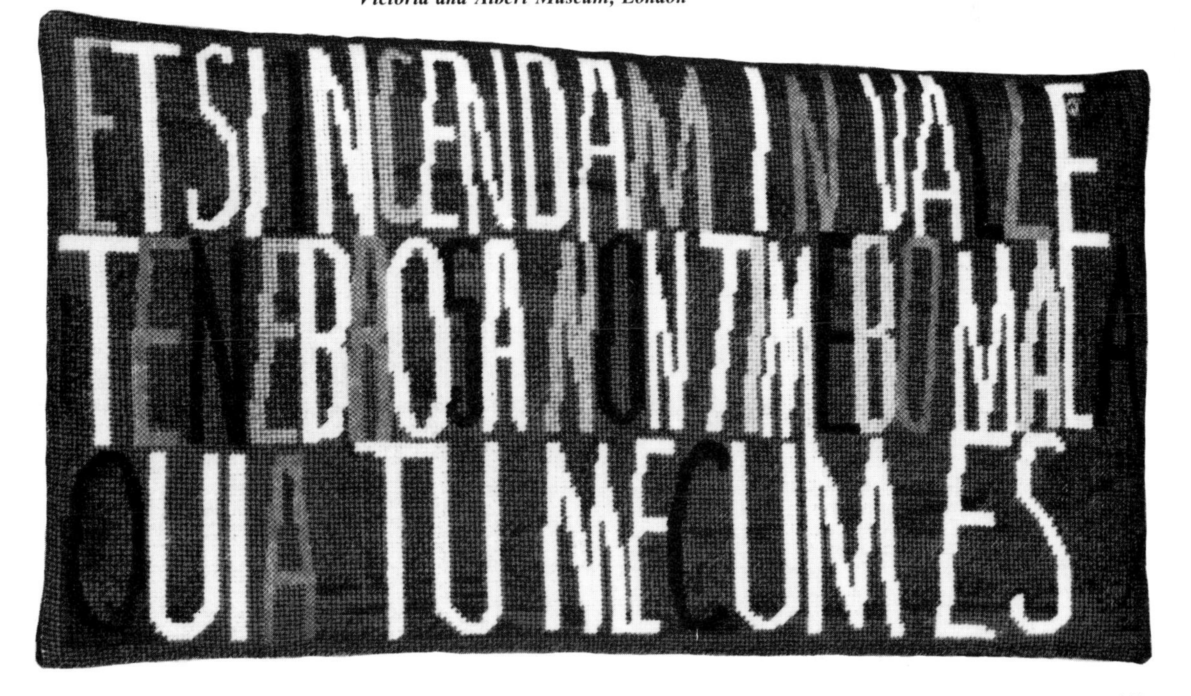

116 1958 – E Kay Norris. *Mother and Child.* A panel, approximately 20 in. (50 cm) high, on dark mulberry fabric, showing a variety of techniques, including patchwork, padding, beading and metal thread embroidery. Among the textures used are reds, cream, dark plum and orange applied fabrics in velvet, satin, cotton

117 Far right: 1958–59 – Constance Howard. Mothers' Union banner designed and worked by Constance Howard, assisted by Kay Norris. The ground is a creamish yellow thick silk with blues, blue-greens, creamish whites and dull pink fabrics applied. Hand stitching in filoselle silks. *Lincoln Cathedral. Photograph by George Tokarski*

118 1958 – Patricia Beese. *Pigeons on a Pavement.* A panel approximately 22 in. high × $18\frac{1}{2}$ in. wide (56 cm × 47 cm). Inlay and padded appliqué using a variety of fabrics including wool, satin, printed cottons, net and nylon organza, with details in hand embroidery and beads. Colours: greys, purples, black, cream and turquoise

119 1959 – Pamela Rooke. Detail of a wedding veil in machine embroidery – white thread on white single and double organza

120 1958–59 – Constance Howard. *Harlequin.* 48 in. × 52 in. (128 cm × 130 cm). The design is developed from a printed Finnish cotton fabric of elongated triangles. Appliqué hand embroidery including couching and running stitches. Colours dull yellows, reds, blues and others. *Was in Rachel McMillan College of Education now at Goldsmiths' School of Art Textile Department. Photograph by Burwoods*

121 Right: Late 1950s – Student, Goldsmiths' School of Art ATC course. A dossal,approximately 5 ft × 2 ft (158 cm × 60 cm), in appliqué in various fabrics, including silks, velvets and chiffons, in contrasting colours

122 1958 – June Tiley. A panel in black, white and subtle colour, using hand and machine stitching

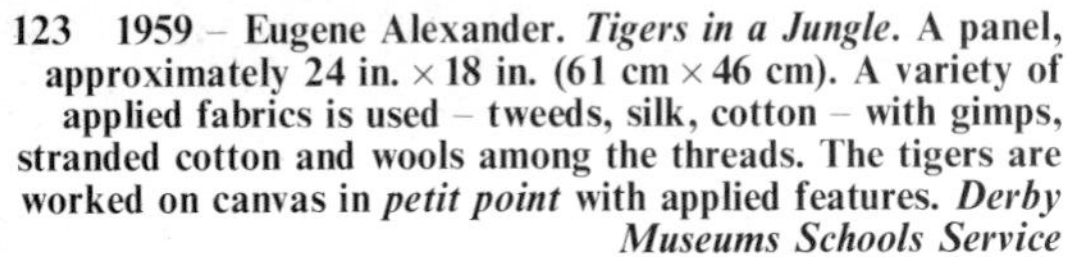
123 1959 – Eugene Alexander. *Tigers in a Jungle.* A panel, approximately 24 in. × 18 in. (61 cm × 46 cm). A variety of applied fabrics is used – tweeds, silk, cotton – with gimps, stranded cotton and wools among the threads. The tigers are worked on canvas in *petit point* with applied features. *Derby Museums Schools Service*

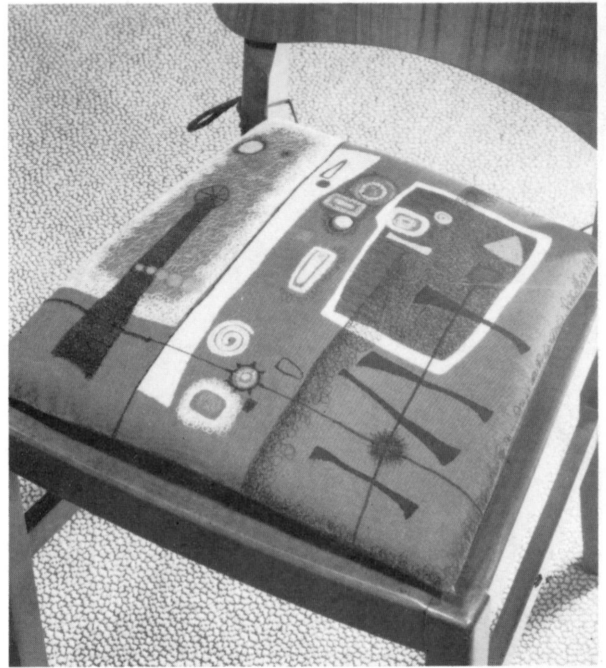

124 Right: 1959 – Eric Lownsback. Designed by him and worked in machine embroidery by Pamela Pavitt. Chair seat in grey with applied fabrics. *Victoria and Albert Museum, London*

125 Far right 1959 – Averil Colby. Blue Diamond Honeycomb Coverlet, 106 in. × 84 in. (265 cm × 210 cm), built on the plan of an eighteenth century example, but modified in pattern to suit a single bed in size. The colour plan was controlled as the scraps for the patches were collected by those who made the coverlet from dress and furnishing cottons mainly in blues. Flowered prints, spotted, striped and checked ginghams in blue, red and pink were selected for the patterns. Dark blue poplin and linens for the dark areas and white linen, calico, piqué, damask and casement made the background area of the coverlet. A number of people worked sections in their own homes. *Photograph by Desmond Tripp Studios*

126 Late 1950s – Susan Riley. *Virgin and Child.* Machine embroidery on a coarse linen ground

127 Right: 1959 – Betty Myerscough. *In the City.* A panel, freely interpreted in appliqué and stitchery, mainly couching

128 Far Right: 1959 – Sylvia Green. *Madonna and Child*, a Mothers' Union banner. Applied blue wild silk, copper coloured silk and crystal nylon, cream nun's veiling and white shantung silk on a gold silk background. Net and open filling stitches give texture. *St Michael's Church, Highgate. Photograph by John Gay*

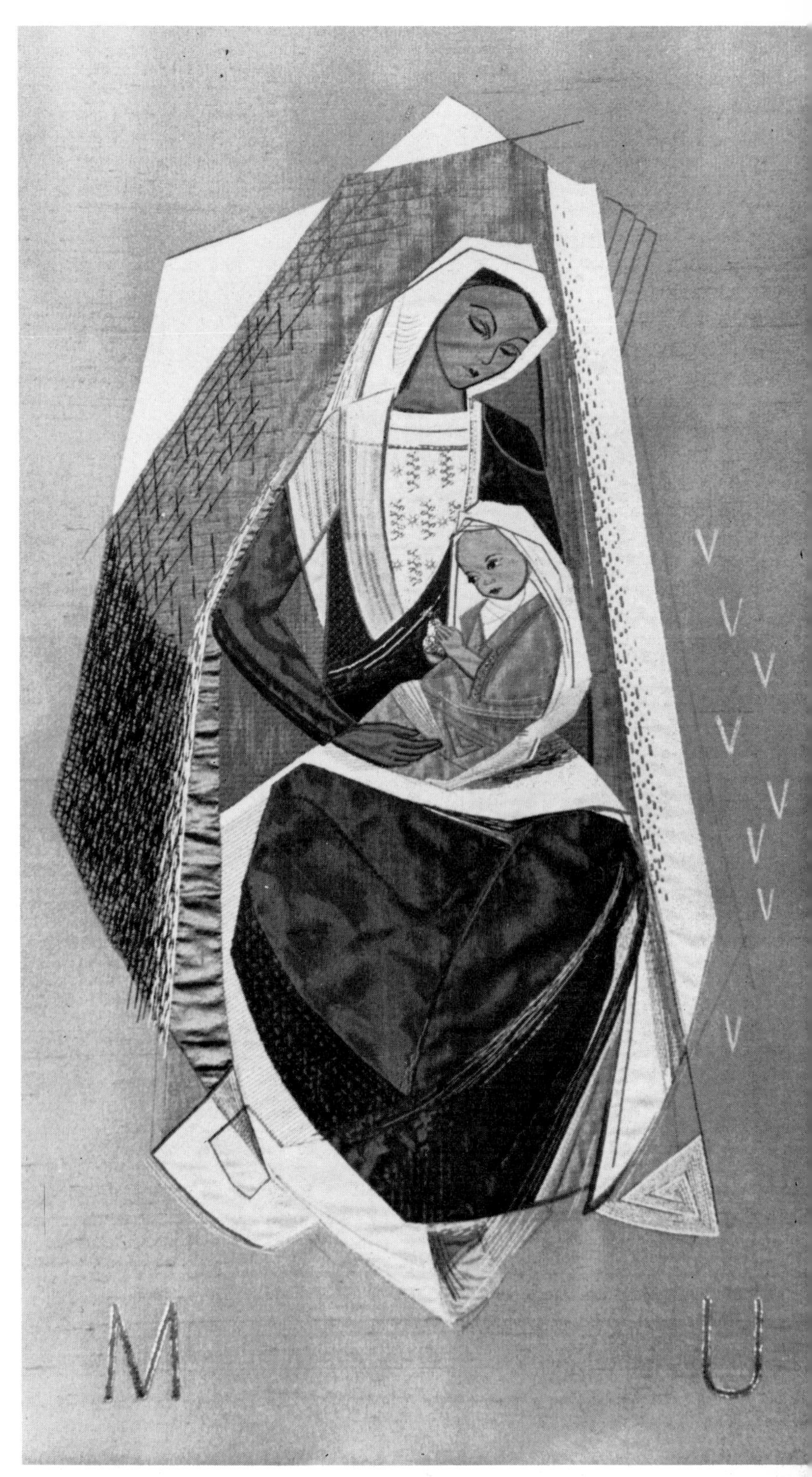
M
U

129 1959 – Lilian Dring. A chasuble, part of a set of green vestments made for Gloucester cathedral, which include the stole, maniple, apparels, burse and chalice veil. Hand and machine stitching, applied fabric of lurex tissue and braids. The back of the chasuble shows symbols of the Chalice and Host, the monogram Alpha and Omega, the Crown of Thorns and the Star of Trinity. A smaller motif decorates the front of the chasuble. The background is a dark, clear emerald fabric made by the Edinburgh Weavers

130 Right: 1960 – Pat Russell. *Capricorn*. A hanging 6 ft × 4 ft (180 cm × 110 cm). The lettering was designed in freely cut paper shapes, arranged to relate to the other design elements. Dates are in Roman numerals. This was the first large hanging made by Pat Russell

CAPRICORN

131 Late 1950s–early 1960s – Maureen Helsdon. Two curtains and the tympanum in Romsey Abbey, Hampshire. These were designed by Maureen Helsdon and worked by both full- and part-time embroidery students at Southampton College of Art. The background is dark violet, with brilliant colours of reds, blues, turquoise and yellows, that give a jewel-like effect, the idea being to obtain a feeling of the quailities of stained glass. Appliqué with hand and machine embroidery. Consecrated October 1963. 13 ft 6 in. × 7 ft 6 in. (4 m × 2.3 m), they are approximately the height and width of the Norman arch. *Romsey Abbey*

132 Late 1950s – Student, one of the men on the ATC course at Goldsmiths' School of Art. The panel, approximately 36 in × 28 in. (90 cm × 70 cm), is in applied fabrics, mainly reds, pinks and several greens, blue green and pale turquoise. Hand and machine stitching

133 1959–60 – Student, one of the men on the ATC course at Goldsmiths' School of Art. *A Woman Hanging out Her Washing*. A panel in appliqué, in plain and patterned fabrics, the design now tending to abstraction

134 1959–64 – Constance Howard, designer, Mrs V Carnegy, embroiderer. A seat cushion for the lower master for Eton College Chapel, showing the Arms of Winchester College and New College, Oxford, flanked by those of Eton College and King's College, Cambridge (representing the 'Amicabilis Concordia' between the four colleges: the tree is intended to suggest that King Henry VI based the scheme of his foundations on the earlier foundations of William of Wykeham). *Booklet on the Eton College Chapel Embroidery Scheme*

135 1959–64 – Elizabeth Andrews, MSIA. A Seat cushion for Eton College Chapel. All the substalls designed by Elizabeth Andrews, depicting the emblems of the four evangelists. St John and the eagle worked by Miss P Jacobson in brilliant reds and golds with shades of green. *Embroidery*, Summer 1964

The early Sixties

General trends

The early sixties continued with the rebellion and anarchy of the fifties. The social climate was geared to the young who had 'money to burn' and were full of ideas and eager to try them out. Permissiveness increased. Interest in pop music was encouraged by the Beatles who dominated the scene from 1961. Foreign films were popular; Italian, French and Japanese among others, many of which influenced British producers. This was a time for young people, many of whom possessed a great deal of talent. Among these were David Hockney, Peter Blake and Alan Jones all painters, as well as young dress designers such as Zandra Rhodes and Jean Muir, all from the Royal College of Art. Mary Quant opened another shop in Knightsbridge, some people crediting her with the introduction of the mini-skirt. Jeans became a kind of uniform, worn by both sexes and all ages, during the sixties although they had first been seen around 1946. The tee-shirt, too, became a symbol of youth with amusing mottoes printed on it, becoming universal wear by the seventies. High boots became the rage from this decade onwards and a fashion feature both in winter and summer. The *couture* houses began to decline with a lack of custom, while small boutques sprang up like mushrooms. Biba, in London, a large edition of the boutique-like shop, became well known for its cheap, trendy clothes.

The conventions and conservatism of the fifties were disregarded in favour of greater licence in behaviour and in fashion and by the end of the decade anyone could wear anything. As time advanced during the decade, beaded twenties' dresses became fashionable, and all kinds of garments of earlier times were re-appearing, including military and other uniforms, bought in street markets, second-hand clothes' shops, and later in those that began to specialise in old uniforms. Long hair for men was 'in', the 'hippy' and ethnic look was beginning in the early sixties and by the end of the decade, the sheepskin coats embroidered in silk and metal threads, from Morocco and Afghanistan, were favourites of the young. Ethnic garments with their richly embroidered embellishments were brought back from India, Morocco, Afghanistan and other places by the 'flower-power' wanderers, the hippies, who could not fit in with life in their own environments. The kaftan, originally from Morocco, became almost a uniform but was a simple garment suited to decoration with embroidery. Lavishly worked bodices and skirts, both old and new, from India, scintillating with mirror glass were seen later on in the boutiques that sold a medly of garments and knick-knacks from abroad. Embroidery was cut from some garments and re-applied to others, often styles being mixed as they came from different areas. These clothes with long skirts were worn by the young during the day, in fact long or short skirts were acceptable for any occasion.

In comparison with the rather rigid geometrically patterned space-type garments of the mid-sixties, the romantic nomad style appeared rich and colourful. Towards the end of the sixties a mixture of pattern with pattern was seen everywhere and Great Britain became a fashion centre where a motley collection of every style and type of garment might be worn. Embroidered clothes, patterned fabrics and a layered look with one garment worn over another, each of a different length, were favoured by the young.

Gawthorpe Hall

At this time, Gawthorpe Hall with its collection of embroidery and lace from all over the world, and a good library, was offered to the National Trust. The intention was that it would be a centre for study and research, also for courses on embroidery and lace, and for periodic exhibitions of historic examples and a variety of textiles from the collection.

Interest in embroidery increases

Events in the sixties that furthered the general interest in embroidery were the Diamond Jubilee Exhibition of the Embroiderers' Guild, with its special issue of *Embroidery*, in 1966, and the exhibition of ecclesiastical embroidery in the crypt of St Paul's Cathedral in 1968. Perhaps the most significant development that raised the standards of embroidery considerably during the decade was the introduction of the National Diploma in Art and Design, giving a greater freedom in planning their own courses in selected colleges of art and the polytechnics with art and design departments. This allowed for more individuality than the examination for the National Diploma in Design, which was previously taken by the students in the colleges and had a set syllabus with set examinations for the whole country and although sound, was restricted in outlook.

It is difficult to see the 'wood for the trees' the nearer we are to our own time, but I would say that embroidery in the sixties developed more rapidly than at any time since the Second World War. Apart from the new examinations – several other factors contributed to this: the inclusion of embroidery in various educational establishments, which created a wider interest in the subject; the manufacture of many more materials; and the formation of new groups of embroiderers, such as the '62 Group in February 1962 and in 1968 the New Embroidery Group. The Embroiderers' Guild ran courses and classes which were well attended, part-time adult classes were sponsored by local education authorities, while exhibitions of embroidery appeared to cause great interest, even controversy, with the emergence of abstraction in design and a greater freedom in the use of mixed media. Ecclesiastical embroidery was becoming popular in colleges of art among both full-time and part-time students, as well as in other educational establishments where embroidery was studied.

Machine embroidery

Machine embroidery continued to horrify some of the traditionalists but was firmly established in the colleges of art, and **Jennifer Gray** organised an exhibition in Kingston-upon-Hull at the Ferens Art Gallery in the autumn of 1959. She was one of those showing embroidery in the Gallery, the majority of items being machine stitched, although hand and machine techniques were sometimes mixed in one piece of work. The exhibition was to demonstrate the use of the domestic sewing machine for embroidery and to show ways in which many different materials could be employed. Jennifer Gray emphasised the possibilities of embroidery for walls and hoped through the exhibition to create interest in the free interpretation of design by machine embroidery.

More articles appeared on machine embroidery; Margaret Nicholson writing on design for hand and machine techniques stressed that in design 'contrast is the essence'. She said in her article (*Embroidery*, summer 1961) that '. . . there is a sincere desire that embroidery should not merely survive, but should take its rightful place in our artistic life . . . as it did in medieval times. Women's organisations everywhere are showing an increasing interest in how they may achieve a more creative approach to embroidery'.

Pamela Pavitt commenced a series of four articles on 'Machine Embroidery for the Home' for *Embroidery* magazine (spring, summer, autumn and winter, 1960) in which she says 'machine embroidery is not just imitating hand work by the use of a machine; it is using a mechanical needle which is guided by hand. . . . I feel one should explore the natural techniques of the machine, rather than force the machine to slavishly imitate something which is far better done by hand'.

Betty Frazer also wrote some articles on machine techniques, 'Creative Experiments by Machine' (*Embroidery*, spring 1961) and 'Machine Embroidery and Handwork' (*Embroidery*, summer 1961), in which she gave instructions on combining hand and machine techniques. She said that 'machine embroidery should never try to imitate hand embroidery nor should designs for hand embroidery be used'.

Hammersmith College of Art and Building

Embroidery at the Hammersmith College of Art and Building in the early sixties produced a distinctive style consisting of fine lines of straight stitching, mainly curved and creating movement by their swirling character. These lines were often in black thread alone, or used for stitching down applied shapes in a variety of fabrics and bright colours. Heavy, hand-couched outlines in black rug wool were seen too, similar to the leading in stained glass.

Ecclesiastical embroidery

Large hangings, banners and embroidered copes incorporating machine and hand stitching, altar frontals and throw-overs, burses and veils, stoles, in fact all types of ecclesiastical work became popular as articles for embellishment during the early sixties. A continuing demand for classes in ecclesiastical embroidery and a growing interest in gold work and all things ecclesiastical, increased in the sixties in colleges of art and among groups of embroiderers conserving or working new textiles for the Church. The clergy became interested, too, having been exposed to Beryl Dean's pioneering work. This interest led to a fresh approach and a broader attitude to ecclesiastical embroidery. The Church began to give more commissions than previously to artists working with fabrics, also to some students. Margaret Kaye carried out work for the Church during this time (175); I designed and worked embroidery for Lincoln Cathedral, and Beryl Dean continued to carry out work (156–158), and wrote another book on Church embroidery. A reappraisal in the designing of vestments and furnishings, a less restrictive use of colour and symbolism and a great use of metal threads, gold kid and even synthetic metal threads and plastic 'kid' appeared. Non-traditional materials, perhaps sometimes unsuitable, were employed instead of the usual brocades and damasks associated with Church embroidery. Nets, chiffons, beads and plastic fabrics were used for experiments in promoting new approaches to a wide subject.

Among artists beginning to specialise in designing for ecclesiastical textiles during the sixties was **Pat Russell**, originally a calligrapher, who started to design and execute works in appliqué with machine stitching. She was versatile in her choice of subjects and in her scale of work, from small panels to hangings of several feet in height. In the summer of 1960 she showed a number of embroideries at the Crafts Centre, mainly in machine embroidery.

Later she produced ecclesiastical vestments and furnishings, incorporating lettering in some of this work (155, 173 and colour plate 9) and since then has designed and made a great many vestments, frontals, stoles and banners, but has never professed to be an embroiderer as she uses the machine mainly to stitch down the applied fabrics and to emphasise linear forms. Her design is varied in concept; it is sometimes geometric, sometimes large patchwork, with a sense of scale appropriate to the buildings for which she is designing.

Communal projects for the Church

At Hammersmith College of Art and Building, students in Beryl Dean's part-time ecclesiastical embroidery classes continued to work on the cope begun in 1958, designed by Susan Riley. The design contained figures of martyrs, saints and angels arranged in a more or less semi-circular pattern in three rows. Machine and fine hand embroidery were combined, some of the figures were worked by machine and then applied to the background and further decorated with hand embroidery.

Another project was being carried out by students in the embroidery department of Southampton College of Art. This was for curtains for the Great West Door of Romsey Abbey, designed by Maureen Helsdon, worked by full- and part-time students (131). As the architecture was of the Norman period, she gave to the figures a Romanesque style. There were 12 of these, each of which were in hand and machine stitching by a different student. The curtains were completed within a year but the tympanum was worked later, all the embroidery being finished by 1963.

Design sources

Designs for ecclesiastical vestments and furnishings were often a combination of geometric and symbolic forms, but those embroiderers working small panels or decorating dress with metal threads, sometimes incorporating gold or silver kid, developed ideas from plants, particularly from bark, which became a favourite source of design for a number of years. The roughness of much of the bark led to more textured embroidery in heavier threads than the usual cottons and silks. Stitches were piled up over one another to give depth. Colours were usually dull, in dirty brownish-greens, blacks and browns with dirty brownish-pinks to give relief.

Design based on cellular structures was seen towards the middle of the decade; this subject lasted well into the seventies among some amateur embroiderers. Growths of small shapes were built up to larger structures, similar to holes seen in sponges. Exploded forms, with ray-like shapes shooting from central or near central points were carried out on a small scale with stitchery, beads and sequins, on a larger scale in appliqué again with stitches, beads and sequins. Overlapping circles, circles, circles within circles and parts of circles, in outline, in appliqué and embroidery, were also favourite motifs, possibly a development of the cellular structures. Cardboard tubing of 1 in. to 3 or 4 in. (2.5 cm to 7.6 or 10 cm) in diameter and from $\frac{1}{2}$ in. (13 mm) to several inches (centimetres) in depth was covered in wool, raffia and other kinds of thread then stuck or sewn to background fabrics, also embroidered, the aim being to integrate the tubes with the stitchery. The idea continued to be used in schools long after its inception in adult education. Figurative subjects were still a source of design, although the abstract and geometric styles were predominant during the 1960s.

People were becoming more design conscious now and I gave a series of three talks in the Victoria and Albert Museum to members of the National Federation of Women's Institutes. These were entitled 'Gathering ideas for Embroidery', and members came from different parts of the country to study historic examples of crafts in various sections of the Museum. They made notes with sketches suitable for design ideas for embroidery, the lectures and the practical study creating a great deal of enthusiasm once the students found out 'how to look'. (*Home and Country* magazine, November 1960.)

The Embroiderers' Guild

The Embroiderers' Guild acquired new premises in 1960, which enabled them to re-house their collection of historic examples, to put their library into less cramped quarters and to have space for lectures and the displaying of small exhibitions.

Kathleen Harris retired at this time from her editorship of *Embroidery*. Enid Jackson, and later, Nora Jones with a small committee took over the editorship of the magazine.

Embroiderers' Guild exhibition 1961

In June 1961 the Embroiderers' Guild mounted a major exhibition at the premises of the Royal Watercolour Society. This received mixed reviews and was said to be overcrowded from lack of rigorous selection, with poor layout, although some interesting work by schools and well-known embroiderers was shown, with hangings and framed pieces using hand and machine embroidery. Design appeared less pictorial in these but more so in banners and panels for the Church. Beryl Dean showed among other articles, a banner; some of her students also showed work, Sister Kathleen's being outstanding (164). Alison Liley exhibited a highly stylised panel with many fine black lines enclosing darning and pulled work patterns (163), and Margaret Nicholson showed an angel, finely worked in machine embroidery (colour plate 8); Kay Norris showed a hand-embroidered pulpit fall with a sunburst. Several well-known embroiderers wrote comments on particular sections of the exhibition (*Embroidery*, autumn 1961).

Other exhibitions

In July 1961 the American Museum in Bath, Claverton Manor, opened with a superb collection of traditional patchwork quilts on exhibition.

An exhibition at Messrs Foyles in London, 'The Materialists' exhibition shown in 1962, was by a group from Goldsmiths' School of Art, both past and present students with a few staff. A review of the show said that it was 'stimulating and controversial' with a wide range of work. Both hand and machine embroidery were represented and although the show was small the individuality of each exhibitor's work was noticeable, showing the possibilities for 'original and creative embroidery'; it was also a reminder that finish and presentation were a part of a piece of work. Among the exhibitors, Eirian Short showed *The Wave* (165), Marjorie Kostenz's work was vigorous, while I exhibited two fish panels, one in gold kid and beads, the other in heavy black stitching with appliqué in small pieces of blue and green fabrics (illustrated in *Inspiration for Embroidery*).

Embroidery and Education

The National Diploma in Design continued until 1965 for those few students who had passed the Intermediate examination in 1963, its last year. The City and Guilds of London Institute examinations continued to be held in a number of centres. The Embroiderers' Guild was given permission to hold evening classes by the London County Council, and evening classes in schools of art, for part-time adult students, continued to expand as did part-time day classes and embroidery in schools, encouraged by the Challenge Cups and other competitions fostered by the Embroiderers' Guild. Exhibitions of embroidery were usually on show at the end of the summer term in colleges of art, colleges of education and further education establishments and were well attended, as the craft continued to cause considerable interest. An exhibition that had been established in the early years of the examination for the National Diploma in Design was held in London in September each year, sponsored by the Ministry of Education; it showed the best examples of work produced at all levels during the current tests. This show was a major event for both teachers and students, giving them some idea of the standards of art and design throughout the country, prevalent trends, different approaches by colleges of art and sometimes new ideas. A selection of work from these exhibitions was shown later in the provinces. With the demise of the NDD examinations, this exhibition ended.

The Royal School of Needlework

When the Royal School of Needlework closed its Diploma course in 1961, a two-year apprenticeship training was started. The scheme was for 16- to 18-year-old students, no special ability being required although drawing skill was an asset. The course was planned for those keen on embroidery to learn and to understand the many kinds of stitchery and their application to a standard of workmanship for which the school had become known. The article says that 'An apprentice does what she is told and in the first six weeks spends four days a week on set samplers, after the six weeks, two days, and if she wishes, may spend one day a week at the London College of Fashion, to learn a different approach to design and embroidery. The City and Guilds of London Institute Examination Part I in embroidery could be taken at the end of the two years. Museum visits once in two weeks with visiting lecturers have been included recently. The course takes forty weeks, the remaining time being spent in the workrooms. A certificate with two grades of efficiency is given at the end, the aim of the training to go into the workroom'. (*Embroidery*, Volume 29, summer)

The Needlework Development Scheme

In 1961 the Needlework Development Scheme was discontinued, having had a considerable influence on embroidery in education. Dorothy Allsopp said that 'it had set standards for all interested in the craft of embroidery, whether a beginner or an accomplished artist, and that others . . . must make quite sure that embroidery takes its place . . . with the major crafts of our time'.

Until its closure, Iris Hills continued as 'expert in charge' of the Scheme, developing more ideas, arranging educative exhibitions and generally promoting the craft of embroidery throughout Great Britain.

Elizabeth Grace Thomson retired from her post with the Inner London Education Authority and Dorothy Allsopp, in 1961, took her place and became an Inspector of Further and Higher Education (Fashion and Creative Studies) for the Inner London Education Authority. Her post of Senior Lecturer in charge of fashion, embroidery and textiles at the Hammersmith College of Art and Building, now vacant, was filled by Iris Hills, who stayed until she joined the Inspectorate with Dorothy Allsopp.

Dress

An article on dress embroidery in 1963 (*Embroidery*, Volume 114, spring) says that 'the couturiers are using rich embroidery, mainly beads on their evening garments – small closely crowded bead patterns, almost geometric are fashionable, flowers and foliage are not fashionable. Mr Lock designs many motifs, at present a honey-comb effect of silver thread, worked on the Cornely machine with continental beads and jewels hand sewn in between. Norman Hartnell also uses similar ideas with paillettes and for the Queen's tours many garments are very richly embroidered with beads and jewels'.

Stanley Lock now designed embroidery and beading for television plays, for the decoration of garments produced for well-known personalities, and continued with his design for stage and screen costumes as well as for the *couture* houses.

The '62 Group

The '62 Group was established in February 1962, the idea for this group having been thought out by Alison Liley and Jennifer Gray, who were responsible for its formation. They, with a number of other people, were concerned 'at the number of young talented embroiderers who left embroidery almost as soon as they were qualified' and the aim of the Group was to bring professionalism into the creative side of embroidery. In their first year five main objectives were set, all to further 'the image of embroidery and to bring it to the notice of as many people and interested bodies, as possible'. The Group held its first exhibition in February 1963 at the Embroiderers' Guild, under whose aegis it was causing much interest. A variety of styles, techniques and subject matter was shown, mainly pictorial, with the emphasis on machine embroidery. Paillettes, glass buttons, nets, hessian and other materials were used and pages from sketch books contributed to this exhibition.

Embroiderers in the early sixties

The sixties produced a number of embroiderers who contributed to the liveliness and advancement of the craft. Among these were several who started to teach in and around 1960, full time and part time, in colleges of art, in adult education and further education. Each continued to develop her own work too, in most cases having attended a college of art for a period.

Alison Barrell taught in a comprehensive school, having developed her interest in embroidery on the ATC course. She continued to embroider in evening classes, carrying out experimental pieces in mixed media, using beads, found objects and various techniques in early works (187).

Patricia Foulds taught at Bourneville School of Art, where she was in charge of printed textiles and weaving. Later she obtained a post in the West of England College of Art (now Bristol Polytechnic), which she built up from an almost non-existent embroidery department, developing decoration for dress. This was of particular interest to her as many of the students in the textile department were on fashion courses. She worked also with the ATD students, which provided her with a secondary interest related to education. She continued with her own embroidery, sometimes for ecclesiastical purposes, sometimes for secular ones.

Elspeth Crawford lectured at Grays School of Art, Aberdeen, in both embroidery and weaving. She produced hand embroidery and machine appliqué which was influenced by primitive and peasant examples (161). She also painted.

Leslie Miller who trained in Glasgow School of Art started to teach too, going as far as the Orkney Islands.

E Kay Norris who had embroidered for some time taught part time in several posts, taking charge of and building up embroidery at Chippenham Technical College, Wiltshire from 1960; eventually instituting and organising a College Diploma in embroidery. She continued to carry out her own work and also assisted Constance Howard part time, on commissions. See also figures 28 and 116.

Beryl Chapman did not teach and was originally a wood-engraver and illustrator. She became interested in embroidery in 1960, starting to exhibit in 1963. Her former interest in the work of Vasarely, with his permutations of colour and illusions of three dimensions led to her geometric design. She obtained three-dimensional effects with appliqué and hand stitchery (154).

Moyra McNeill continued to work on her own while teaching in several places part time. She produced many types of embroidery including canvas work as shown in figure 180.

In 1962 **Gay Swift** was teaching embroidery in Harrogate School of Art, while in 1963 **Joan Cleaver** was appointed to take charge of embroidery in the Birmingham College of Art. **Anne Butler**, meanwhile, became a lecturer at Goldsmiths' School of Art in the Textile Department. **Lilla Speir**, who had taught in a number of colleges of art, was in charge of embroidery in Manchester College of Art while **Alison Liley** was now appointed to take charge of embroidery at Loughborough College of Art having taught previously in other colleges of art.

Exhibitions

National Exhibition of Children's Art

In 1962 the crafts chosen for the National Exhibition of Children's Art were embroidery and fabric printing. In the commentary on these crafts it says that both were concerned with the enrichment of an already existing fabric, so that they were not as fundamental as working in clay or paint as far as the child was concerned. Valerie Cliffe, one of the craft committee members says further: 'Patterns of rich and varied design can be worked by hand or machine. Younger children take the pictorial in their stride and their needlework is as fresh and direct as their painting, but the dead weight of the old tradition of domestic embroidery, with samples, finicky stitchery and all that is implied by "fancy needlework", still hangs heavy even now. It is time that embroidery was finally freed from this dependence on traditional stitchery. . . . It has often looked backwards to peasant crafts rather than outward to the competitive world at large. . . . Embroidery still needs revitalising – a beginning could be made in the schools . . . but it is a great craft and long due for serious reassessment'. (Catalogue, National Exhibition of Children's Art, 1962.)

Kathleen Whyte's students

Work by the former students of Kathleen Whyte was shown at the Embroiderers' Guild in April 1963. Hand embroidery predominated, showing a wealth of ideas and subject matter. One I remember, as it impressed me at the time, was by Kathleen Whyte of red poppies in layers of transparent, folded fabrics, mounted between two pieces of glass to allow the light to shine through (186). Other impressions that I still have were of strong design with individual interpretations of figurative subjects, bird forms and buildings.

Opus Anglicanum

Another exhibition, at the Victoria and Albert Museum during September to November 1963, of the mediaeval *Opus Anglicanum* embroideries, was magnificent with examples lent from other European countries who had acquired them in the past as gifts. This exhibition may have helped to recreate an awareness of medieval techniques, such as underside couching, and the *or nué* technique of working over gold threads laid down and couched in patterns with coloured silks.

National Diploma in Art and Design

The new art examinations were inaugurated in 1963, the National Diploma now superceded by the National Diploma in Art and Design, under the control of the Council for National Academic Awards. A report on art education had been issued in 1960, by the National Advisory Council, with a proposal for a New Diploma of Higher Education. To study for this examination it was agreed that the general education of a candidate must be satisfactory, with five 'O' Level subjects or three 'O' Level subjects and one 'A' Level. The Diploma was to cover three years after the candidate had reached a standard of work comparable with that of the Intermediate examination in art, or had taken a pre-Diploma course of one year in a college or school of art. It was suggested that some secondary schools might be able to supply introductory courses of a similar standard. Art schools were to be free to create their own pre-Diploma courses and to work out their own ideas for the advanced courses. Among subjects approved when the Diploma in Art and Design was inaugurated in 1963, textiles/fashion were included with printed and woven textiles and fashion, but no embroidery. Although embroidery was not part of this new examination until 1964, it seems reasonable to end this volume here as the outlook in colleges of art was completely changed when recognition was given for the Diploma. Through this change, teaching and the approach to the work of students and consequently the approach by students to art and design altered. This in turn had an effect on the work and attitudes of students on the Art Teachers' Certificate and Art Teachers' Diploma courses and later, on their teaching when they entered the schools or taught in further and higher education. Gradually the new ideas and ways in which embroidery was interpretated, infiltrated into different educational establishments, from junior to adult classes. Greater freedom by the selected colleges of art and polytechnics to make their own curricula and with this a more experimental attitude, led to wider uses of mixed media, to a more catholic choice of fabrics and threads and a general raising of standards. The fact that the crafts were now regarded as on the same level as Fine Art, that drawing was a common basis as well as art history, to be studied by every student on the new course, aided and abetted this standard.

Summary 1960–1963

Prominent people

Joan Cleaver
Elizabeth Crawford
Barbara Dawson
Patricia Fouldes
Rosalind Floyd
Diana Jones
Moyra McNeill
Betty Myerscough
Pat Russell
Lilla Speir

Societies, schools, exhibitions, events

1960 The lease of 73 Wimpole Street was purchased by the Embroiderers' Guild
1961 The Beatles emerged
1961 The Diploma of the Royal School of Needlework was discontinued
1961 The Needlework Development Scheme closed
1961 The American Museum in Bath was opened at Claverton Manor
1961 The Arts and Crafts Exhibition Society changed its name to The Society of Designer Craftsmen
1962 The '62 Group was inaugurated, the idea of Alison Liley and Jennifer Gray
1963 The Glasgow Embroidery Group held its first exhibition at the headquarters of the Embroiderers' Guild in London
1963 The new art examinations commenced, for the National Diploma in Art and Design

Main types of embroidery

Interest in metal thread embroidery
Ecclesiastical design
Great use of gold kid
Plastic fabrics tried out
Larger hangings
Panels also popular
Mixed techniques
The circle
Cellular structure } All much used as a basis of design
Bark
Appliqué and surface stitchery

Magazines and books

1960 *Canvas Embroidery*, Hebe Cox

1960 *Let Me Embroider*, Winsome Douglas

1960 *The Basic Stitches of Embroidery*, N Victoria Wade (Victoria and Albert Museum)

1960 *English Historical Embroidery*, Barbara Snook

1960 *Learning to Embroider*, Barbara Snook

1960 *And So To Embroider*, Needlework Development Scheme

1960 *Handbook of Crafts*, edited by Grizelda Lewis, with articles on aspects of embroidery by Constance Howard, Hebe Cox, Christine Risley, Averil Colby and Margaret Kaye

1961 *Church Needlework*, Beryl Dean

1961 *Machine Embroidery*, Christine Risley

1961 *Design for Flower Embroidery*, Elizabeth Geddes

1961 *The Craft of Embroidery*, Alison Liley

1962 *Victorian Embroidery*, Barbara Morris

1963 *Embroidery Stitches*, Barbara Snook

1955 *Discovering Embroidery*, Winsome Douglas

1963 *Linen Cut Work*, Oenone Cave

Magazines; Embroidery; Stitchcraft; Fancy Needlework; Needlewoman

Catalogues of exhibitions

136 Left: Early 1960s – Marjorie Kostenz. ***Saintes Maries de la Mer, Camargue.*** A panel with a navy tweed background, and appliqué in many different fabrics and colours for the figures and environment. The foreground figures are brown-skinned, the two women have white faces, the horse also is white. Waves are bright blue cotton, the sky is in blocks of orange and bright blue. Outlines in couching are in brilliant coloured threads. The design is based on the custom that 'once a year gypsies gather from all over the world to join in a pilgrimage when the statues of the two St Marys and of St Sarah are carried out into the sea where they are submerged' (catalogue of an exhibition, Gunnersbury Park Museum, December 1981 – January 1982). ***Loaned by Luke Gertler and John Guilfoyle. Photograph Hawkley Studios***

137 Right: 1960 – Jennifer Gray. Table runner, 64 in. × 104 in. (163 cm × 264 cm) in hand stitching. Slate blue and grey linen with houses on each end in black and white stitching with some grey and turquoise. Yellow linen windows are let into the ground fabric. ***Formerly belonged to the NDS. Loaned by the Embroiderers' Guild. Photograph by Nick Nicholson***

138 Left: Early 1960s – Constance Howard. *Ophelia.* A panel in hand stitching and appliqué. Velvets and silks in blues and greens, black net, with black outlines in couched threads, backstitched and knotted wheels in yellow greens, green and blue threads and others. *Owned by Kit Pyman. Photograph by Robert Cuthbert*

139 Right: 1960 – Maureen Helsdon. *Comus.* A panel, 36 in. × 15 in. (90 cm × 37.5 cm) exhibited in Stuttgart in 1963. Appliqué with machine and hand embroidery. The background is a dark blue printed furnishing cotton from Heals, with stitching in greens, blues, black, lime yellow

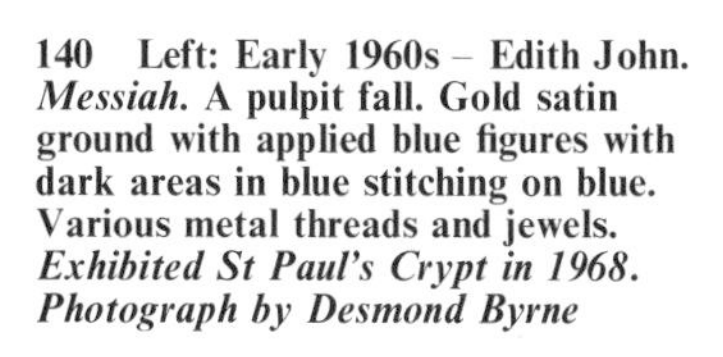

140 Left: Early 1960s – Edith John. *Messiah.* A pulpit fall. Gold satin ground with applied blue figures with dark areas in blue stitching on blue. Various metal threads and jewels. *Exhibited St Paul's Crypt in 1968. Photograph by Desmond Byrne*

141 Above: Early 1960s – Joy Clucas. *Nuclear Fission.* A panel, 31 in. × 21½ in. (78.5 cm × 55 cm), with fine machine embroidery in straight and satin stitch on a black cotton ground. *Loaned by the Embroiderers' Guild. Photograph by Nick Nicholson*

142 Right: 1960 – Fiona Isbister. *Javanese Puppets.* Chair seat designed and worked by a student on the Art Teachers' Certificate course at Goldsmiths' School of Art, London. The seat is worked on canvas in various stitches in muted colours of pinks, greens and yellowish greens. *Photograph by Hawkley Studios*

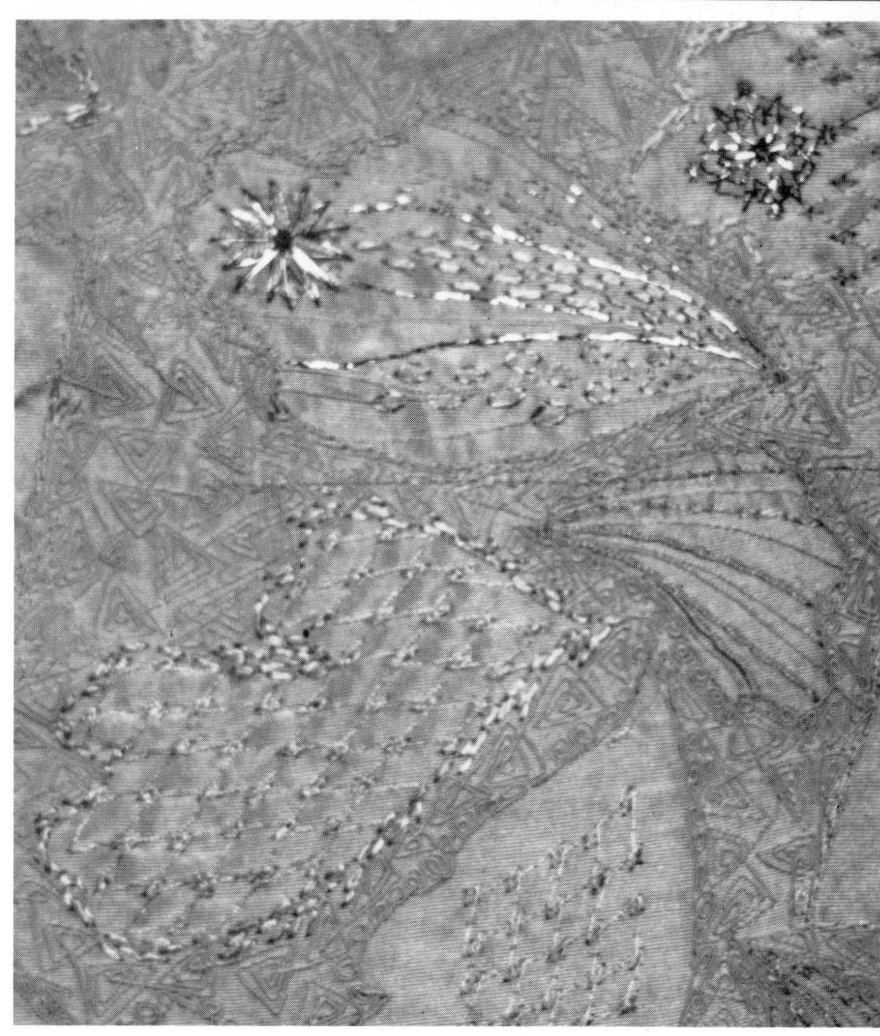

143 Right: Early 1960s – Esther Grainger. *Moissac Remembered.* Embroidered collage 24 in. × 20 in. (61 cm × 51 cm) with silks and chiffons on linen, worked in stranded cottons. *Derbyshire Schools Museum Service*

144 Above: A display case showing a machine embroidered christening robe and a grey silk machine embroidered waistcoat. Birmingham College of Art. *An exhibition of embroidery for the Victoria and Albert Museum Loan Collection*

145 Right: 1960 – Rita Allen, student at Birmingham College of Art. Detail of a waistcoat submitted for the National Diploma in Design. Machine embroidery examination. The background is a pale grey silk, with stitching in lurex and other threads

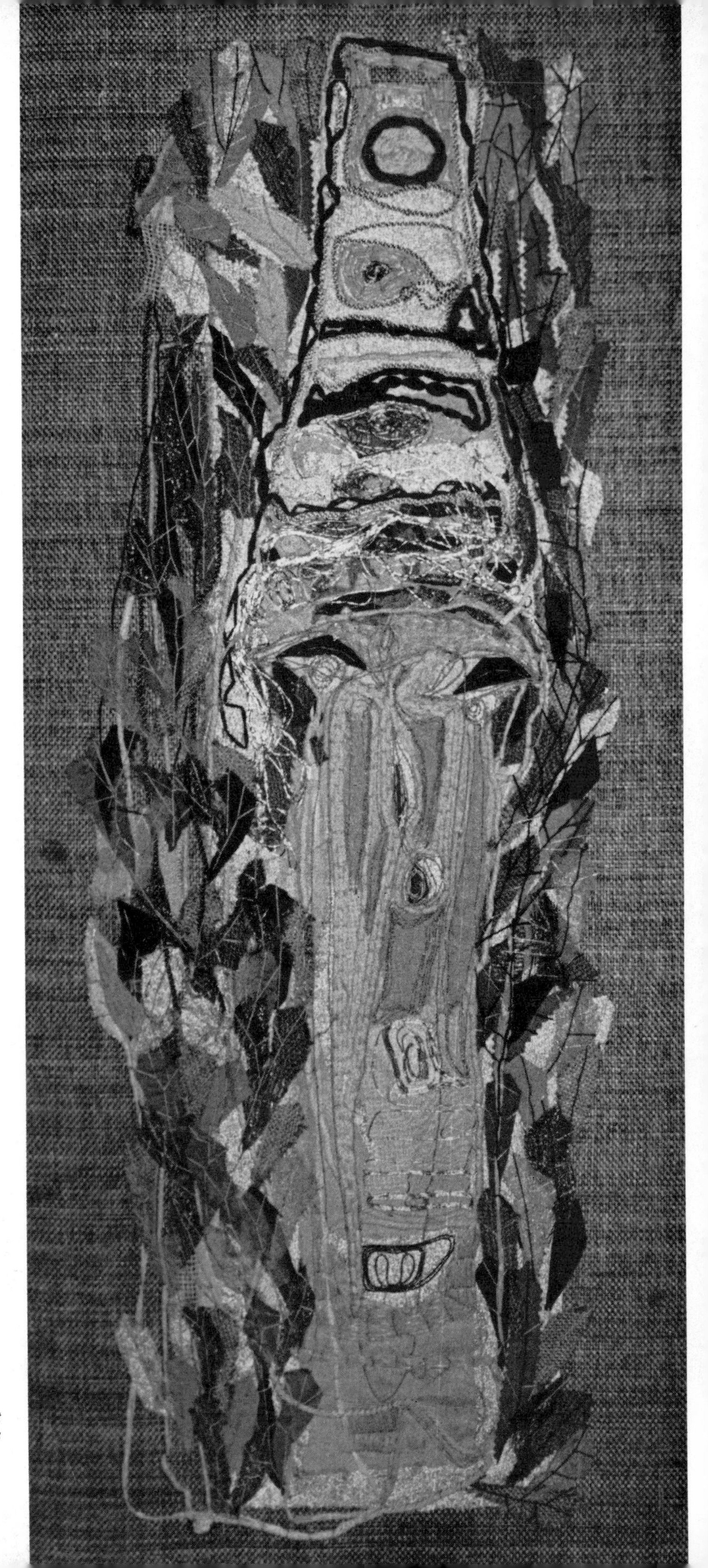

146 1961 – Betty Myerscough. *Chestnut Princess*. A panel 16 in. × $36\frac{1}{4}$ in. (41 cm × 92 cm) on coarse furnishing fabric with appliqué and free surface stitching, mainly couching

147 Far right: Detail of the *Chestnut Princess*

148 1960 – Constance Howard. Altar frontal. The idea developed from a Luo wall painting. On a background of scarlet linen, with orange bands across the top and bottom, also linen, orange flames are applied, stitched in white. The white shapes and the cross are applied, with mosaic-like areas in oranges and pinks. Stitching is in black, white, orange and pink. ***In the chapel of St Francis, Makerere University College, Kampala, Uganda***

149 1961 to the early 1970s – Guy Barton. One of a set of hangings for Lancaster Priory, *Nicholas of Myra*, in cross stitch, *petit point* and other canvas stitches, worked in a variety of patterns with brilliant blues, reds and golds predominant, and purples, turquoise and pinks for emphasis. *Reproduced by permission of Canon Geoffrey Tomlinson, Vicar and Rural Dean of Lancaster. Photograph by Stuart Watson, BA, and Keith Lawson, BA*

150 1960 – Esther Grainger. *Abercanaid.* A fabric collage with a variety of fabrics, emphasised with freely worked hand stitching

151 1961 – Margaret Turner, teacher of adult students in Women's Institutes and village community centres. Student at Chippenham Technical College, Bath. A book cover, $9\frac{3}{4}$ in. × $14\frac{1}{2}$ in. (24.3 cm × 36 cm) worked for the Advanced examination in embroidery of the City and Guilds of London Institute. Pale green and cream fabric, some appliqué, gold thread, assorted beads, gold kid

152 Below: 1959–1960 – Pamela Pavitt. A tablemat in nylon, worked on the Irish machine. A repetitive pattern obtained by geometry, illustrating her first article on machine embroidery for *Embroidery*, Spring 1960

153 1961–2 – June Tiley. A collage of buttons, wood and fabric on a brown ground, in turquoise, light brown, grey, with yellow stitching

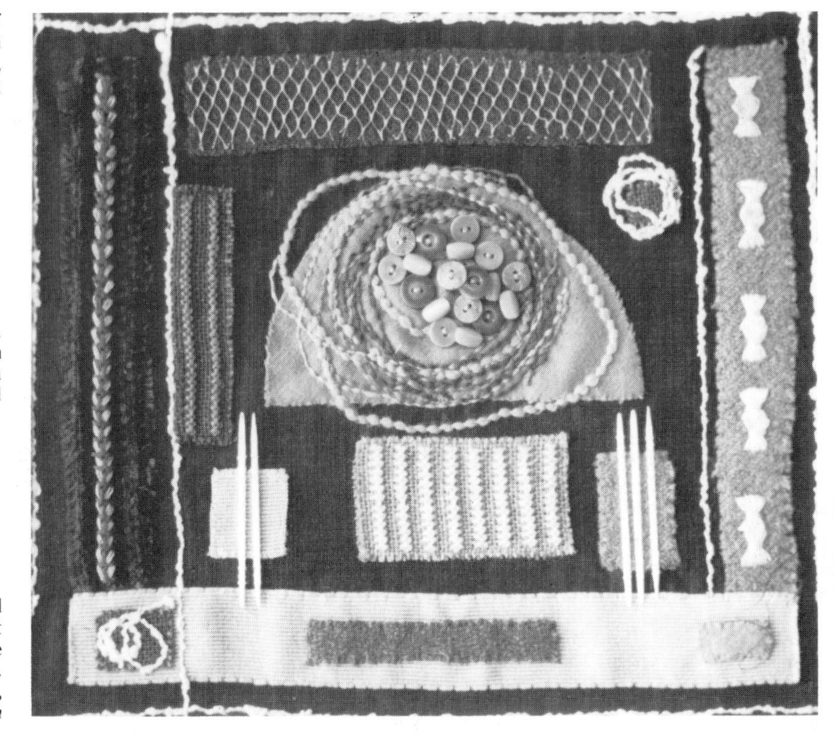

154 Below: 1961 – Beryl Chapman. *Shadows of Trees and Birds*. A panel in varying tones and textures of blue on a brown linen ground

155 Far right: 1961–62 – Pat Russell and Elizabeth Ford. Frontal in different textures of fabric, with machine stitching and a little hand stitching. *Chapel for the deaf, Alban-Neve Centre, Luton*

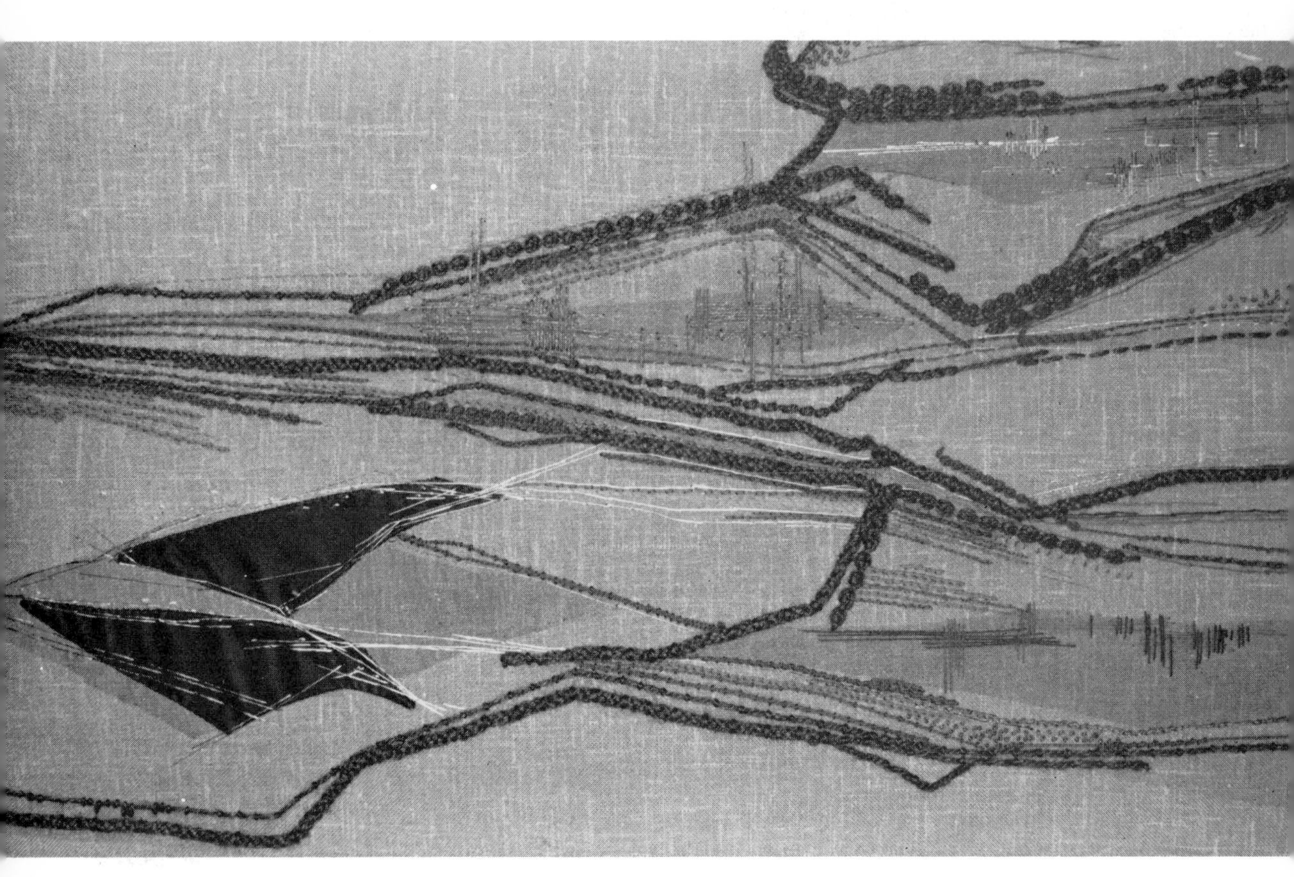

156 Below: 1961 – Beryl Dean. Altar frontal for Emmanuel College, Cambridge, designed and embroidered by her. Aluminium threads, synthetic gold braid and Jap gold and applied fabrics on a silver-grey ground. The Chi-Rho is in aluminium threads, patterned over string and silver kid, with lurex fabric over padding. Black chenille gives an appearance of depth to the forms. Behind the Chi-Rho a sun is applied in orange fabric and gold metallic fabric. Metal threads, synthetic gold thread and Jap gold are used for the stitching

157 Above: Early 1960s – Beryl Dean. A cope for Guildford Cathedral, inspired by the archways and windows of the Cathedral. The background is plum-coloured Thailand silk, the applied shapes are in cloth-of-gold, all of one piece of fabric 50 in. (125 cm) in width. The leaves are outlined in Jap gold, the arches inside are in orange threads couched down with vermilion, each taken from the cotton furnishing fabric of the hood and orphrey

158 Left: Detail of cope

159 Early 1960s – Beryl Dean. Front of the bishop's mitre for Guildford Cathedral. Cloth-of-gold, with the Ankh cross padded and embroidered in Jap gold

160 Above: 1960–61 – Joy Clucas, Flower panel, mainly in reds, orange and yellow, with touches of blues and greens. Small leaves are in dull greens, greys and browns, all on the dull side of black satin. Machine and hand embroidery. *This panel was illustrated in an article by Joy Clucas in the summer number of* Embroidery, *1963. It was also in the Embroiderers' Guild exhibition of 1961*

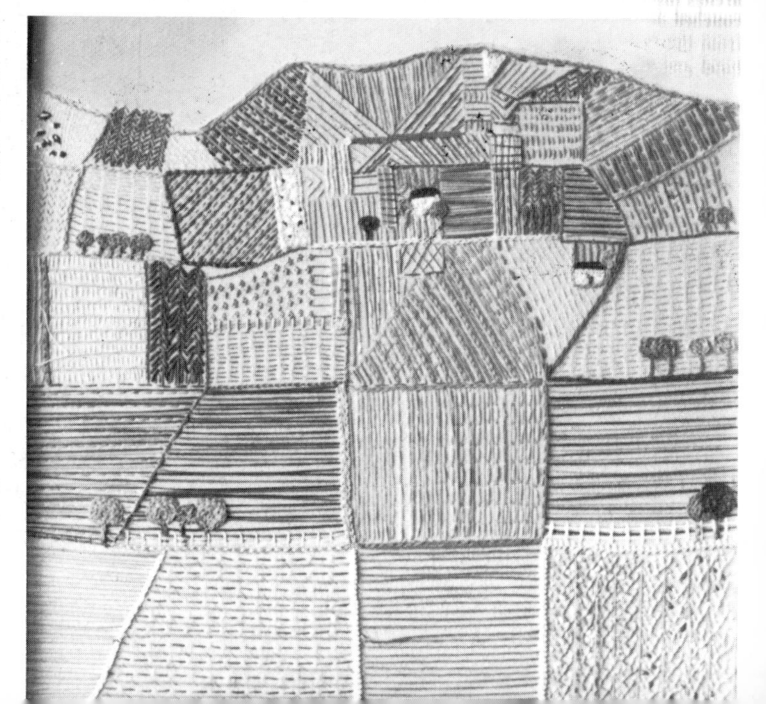

161 Right: Early 1960s – Elspeth Crawford. *Landscape.* A panel, hand stitched in textures, on a pinkish yellow ground, with a number of coloured threads that appear to change the background when worked closely together

162 Right: Early 1960s – Margaret Kaye. *Cock and Swan.* A panel, 4 ft × 2 ft (120 cm × 60 cm), collage of mixed fabrics, with some stitching

163 1961 – Alison Liley. *The Magi.* A hanging worked on evenweave linen, in cream, steel and red. Darning patterns, pulled work and inventive stitchery give richness to the embroidery. This panel was awarded a shared second prize in the Ecclesiastical Embroidery section of the Embroiderers' Guild exhibition in 1961. *Embroidery*, Autumn 1961

164 Right: 1961 – Sister Kathleen. *The Good Shepherd.* A banner designed by Patricia Scrase, worked by Sister Kathleen. The background is oyster silk furnishing fabric, worked in floss silks in laid work, long and short stitch and some gold threads. This banner was awarded first prize in the Ecclesiastical section of the Embroiderers' Guild Exhibition in 1961. *Embroidery*, Autumn 1961

165 Top: 1960 – Eirian Short. *Wave*. A panel of applied fabrics on a dark background, some folded and some corded, with handstitching. *Exhibited at 'The Materialists' show at Foyles*

166 Above: Early 1960s – Eirian Short. Pincushions, patchwork and other methods of construction. Patterns are made with pins or pins fixing beads down. A variety of materials has been used for these pincushions, satin, gold kid, plastics, velvet and others

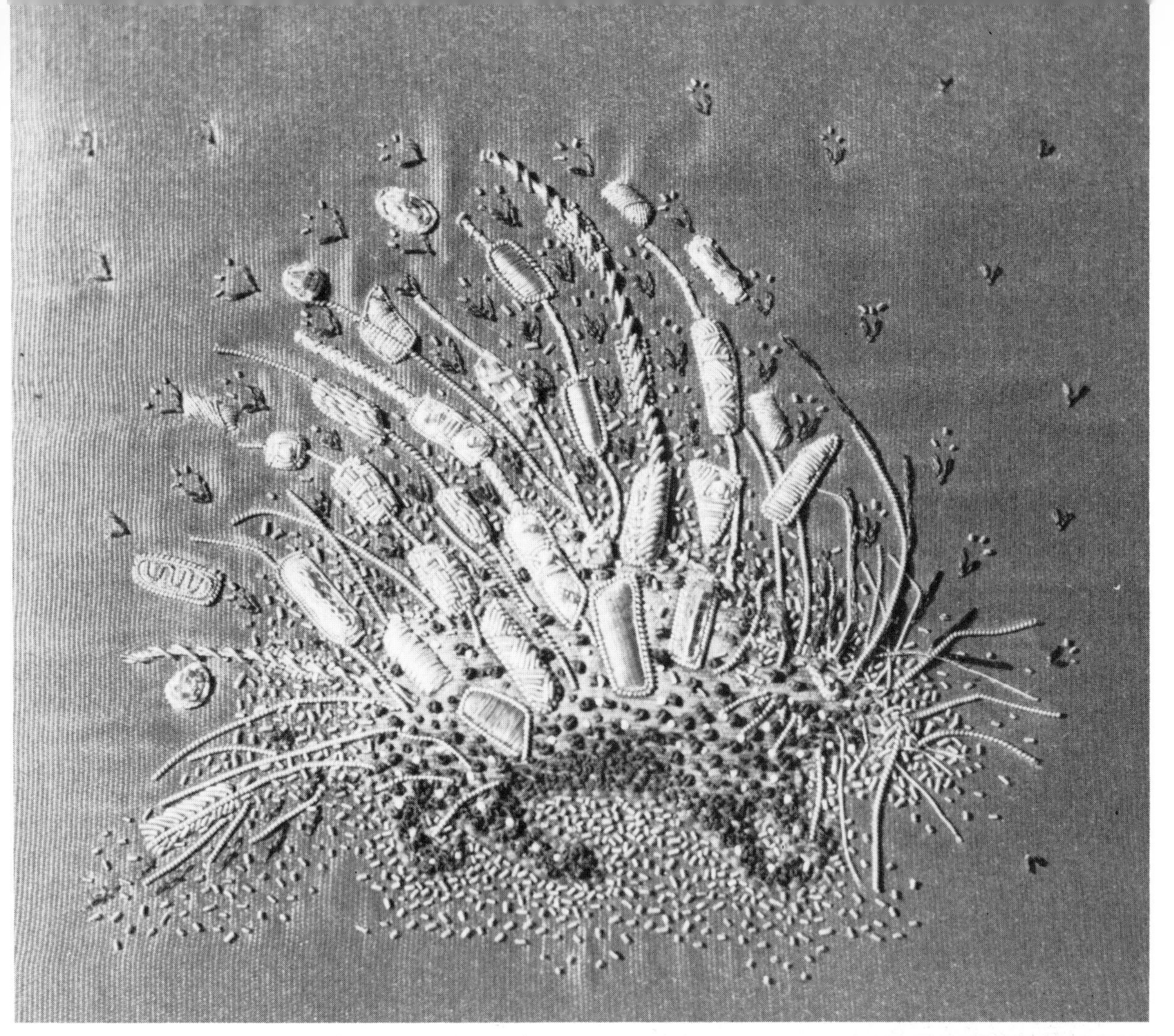

167 1961 – Barbara Dawson, Goldsmiths' School of Art. A panel of a porcupine in gold work and silk embroidery, on a brown background

168 Right: Early 1960s – Joy Clucas. *Blaze*. A panel in hand and machine embroidery. Applied nets on a tomato coloured woollen ground

169 1961 – John Hamilton, student at Goldsmiths' School of Art on the ATC course. Panel in applied white fabric dyed in greens in parts. The figures are stitched in red threads. The background is in machine zigzag stitch in yellow on brown, with straight stitching in red on blue

170 Above: 1961 – Jill Cunnell. *Mermaid.* A panel worked by a student at Goldsmiths' School of Art for the National Diploma in Design, special level hand embroidery. A variety of textured fabrics is applied to a bright blue shiny background. A number of stitches include running, couching, cretan and fern stitch

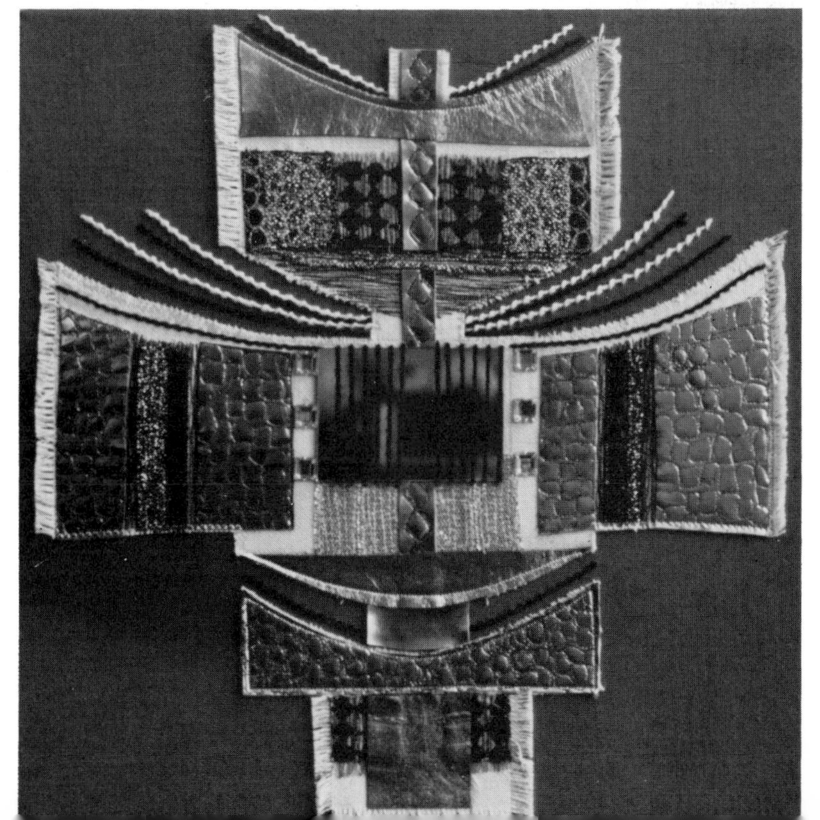

171 Right: Early 1960s – Maureen Helsdon. Small panel on a bright blue ground. Various textures are embroidered, in black and white, silver and gold. Machine and hand stitching

172 1961 – The enthronement robe for the Archbishop of Canterbury, the Most Reverend Right Honorable Michael Ramsey PCDD, worked by Mary Ozanne. The corded pattern is designed by Stephen Dykes Bower FRIBA. The cope is in lurex cloth-of-gold with deep red damask orphreys. The coats of arms indicate the places where the Archbishop has served. The clasp was worn by Archbishop Howley on his vestment at Queen Victoria's Coronation in 1838

173 Far right: Early 1960s – Pat Russell. A panel, 30 in. × 45 in. (76 cm × 114 cm), in cut net, mounted on Japanese paper. 'Out of a misty dream our path merges for a while then closes within a dream'

OUT OF
A MISTY
DREAM
OUR
PATH
EMERGES
FOR
THEN

174 1963 – Isobel Clover. Altar frontal worked for the NDD examination. It is in natural curtain sheer with applied white wool and chiffons, and embroidered in white wool, camel hair woven with white raffine and gold threads. The idea symbolises The Trinity. ***The frontal is in the Church of St Michael and the Holy Family, Kesgrave. Reproduced by permission of Mrs D Rope. Photograph by M Saunders***

175 Below: Early 1960 – Margaret Kaye. Altar frontal, Marlborough College Chapel, designed and worked by her. Blue purple Thai silk with applied black velvet, white satin, blue, cerise-pink satin, black fine veiling, Indian gold fabric. Stitching in cotton and silk, with some metallic threads. *Embroidery*, Autumn 1964

176 Left: 1961 – Susan Riley. *Three Kings* or *The Adoration of the Magi.* A hanging on a gold lamé background. Applied black and pale purple gauze, red and blue nylon fabric. Machine stitched in many colours of thread, including white, black, purple, crimson-purple, in cotton and woollen threads, gilt covered cord. *Exhibited at Coventry, originally belonging to the Needlework Development Scheme. Acquired by the Royal Scottish Museum, Edinburgh 1962. Embroidery*, Autumn 1964 and the Catalogue of Embroideries. *Given to the Museum by the NDS*

177 Above: 1962 – Esther Grainger. *Rock Face.* Fabric collage in a variety of fabrics, including nets and sheers, with hand stitching. *Private Collection*

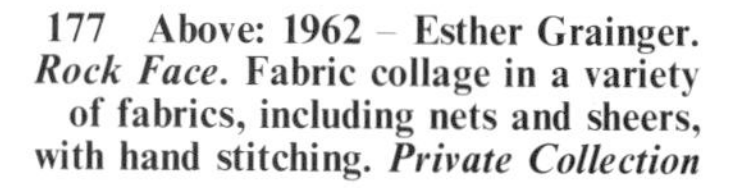

178 Right: 1962 – Lilian Dring. Hand and machine stitchery and appliqué of different fabrics. *For Sir William and Lady Worsley, Hovingham Hall, near York*

179 1962 – Hebe Cox. *Obelisk and Roses.* Canvas embroidery, 25 in. × $14\frac{1}{2}$ in. (62.5 cm × 35.2 cm), in tent and Gobelin stitch. Two grey and white vases with red and pink roses. Grey obelisk, with a background of dark red, grey and black tones

180 Right: Early 1960s – Moyra McNeill. *Sunflower.* Approximately 14 in. × 12 in. (36 cm × 30.5 cm). In canvas work. The flower is in cross stitch in gold, yellow and white wools. The background is in reds and browns and the leaves are in blue and grey canvas stitch. Stamens are couched gold wool. *Loaned by the Embroiderers' Guild. Photograph by Nick Nicholson*

181 Left: Early 1960s – Margaret Kaye. *Owl.* Collage panel approximately 22 in. × 15 in. (55 cm × 37.5 cm) using a variety of textured fabrics and threads, including gimps and slubs. *The Embroiderers' Guild*

182 Above: 1961–62 – Richard Box. *Cows.* A panel, approximately 2 ft 6 in. (75 cm) square. A blue background with cows applied in a black pile fabric and a mauve velvet. Machine stitched outlines in a lighter mauve add dimension to the paler cow

183 1961–62. One of a set of six copes, designed by Ceri Richards, a painter, carried out by Margaret Forbes, assisted by Freda Colebourne and Mrs Halligan, at the Colebournes' studio in Downe, Kent. The copes were designed in the cut paper method, influenced by the cut out designs of Henri Matisse. The backgrounds of the copes are in off white curtaining silk, with flowing applied shapes in light gold lurex. The orphreys are of canary yellow velvet for two of the copes, of sky blue velvet for two and for the other two, rust velvet. The hoods each have different designs, using a variety of fabrics, rayon, suede, and velvet, with borders in gold and silver lurex. *Information supplied by Margaret Forbes. Reproduced by permission of the Very Reverend Robert T Holtby, Dean of Chichester. Photograph by Hawkley Studios*

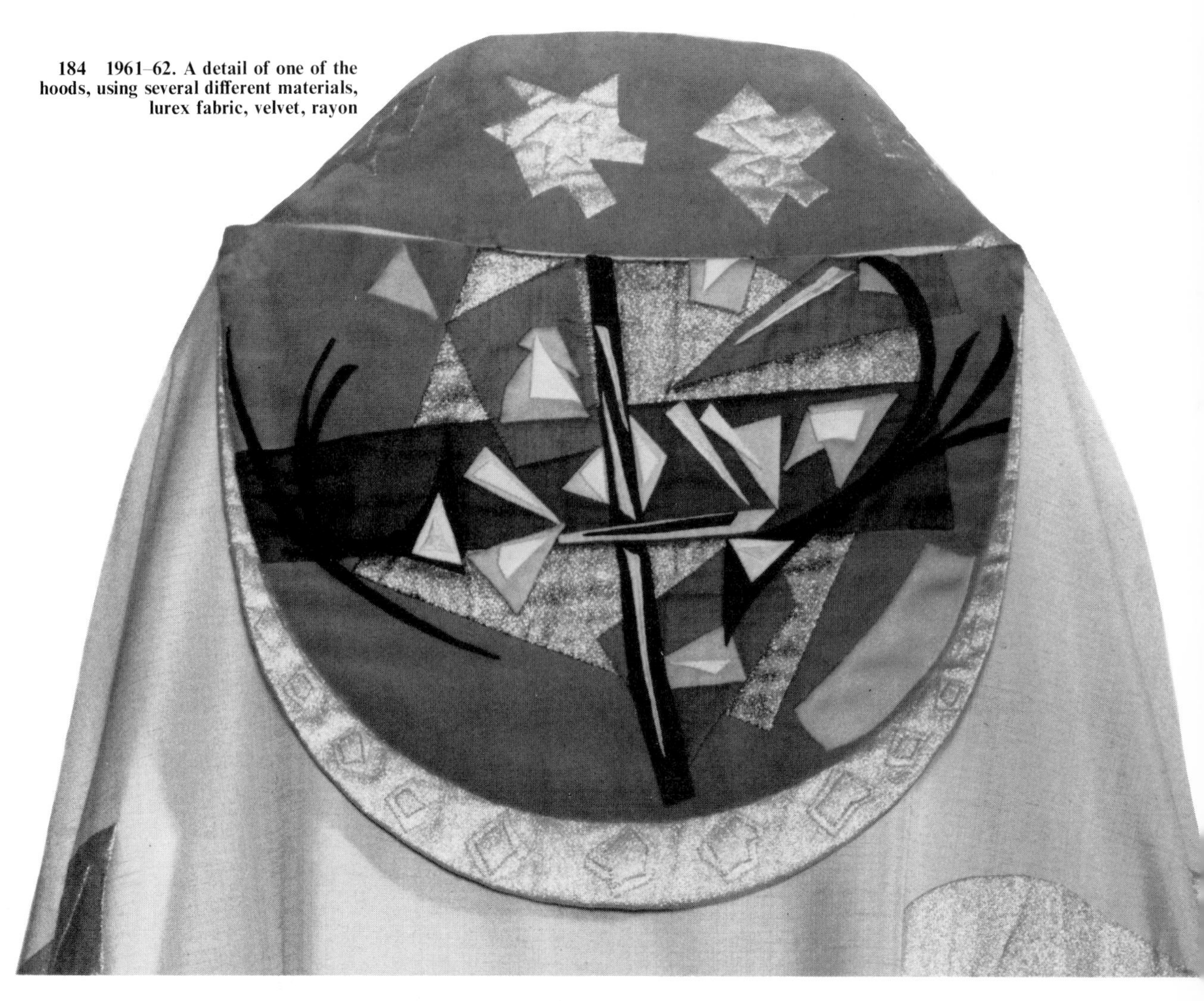

184 1961–62. A detail of one of the hoods, using several different materials, lurex fabric, velvet, rayon

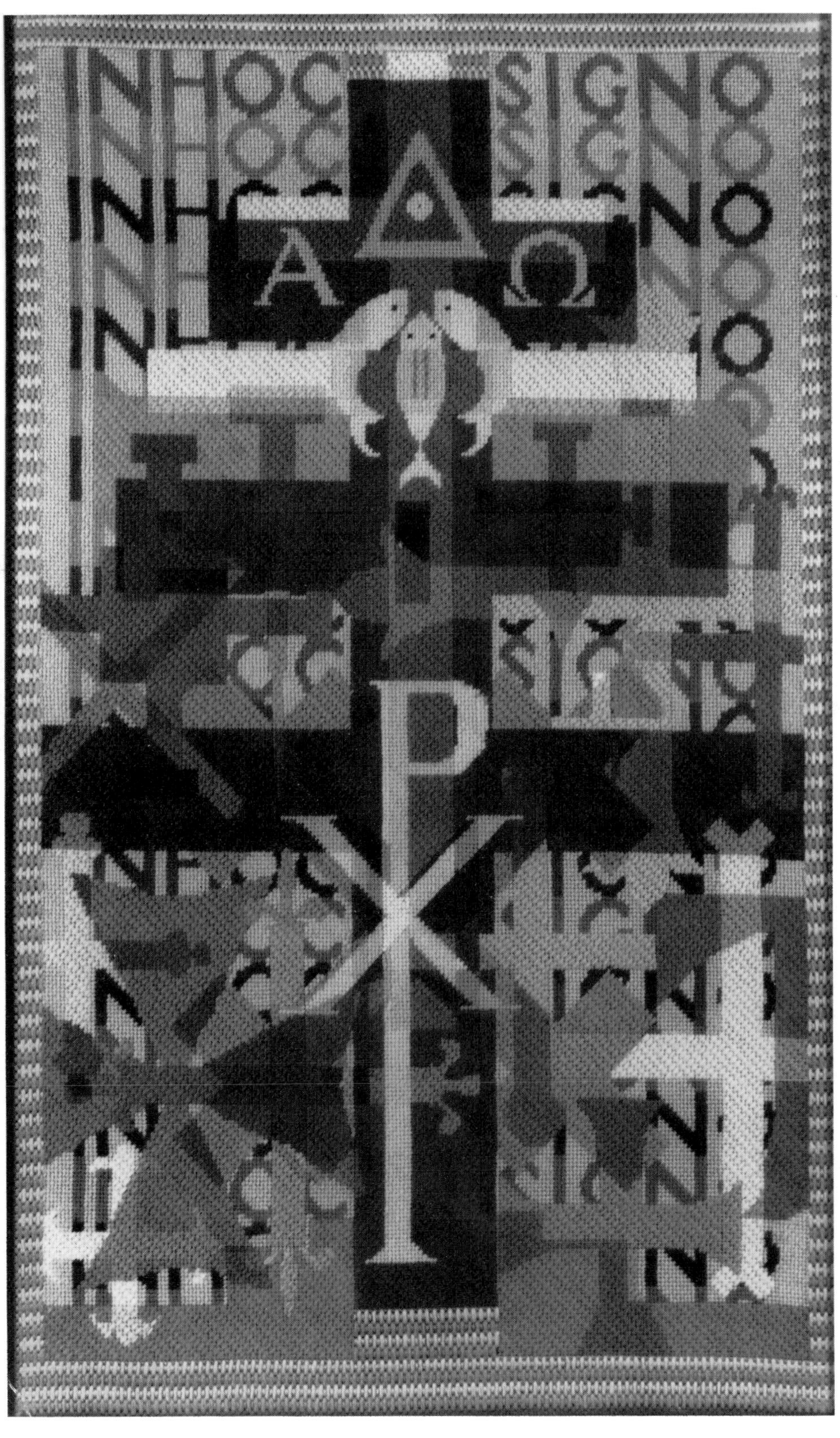
INHOC SIGNO
A Ω

185 Far left: 1961–63 – Marjorie Dyer. A panel in canvas embroidery, *In Hoc Signo*, inspired by a gift of a mixed bag of Swedish wools, with the problem of unifying the colours. Sixteen different cross shapes, each of a different colour are superimposed, so that the overlapping produces many different colours. *Photograph by Hawkley Studios*

186 Above: 1963 – Kathleen Whyte. *Poppies*. A fabric collage in crystal nylon, chiffon, net and coloured silks. *Victoria and Albert Museum, London*

187 Left: Early 1960s – Alison Barrell. A small blackwork sampler, showing a variety of filling patterns

Biographies

Abbreviations

ARCA = Associate of the Royal College of Art
ATC = Art Teachers' Certificate
ATD = Art Teachers' Diploma
DA = Diploma in Design
C & G = City and Guilds of London Institute
FSDC = Fellow of the Society of Designer Craftsmen
FSIA = Fellow of the Society of Industrial Artists
NDAD = National Diploma in Art and Design
NDD = National Diploma in Design
Dip AD = Diploma in Art and Design. This was a shortened form of NDAD and known by students as Dip AD until 1975

Dorothy Allsopp ARCA ATD 1911–

1929–31 Training at Chelsea School of Art
1931–35 The Royal College of Art – Design School and ATD
Teaching 1935–49 West Hartlepool College of Art – full time lecturer in charge of women's crafts
1949–54 Expert in charge of the Needlework Development Scheme
1954–61 Senior lecturer in charge of fashion, embroidery and textiles – Hammersmith College of Art and Building (now part of Chelsea School of Art)
1961–76 Inspector of further and higher education (Fashion and Creative Studies) ILEA
1976 Retired from the Inspectorate
1978 Chairman of the Examinations Subject Committee for Creative Studies for the City and Guilds of London Institute

Work purchased by the Victoria and Albert Museum

Dorothy Angus 1891–1979

Training at Edinburgh College of Art – painting and embroidery.
Assisted Louisa Chart in restoration work at the Palace of Holyroodhouse

Teaching 1916 Appointed to Carnegie Trust Craft School, Dunfermline
1920 Lecturer in embroidery, Grays School of Art, Aberdeen
1955 Retired from the school

Commissions For the Needlework Development Scheme. A heraldic bedspread for Lord Glentar

1939–40 Panel – War Impressions owned by Dr Helen Russell. Also many others in private collections

Eugenie Alexander NDD ATC 1919–

1936–38 1946–50 Training at Chelsea School of Art – illustration NDD, taught by Henry Moore and Graham Sutherland

1950–51 Goldsmiths' School of Art, University of London – embroidery, etching and lithography

Teaching 1954–58 Visiting lecturer, Goldsmiths' School of Art; also lecturer for ILEA courses for teachers

Exhibitions

1955 One-man show, Arthur Jeffress Gallery in London

1967 and 1969 William Ware Gallery

1977 Medici Gallery

Group shows Society for Education through Art; Pictures for Schools; Society of Designer Craftsmen; Women's International Art Club; Whitworth Art Gallery and others, including Arts Council travelling shows, and abroad

Publications *Art for Young People*, Mills and Boon, 1958
Fabric Pictures, Mills and Boon, 1959 (six reprints)
Museums and How to Use Them, Batsford, 1974
Works reproduced in a number of magazines and reviewed in newspapers – *Sunday Times*, *Guardian*, etc
Pictures shown several times on television

Films 1955 Pathé Pictorial on embroideries

Works purchased by National Museum of Wales; Derby Museum and Art Gallery; US Embassy; and education authorities as well as by private clients including Helena Rubenstein

Doris Anwyl FSDC 1912–

1930–34 Training at Croydon School of Art

1942 City and Guilds of London Institute, Teacher's Certificate

Teaching 1934–38 Southern College of Art, Portsmouth

1938–45 Sutton and Guildford Schools of Art (part time)

1945–49 Sutton School of Art (full time)

1949–72 Benenden School, Kent

1981 Teaching disabled at Tenterden Day Centre

Commissions, etc

1974 Chess set in leather

1977 Re-mounting and repairing the Queen's State Colours, belonging to the Scots Guards

1980 Laudian altar frontal for St Mildred's Church, Tenterden, Kent, in collaboration with a weaver

1981 Four-fold screen, 'The seasons as seen through a chestnut tree'

Since 1972 Projects organised for the East Kent Embroiderers' Guild

Joan Archer (née Hughes) NDD DA (Manchester) 1931–

1948–53	Training at Manchester Regional College of Art – printed textiles, embroidery
1953	ATC
1958	Travelling scholarship – Edward Cadbury Travel Fund – to Italy
Teaching 1953–58	Friends School, Saffron Walden
1960–64	Part time at Altrincham Grammar School for Girls
1973	Part-time adult teaching at Sale Adult Centre, South Trafford College of Further Education, Manchester College of Adult Education
1977	Organised biennial exhibition 'Textiles and Stitchery' in Manchester
	Work sold to education authorities and private clients
Commission	
1959–60	Four panels of embroidery, with symbols of the Evangelists for White Moss Methodist Church, Manchester. Now in Chain Bar Methodist Church, Manchester

Alison Barrell NDD ATD 1939–

1957–59	Training at Ealing College of Art – Illustration NDD
1960	Hornsey College of Art – ATD
	Part-time evening classes – Goldsmiths' School of Art, embroidery
	City and Guilds of London Institute examination in hand embroidery
Teaching 1960–64	Crown Woods Comprehensive School
1967	Part-time tutor at Beckenham and Penge Adult Education Centre where the Textile Studio was founded, with Margaret Forbes, Tutor in Charge of the Studio
1967	Member of the Embroiderers' Guild. On executive committee
1968	Joined '62 Group
1969	In charge of the Textile Studio
1975–77	Chairman of the '62 Group
Exhibitions	Textile Studio; SDC; New Embroidery Group and other shows
	Works purchased by education authorities, private collectors, museums and foreign collectors

Guy Barton 1907–81

	Training at King's College, Cambridge – Degree in modern languages
Teaching 1932–40	Art master at Bedford School
1940–45	Served in the Royal Corps of Signals – became a Captain
1946–66	Art master at Marlborough School
Commissions, etc	
early 1950s	Started to design for embroidery
1961	Commenced scheme for Lancaster Priory. This led to designing embroideries for a number of churches
1966	Retired from Marlborough and concentrated on painting and designing for church embroideries

Valerie Bayford ?–1958

Training at Slade School of Fine Art – painting and drawing
Croydon School of Art, Board of Education – industrial design, embroidery

1933 C & G Embroidery I

1935 Part-time lecturer – Croydon School of Art. Also part-time lecturer, Royal School of Needlework

Late 30s Full-time lecturer, Reading University, Fine Art department
Chief examiner for the C & G of London Institute (embroidery) until her death

Vanessa Bell 1879–1961

Worked with Duncan Grant
Training as a painter at the Slade
A mural designer and interior decorator and designer for embroidery

1913–19 Worked at the Omega Workshops with Roger Fry
A member of the Bloomsbury Group

Dorothy Benson 1902–1977

1916 Entered Singer Sewing Machine Company. Carried out odd jobs. Later began training as a machine embroiderer and teacher of machine embroidery

1937 Appointed examiner as a machine embroidery specialist for the Board of Education Industrial Design examination

1939–45 In charge of the embroidery section in Singer

1947 Continued as an examiner for machine embroidery for the new Ministry of Education examination, the National Diploma in Design, in which machine embroidery was a separate subject

1958 Appointed to take charge of the complete department at Singer

1962 Retired from Singer

1965 The National Diploma in Design ceased

Publication *Your Machine Embroidery*, Sylvan Press, 1952

Angela Bradshaw

1924–29 Training at Manchester Municipal College of Art – textiles. Whitworth Scholar. Prizes for textile and theatre design – Royal Society of Arts

1929–34 Conducted own studio. Contributed articles and ideas to national newspapers and magazines, including the *Guardian, Glasgow Herald, Homes and Gardens* and Swedish papers

1934–50 In charge of women's crafts, Dundee College of Art

1950 Manchester College of Domestic Economy – lecturer

Commissions Designer for the Daily Express Coronation Pageant, City of Dundee
Pulpit fall – Glamis church, and others

Constance Brown (née Stone) ARCA 1881–1978

Training at Bristol College of Art
The Royal College of Art

1912 Head of Embroidery – Cambridge School of Art

1914 Embroidery accepted and hung in the Paris Salon – petit point roundel

1914 Award of Merit – Cambridge Arts and Crafts Society

1959 Retired to Bristol

Louisa Chart ?–1963

	Training at The Royal School of Art Needlework
1906	Founder member of the Society of Certificated Embroideresses
1911–13	Appointed to teach embroidery at Wimbledon School of Art and Kingston-upon-Thames School of Art
1913	Lecturer in Embroidery, Edinburgh College of Art
1944	Retired from the College
Commissions	Repairing old embroideries – Palace of Holyroodhouse
	Set of Chair seats – covers – for the Palace of Holyroodhouse
	A Bible Cover for Edward VII
	A Coat of Arms for George Watson Boys' School, and other works

Joan Cleaver NDD 1927–

1947	Training at Durham University, Fine Art BA course
1948	Birmingham College of Art – NDD in printed textiles and embroidery
Teaching 1963	Appointed head of School of Embroidery, Birmingham College of Art (now in the City of Birmingham Polytechnic)
Lectures	In Great Britain to students at colleges of further education and in adult education establishments
Exhibitions	Red Rose Guild, Peter Dingley Gallery, Stratford-upon-Avon and other Galleries, Pictures for Schools
Commissions	Ecclesiastical and secular work, including an altar frontal, St Thomas's Church, Wednesfield, Staffordshire; pulpit fall, Trinity Methodist Church, Wandsworth
1977	Frontal designed for St Michael's church, Boldmere, worked by parishioners
	Work sold to public and private collectors, including the Oxford and Warwick museums
	A panel for a new office block, for Chamberlaine and Hill, Iron Founders, Walsall
Publications	Articles for magazines, and book reviews for *Embroidery* magazine
	Appliqué, Search Press 1978

Isobel Clover 1941–

1960–63	Training at Hammersmith College of Art and Building
1964	Art Teachers' Certificate, London University
1965	Won the Jubilee Silver Medal of the Embroiderers' Guild
Teaching	In a number of places, including secondary and further education
1967 on	Lecturer at Ipswich College of Higher and Further Education
1972 on	Assessor for the C & G examinations
Professional work	Ecclesiastical embroideries, many in East Anglia, frontals and hangings
	A cope in Dedham
	A frontal in North Wootton Church, King's Lynn
	1980 White dossal – Kesgrave, Ipswich
	1981 White burse, veil and stole – Kesgrave, Ipswich
	1982 Red vestments – designed and supervised – N. Cadbury, Somerset
	1982–3 New Advent dossal – Kesgrave
	Founder member of the Suffolk Craft Society
Exhibitions	Work shown in London, East Anglia and a number of other places

Beryl Chapman 1908–

1933 Training at Royal College of Art – wood engraving part time

1960 Part time – embroidery, Goldsmiths' School of Art

Exhibitions

1963 on Pictures for Schools

'62 Group and others

Commissions Engraving bookplates and illustrating the Penguin New Writings

Joy Clucas (née Dobbs) NDD ATC 1931–

1948–50 Training at Southampton School of Art

1950–52 Bromley College of Art – fabric printing by hand, machine embroidery

1952–53 ATC course at Brighton College of Art

Teaching and other work

1953–56 A number of jobs including teaching and self-employment

1956–58 Lived in Nigeria, working in a commercial art studio; also designed textiles

1958–63 Freelance

1963–69 Art and craft teacher part time at Bishop Simpson's Church of England Secondary School for Girls

1968–70 Part time in several colleges of art

1970–72 London College of Fashion, the Stanhope Institute and the Royal School of Needlework; also part-time courses for teachers and others throughout the country

1977, 1978, 1979 Visits to the USA

Exhibitions Work sold to public and private clients

Averil Colby 1900–1983

1918 Training at Horticultural College of Education

Worked temporarily restoring neglected gardens. Then on a farm and in the garden.

Illness led to quieter life. Went to Hampshire. Helped the Women's Institute with a patchwork bedspread, planned by Muriel Rose who became Craft Officer to the British Council.

1932 Interest in patchwork developed. Returned to the farm

Publications *Patchwork*, Batsford 1958, paperback edition 1976

Samplers, Batsford 1964

Patchwork Quilts, Batsford 1965

Quilting, Batsford 1972

Pincushions, Batsford 1975

Articles for magazines and journals

Hebe Cox 1909–

1931–34 Training at Central School of Arts and Crafts, C & G II

On the staff of the Royal School of Needlework.

Textile studio assistant.

Worked for and advised the National Federation of Women's Institutes with lectures and courses.

Founder member and trustee – Crafts Centre of Great Britain

Member of the Arts and Crafts Exhibition Society

Publications *Simple Embroidery Designs*, Studio Vista 1948

Embroidery Technique and Design, Dryad, 1954

Canvas Embroidery, Mills and Boon, 1960

Fifteen Craftsmen on their Crafts, Sylvan Press, 1945 (contributor)

Contributed to *Oxford Junior Encyclpaedia*

English and Swedish Journals

Elspeth Crawford (née Younger) DA 1936–

1953–57 Training at Glasgow School of Art – embroidery and weaving Diploma

1957–58 Post-Diploma course

1958–59 Jordanhill Teachers' Training College

1959 Travelling Scholarship

Teaching 1960–66 Lecturer in embroidery and weaving at Grays School of Art, Aberdeen

Exhibitions One-man shows

1965 57 Gallery, Edinburgh

Lane Gallery, Bradford

1969 Arts Centre, Aberdeen – oil pastels

1971 Arts Centre, Aberdeen – painting

1973 Senior Common Room, University of Aberdeen – embroidered wall hangings and paintings

Group shows with:

Aberdeen Artists' Society

Society of Scottish Artists, Edinburgh

Arts Council Travelling Shows

1958–76 Glasgow School of Art Embroidery Group

Works purchased by Dundee Art Gallery, Dundee Education Authority

Barbara Dawson NDD 1922–

1946–47 Training at Hornsey School of Art – dress design

1948–51 Royal School of Needlework

1963–64 Goldsmiths' School of Art, NDD embroidery

Teaching 1950–51 Nottingham School of Art

1946–61 Hornsey School of Art and the Royal School of Needlework

1965–75 Full-time lecturer, Goldsmiths' School of Art

Organised short courses in England and Scotland; also visiting groups from the USA for specialised courses at Goldsmiths' College

1975 Represented the Embroiderers' Guild at the Conservation Centre at Hampton Court Palace

1975–82 Senior lecturer and curator of collection of textiles at Goldsmiths' School of Art

Commissions

1966–72 Chelmsford Cathedral – vestments and hanging

Deptford – hanging for a church

1968– Downing College, Cambridge – vestments

1974–81	Manchester Cathedral, Truro Cathedral – vestments
1979–80	Work for Llandaff Cathedral, Downing and Jesus Colleges, Cambridge, Mountain Ash, Wales, and Truro, Cornwall
	Work purchased by education authorities in Great Britain, the Department of the Environment, and by private buyers both in Great Britain and abroad
Exhibitions	
1962 onwards	In various parts of the country including the Crafts Council of Great Britain, Embroiderers' Guild, Pictures for Schools, and St Paul's Cathedral, and also in the USA at the Smithsonian Institute and the Chicago Institute of Fine Art, Switzerland, Africa and Canada
1964–68	Pictures for Schools
1973	British Craftsmen, Victoria and Albert Museum
1977	Department of the Environment
1981	Master Craftsmen, Victoria and Albert Museum
1983	Guildford
1983	Goldsmiths' Gallery
	Member of Society of Designer Craftsmen
	Member of Crafts Centre of Great Britain
	Member of British Crafts Council
	Member of Embroiderers' Guild
	Member of National Society of Art and Education
	Work purchased by private clients
Publications	
1968	*Metal Thread Embroidery*, Batsford
1976	New edition, Batsford. Paperback edition 1982

Beryl Dean MBE ARCA 1911–

	Trained at The Royal School of Needlework
1930s	Bromley College of Art – embroidery, leather design dress – Board of Education Examinations Royal College of Art Part-time teaching
1937–39	Professional milliner
Teaching 1939–46	Lecturer, Eastbourne School of Art
1946–47	Lecturer, King's College, Newcastle. Own workroom for *couture* clothes
1952	Part-time lecturer, Hammersmith College of Art and Building – embroidery
1958	Ecclesiastical embroidery class commenced Part-time lecturer at Stanhope Institute, London, courses and lectures throughout Great Britain and in the USA
1975	Awarded an MBE for services to embroidery
Commissions include	
1940–45 onwards	Ballet costumes and decor
	Work for the Needlework Development Scheme
	Banner – Chelmsford Cathedral
	Red frontal – Chelmsford Cathedral
	Three frontals – St Margaret's Church, Kings' Lynn
	Set of vestments and frontal – St Martin's Church, Dorking, Surrey
	A cope for Guildford Cathedral
	Frontal – St Giles' Church, Northbrook, Illinois, USA

1974	Five panels – Royal Chapel, St George's Chapel, Windsor
1977	Festival cope designed by Beryl Dean and worked by students of Stanhope Institute
	The Dean and Canon's copes; enthronement of the Archbishop of Canterbury
	Two works for Sir Basil Spence, designed by Anthony Blee, worked by Beryl Dean
	Work purchased by the Victoria & Albert Museum
Publications	*Ecclesiastical Embroidery*, Batsford 1958
	Church Needlework, Batsford 1961
	Ideas for Church Embroidery, Batsford 1968
	Creative Appliqué, Studio Vista 1970
	Embroidery for Religion and Ceremonial, Batsford 1981
	Articles for magazines

Lynette de Denne ?–1981

1939	Trained at the Royal School of Needlework. During the war she gave up her training. Became secretary of a camp for evacuated children. Joined WAAF, later becoming a driver
1947	Continued her training
Teaching	Taught in several schools – embroidery and needlework Five years at Messrs Foyles. Started a handicraft shop
1956	Part time with the Guild. Continued to teach
1969–70	Joined the Embroiderers Guild full time
Exhibitions	Organised many exhibitions, the first one 'Elegance and Embroidery'
1971	'Thousand Years of Embroidery' – Celanese House
1972	Commonwealth Institute Art Gallery
1973	The Ideal Home
	'Monarchy 1000' – Bath
1974	'Young Embroiderers' at Celanese House, the first national exhibition of children's work
1976	Commonwealth Institute exhibition. Led a party to Iceland
1977	'Hands of the Craftsman' – St Alban's Cathedral
1977	Designed and organised the Silver Jubilee Exhibition for the Royal School of Needlework at the Royal College of Art
1978	'Colour Through the Needle' Horniman Museum then at Gawthorpe Hall
	Became the Secretary of the Embroiderers' Guild
1979	Ill and in hospital
Commissions	A new banner for the Worshipful Company of Broderers
	A masonic banner and other embroideries
Publications	
1968	Joint editor with Nora Jones of *Embroidery* magazine
	Decorating with Stitches
1979	*Creative Needlework*, Sundial Press

Joan Drew 1875–1961

Training uncertain, probably self taught. Carried out some book illustration in her youth. Gave a great deal of help to the Women's Institutes. Held classes in her own studio and also taught children.

Teaching 1920–22	The first classes in embroidery held at the Victoria and Albert Museum
1926	Had portfolios of designs published by Pitman as an aid to the non-designer
1930s	Produced hand-embroidered rugs, banners and hangings Won the Embroiderers' Guild Challenge Cup
1978	Research by Kathleen Aldworth, assisted by Joan Edwards, in setting up an exhibition of her work at Loseley House, by permission of Mr and Mrs Molyneux, Guildford

Lilian Dring ARCA FSDC 1908–

1922–26	Training at Kingston-upon-Thames School of Art
1926–29	Royal College of Art
Work 1930	Commercial artist, Fleet Street
1931	Started to embroider
1935	Invited to joint the Arts and Crafts Exhibition Society
1939–45	Worked for educational publishers, ideas for evacuees
1946	Illustration and commercial work
1947	Founder member, Crafts Centre of Great Britain
1950	Prize awarded in poster competition
1965	Part-time teaching
Exhibitions	
1937	Exhibited with Contemporary Georgians
1942	Exhibited with British Council
1955	Exhibited in New Zealand with the Arts and Crafts Exhibition Society
1967	Retrospective one-man show at All Hallows, London Wall (courtesy of Council for the Care of Churches); also work in the St Paul's Cathedral exhibition
1975	Parable II shown at Orleans House Gallery, Twickenham
	Patchwork exhibited – community project organised by Lilian Dring in 1951
1977	Patchwork at the Victoria and Albert Museum – 'A tonic for the Nation'
	Silver Jubilee exhibition of own work – 50 years retrospective, Teddington. 'Silver-Gilt'
Commissions	
1956	First commission for 'a portrait of a house'. Various other commissions for 'a portrait of a house'
1957	First ecclesiastical commission
1962	Vestments for Gloucester Cathedral
1967	Lenten set for St Mark's, Surbiton
1971	Red presentation stole for Vicar of St Mark's, Surbiton

Marjorie Dyer (née Goggs) ATD 1911–

1931–34	Training at the Slade School of Fine Art, University of London – painting
	Part-time evening classes at Central School of Art and Crafts, London – embroidery
1932–33	The Slade Prize for Design
1934	The Slade Prize for Lettering
	University Diploma in the Arts, distinction for portrait heads
1935	Art Teachers' Diploma
Teaching 1935–37	Art at Hunmanby Hall School, Yorkshire

1968 Painting and embroidery, to adult classes in further education

Lectures to art groups

1938–50 Married and in the Far East

Designed the War Memorial Chapel, Rangoon Cathedral

Lettered the Memorial Book for the Burma Campaign – now in Rangoon Cathedral

1950 Returned to England

1963 Joint winner – Embroiderers' Guild Challenge Cup

1975 Member of the New Embroidery Group

1977 Member of the Society of Designer Craftsmen

1978 *The Artist*, 303

Exhibitions

1973 One-man show – Butlin Gallery, Dillington House, Ilminster

1977 Painting – West of England Academy, Bristol

1979 One-man show – Butlin Gallery

Various group shows in Great Britain and abroad

Rosalind Floyd NDD ATD 1937–

1953–57 Training at Mansfield School of Art – NDD in embroidery and printed textiles

1957–58 ATC course – Leicester College of Art

1958 Attended evening classes in embroidery at Goldsmiths' School of Art, University of London

Teaching 1958–64 Sydenham School for Girls, London

1964–65 Shoredith College for the Garment Trade (now part of the London College of Fashion)

1965–77 Rachel McMillan, College of Education

1966–69 Tutor – Barry Summer School, South Wales

1977 Lecturer at Goldsmiths' School of Art

Exhibitions

since 1959 Pictures for Schools

since 1962 Group exhibitions, touring exhibitions including:

since 1964 Comtemporary Hangings

1967 Festival Hall, London

1969 Victoria and Albert Museum, London

1978 Commonwealth Institute – Embroiderers' Guild

'Blue, Black, Silver,' Nottingham – Midland Group Gallery

Works purchased by the Victoria and Albert Museum, Embroiderers' Guild, education authorities and other public and private collectors

Member of the '62 Group

Margaret Forbes 1929–

1947–1949 Training at the Royal School of Needlework

1950 Vicars and Poirson, Commercial Embroiderers

1950–1953 Workroom at RSN, also part-time student for C & G dressmaking course

Teaching 1953–58 Trubweeke School of Domestic Science, Cuckfield, Sussex

1958–59 Hampton School of Embroidery, Twickenham

1959–61 Bromley College of Art

1962–66	Ravensbourne College of Art and Design
1966–71	Beckenham and Penge Adult Education Centre
1969	Set up Textile Studio, under direction of Alison Barrell, 1970
Commissions	
1961	Altar frontal for St Mary the Virgin, Hayes, Kent
1961–62	Set of six copes for Chichester Cathedral designed by Ceri Richards
1966–67	Cope with four hoods for Lady Margaret School, Parsons Green, London, in collaboration with teachers and students
1967	Frontal for Golders Green Crematorium Chapel, designed by Jennifer Campbell

Elizabeth Ford NDD 1925–

1946–50	Training at Birmingham College of Art – hand and machine embroidery
1956–57	Weaving at the Central School of Art and Crafts, London
1951–57	Nottingham College of Art (now part of Trent Polytechnic)
1958	Assisted Gerald Holtom and David Holt – machine embroidery
Teaching 1958–63	Part-time teaching at Oxford College of Art
1963–70	Lecturer in embroidery at Worcester College of Education, later in charge of the Needlework Department
	Collaboration with Pat Russell on a commission for a church for the deaf and dumb, Luton
1970–80	Part time in further education
Exhibitions	
1953	Midland Group Gallery, Nottingham
	Pictures for Schools
1976	One-man show, Gallery 27, Tonbridge, Kent
1978	One-man show, Stoke Polytechnic
1979	One-man show, Ibis Gallery, Leamington Spa
	Turks Head Gallery, Alcester
	Work sold to private and public collectors, including churches at Streetly, Staffordshire, Wylde Green, Sparkhill, Birmingham, Derby, Luton, Peterborough, Bedford

Patricia Foulds (née Beese) NDD ATC 1936–

1954–58	Training at West of England College of Art (now Bristol Polytechnic) – NDD embroidery and printed textiles
1958–58	London University, Institute of Education ATC
Teaching 1959–61	Bourneville School of Art, Birmingham
	Full-time post in charge of Printed Textiles and Weaving
	Intermediate and part-time vocational students
1961–68	Full and part-time teaching posts in charge of embroidery, Diploma Embroidery and Fashion students, ATD and Foundation, also Vocational Fashion
from 1968	Loughborough College of Art and Design Senior Tutor in charge of Embroidery. BA Hons Embroidery students Full-time sandwich and part-time courses for teachers in adult education also vocational fashion
	Many short courses and lectures for teachers in primary, secondary and further education, as well as for the Embroiderers' Guild and other groups of embroiderers
	External examiner for Bristol University Institute of Education

Exhibitions The Crafts Centre of Great Britain, St Paul's Cathedral, York Minster. Royal West of England Academy, various provincial museums

Works purchased by Leicestershire Education Authority. Various private collectors

Publication *Embroidery for the Church*, Studio Vista, 1975

Elizabeth Geddes NDD 1917–

1935–38 Training at Reading University School of Art – book illustration and wood-engraving

1939–47 Land Army and later on draughtswoman for the Ministry of Aircraft Production

1947–49 Maidstone College of Art – NDD in typographical design

1949–51 Bromley College of Art – NDD in hand and machine embroidery

Teaching 1951–78 Part-time lecturer in a number of schools and colleges, including Hornsey College of Art, Bromley College of Art, Hammersmith College of Art and Building, Royal School of Needlework and Stanhope Institute. Assisted on many courses

1953 Full Technological Certificate C & G

1954–58 Freelance work – Needlework Development Scheme. Creative Assistant to Iris Hills

1959–66 Assistant examiner with Iris Hills – C & G in embroidery, both levels

1970–72 Textile conservation – Karen Finch

Commissions

1953–54 Four frontals for Bromley Parish Church – designed by students of the College of Art and carried out by Elizabeth Geddes

1958 Cope – designed by Margaret Treherne, carried out by Elizabeth Geddes

1966–67 Heraldic coat of arms – Lambeth Town Hall

1967 Academic robes for the Royal College of Art – designed by Joyce Conwy-Evans

1969 Designed and worked a frontal for St Margaret's, Putney

1977 Designed and worked an embroidered bed-head for the Queen's bed on the Royal Train

Publications *Design for Flower Embroidery*, Mills and Boon, 1961

Blackwork Embroidery, with Moyra McNeill, Mills and Boon, 1965

Esther Grainger 1912–

1928–34 Training at Cardiff School of Art – painting

Teaching 1934–36 Handicrafts, Pontypridd Settlement and the National Council of Social Services of South Wales

1940 In conjunction with the British Institute of Adult Education, organised art lectures, classes and courses in South Wales

1946–50 Caerphilly Girls' Grammar School; also taught groups of teachers

1950–60 Lecturer in art and art history for supplementary courses for serving teachers of art and crafts; for Cardiff Education Authority

1960–76 Principal lecturer, Art Department, Cardiff College of Education

1976– Retired from teaching

Professional work Work exhibited in a number of galleries and exhibitions, including Pictures for Schools, Welsh Arts Council and abroad. Work purchased by education authorities, Welsh Arts Council, Merthyr Tydfil Museum and Art Gallery, and other public and private collectors in Great Britain and abroad

Jennifer Gray NDD 1931–

1951–53 Training at Bromley College of Art and Design – hand embroidery

1954 ATC Brighton College of Art

Teaching 1954 Appointed to teach hand and machine embroidery at Hull Regional College of Art and Crafts

1981 Retired from teaching

Exhibitions

1953 Artists' House, London ('Still life' of an experimental panel in white thread and fabrics was acquired by the Victoria and Albert Museum)

1955 Anglo-Danish exhibition, City Hall, Hull

1958 Ferens Art Gallery, Hull, joint exhibition

1963 Interiors International, London, joint exhibition

1964 University of Hull

1966 Institute of Advanced Architectural Studies, York Festival

1969 Ferens Art Gallery, Hull and Nottinghamshire Galleries, joint exhibition (variable compositions)

1970 King's Manor, York, exhibition of recent work

1974 James Starkey Galleries, Beverley – recent work

Publications *The Technique and Design of Machine Embroidery*, Batsford, 1973

Canvas Work, Batsford 1974

Commissions

Late 60s Hassocks and kneelers for Girton College

1960s Eastgate Hotel (Trust House) Lincoln

Group projects

1961 St John of Beverley panels depicting his life

1982 Designing and overseeing working of Beverley Minster Festival banners, first hung Whitsun 1982

Sylvia Green ARCA 1915–

1935–38 Training at Royal College of Art, Design School

1936–38 Evening classes, Bromley and Beckenham School of Art

Teaching 1938–46 South West Essex Technical College and School of Art

During this time made costumes for the Ballet Guild

Career 1947 Freelance book illustration

1948 More teaching. Part time, Hammersmith College of Art and Building, where girls from the Mary Boon School attended for 'O' and 'A' Level classes

1969 Left the Mary Boon School. Taught adults for the Inner London Education Authority

to date Courses for the ILEA, Royal School of Needlework, the Embroiderers' Guild and others. Tutor to ILEA, Annual Summer Workshop for craft teachers. Took over Beryl Dean's classes at the Stanhope Institute

Commissions

1954 First commission – ecclesiastical embroidery

1959 Mothers' Union Banner – St Michael's Church, Highgate, London

1963 Stole – St Michael's Church

1964 Green altar frontal, burse and veil all for St Michael's Church, Highgate, London

1969 Red cope for the Vicar of St Michael's, now in St James' Church, Gerlick, Hythe, Kent

1972 Two purple stoles, burse and veil

1976–78 Red altar frontal – St Michael's, Highgate

1979 White stole, burse and veil; Red stole, burse and veil – St Michael's, Highgate

Publications *Canvas Work for Beginners*, Studio Vista, 1970

Patchwork for Beginners, Studio Vista, 1971

Ronald Grierson FSIA 1901–

Training – worked as a designer for industry producing ideas for rugs and textiles

1979–80 'The Thirties' Exhibition, Hayward Gallery, South Bank, retrospective

Commissions (including works purchased)

1932 Fire screen exhibited and purchased by the Victoria and Albert Museum

1950 Large hanging for St Alban the Martyr Church, Charles Street, Oxford

Exhibited at the Arts and Crafts Exhibition, Victoria and Albert Museum

Commissions for woven articles for industry and private purchasers, both for ecclesiastical and secular purposes

Kathleen Harris (née Turner) ARCA 1880–1963

Training at Camberwell School of Art, with Ellen Wright, a pupil of May Morris, and Mary Houston
Specialised in embroidery and pottery

Teaching 1913–21 Lecturer in charge of embroidery, Manchester Municipal School of Art

1921–39 Part-time lecturer, the Royal College of Art
Part-time lecturer, the Regent Street Polytechnic
During the War taught at the James Allen Girls' School

1933 Conducted the first course for the Embroiderers' Guild

1951–60 Editor of *Embroidery* magazine
After retirement became President of the Sussex Branch of the Embroiderers' Guild

Publication A guild book on *Altar Linen*

Freda Harlow ARCA 1909–

1928–31 Training at Northampton School of Art

1931–34 Royal College of Art – textile printing and embroidery

Teaching 1934 Part time

1935 In charge of art and crafts at Frensham Heights School
Queen Ann Grammar School, York
Lawnswood School, Leeds

1975 Retired
Textiles sold to the Rutherston Collection

1982 Member of Quilters' Guild

Maureen Helsdon NDD ATD FSDC 1923–

Training at Haberdashers' School which had a lasting influence on her art due to the interest by the art teacher in the philosophy of Marion Richardson

Ealing School of Art

1950 Hornsey College of Art – illustration for NDD

1951 Embroidery studied on the ATC course. Machine embroidery discovered. Intensive study of embroidery

Teaching 1952–77 Embroidery at Southampton College of Art – in charge of the department. C & G courses

1977	Retired from full-time teaching, becoming part time
Exhibitions	
1960	One-man show at the Crafts Centre, London
1965	Another one-man show at the Crafts Centre and at Southampton University
1970	One-man show at Alwin Gallery, London
Commissions	Curtains for Great West Door of Romsey Abbey *Vulcan* for entrance foyer of EKO building, Woking, Surrey *Comus* – received a special award from an exhibition in Stuttgart Royd's Advertising Agency – series of panels for the Board Room Works sold to education authorities and private clients

Iris Hills ARCA 1913–

1932–35	Training at Royal College of Art Design School – illustration and embroidery
Teaching 1935–36	Part-time lecturer, Bromley College of Art
1936–42	Full-time lecturer, Bromley College of Art
1942–55	In charge of the Craft School, Bromley College of Art, and in charge of embroidery in 1946 also, after Elizabeth Grace Thomson left the College
1955–61	'Expert in charge' of the Needlework Development Scheme
1958–66	Chief Examiner for the City and Guilds of London Institute examinations, assisted by Elizabeth Geddes from 1959
1961–66	Senior lecturer in charge of Fashion, Embroidery and Textiles at Hammersmith College of Art and Building
1967–77	Inspector of further and higher education (Fashion and creative studies) ILEA
Publication	*Introduction to Embroidery*, Victoria and Albert Museum, 1953

Margaret T Holden-Jones ARCA FRSA FIAL (Hon) FSDC 1890–

1913–16	Training at Liverpool School of Art
1916–20	Royal College of Art – embroidery and calligraphy
1919	Royal College of Art – post graduate course
Teaching 1922	Principles of teaching and school management
1923	Visited and taught in the USA Carried out various commissions Elected a Master Craftsman of the Society of Arts and Crafts
1922–23	Part-time lecturer at Blackheath School of Art, London Part-time lecturer at Goldsmiths' College, University of London
1925–58	Lecturer in several schools and colleges
1940–54	Full-time lecturer at North West Polytechnic, London; taught embroidery, pottery, calligraphy
1947	Founder member of the Craft Centre of Great Britain
1954	Retired from teaching
1960	Fellow of the International Institute of Arts and Letters Articles written on embroidery for magazines
Commissions	Include many for calligraphy, also: A colour wood-cut flower and insect book, now in the print room of the British Museum A water colour flower book in the manuscript department of the British library at the British Museum

A petit point embroidered pendant
A small petit point panel
} Both in the Victoria and Albert Museum

Constance Howard MBE ARCA ATD FSDC 1910–

1925–31 Training at Northampton School of Art – embroidery, wood-engraving

1931–35 Royal College of Art – book illustration, wood-engraving

Teaching 1935–46 Full-time lecturer at Cardiff, Eastbourne and Kingston-upon-Thames Schools

1947–75 Part-time lecturer, then full-time senior lecturer and principal lecturer in charge of Textiles/Embroidery, Goldsmiths' School of Art, University of London. Many courses and lectures conducted throughout Great Britain, including those for the Ministry of Education, The Barry Summer School, and the Embroiderers' Guild

1955–63 Examiner for the National Diploma in Design – hand embroidery

1958–69 Examiner for O and A Levels, Joint Matriculation Board – embroidery, dress design

1950s to date Examiner for University Institutes of Education

1973–75 On panel for Council for National Academic Awards

1969–77 Lecture tours to Canada and USA

1975 Awarded the MBE, for services to Art Education

1978–81 Assessor for Council for National Academic Awards

1978 Lecture tour to Australia and New Zealand

1979 to date Canada and the USA

Exhibitions

1945+ Arts and Crafts Exhibitions Society (SDC 1961)

1948+ Pictures for Schools

1968– St Paul's Cathedral, York Minster

mid '70s Hereford and Rochester Cathedrals

1973 Crafts '73 Victoria and Albert Museum

1981 London, Ontario, Canada

1983 Kyoto and Tokyo Fine Art Museums

1983 Guildford House, Guildford

Commissions

1951 Festival of Britain

1950s Altar frontals – Makerere University, Kampala. Also stoles and burses.

Banner – Mothers' Union, Lincoln Cathedral

Designs for canvas work – Eton College Chapel

1960s Throwover altar cover – Lincoln Cathedral

1973 Hanging – Northampton Museum

Other commissions for secular embroidery

Work purchased by public and private collectors in Great Britain and abroad, including the Victoria and Albert Museum

1974 Elected as a member of the Art Workers Guild

Publications *Design for Embroidery from Traditional English Sources*, Batsford 1956

Inspiration for Embroidery, Batsford 1966

Embroidery and Colour, Batsford 1976

Textile Crafts (editor and section on embroidery), Pitman 1977

The Constance Howard Book of Stitches, Batsford 1979

Twentieth-Century Embroidery to 1939, Batsford 1981

Many articles in magazines and booklets, etc, including *Embroidery*

Edith John 1914–

Training at Doncaster School of Art – embroidery

Teaching 1935–47	Taught over a wide area in the old West Riding Institute, Yorkshire
1935–76	Taught also in the Doncaster School of Art (later College of Art)
1972	Nantucket, USA, summer school
	Short courses and lectures for branches of the Embroiderers' Guild
Exhibitions	Work exhibited in many shows in Great Britain and abroad, including:
1962	Foyles
1963–68	Australia
1968	St Paul's Cathedral
Commissions	Commissions include a chasuble worked for the British Artist Craftsmen exhibition – sold to Washington DC
	Work purchased by public and private collectors in Great Britain and abroad
Publications	*Creative Stitches*, Batsford, 1967
	Filling Stitches, Batsford, 1967
	Ideas for Needlecraft, Batsford, 1968
	Needleweaving, Batsford, 1970
	Experimental Embroidery, Batsford, 1976

Diana Jones NDD ATD 1932–

1953	Training at Cardiff College of Art – illustration, embroidery
1953–54	Art Teachers' Diploma
Teaching	Stroud School of Art; Cardiff College of Art; Dyfed College of Art
	Short courses for Glamorgan Education Authority, Barry Summer School, also many other courses
1966	Membership of the '62 Group
1976	Membership of the Society of Designer Craftsmen
Exhibitions	Work exhibited in group shows including:
1957	Victoria and Albert Museum, London
1973	Artist at Work, Colwyn Bay, North Wales
1974	Holborn Museum, Bath
	The '62 Group
1975	With one other exhibitor at the University of Aberystwith – textiles
1977	Textile exhibition, Southampton
	Several Pictures for Schools exhibitions
Commissions	
1965	Banner – church in Wales
1967	Altar frontal
1976	Patchwork quilt – Welsh Arts Council
	Works purchased by Welsh Arts Council, North Wales Association for the Arts, South Wales Association for the Arts, education authorities in England
Publication	*Patterns for Canvas Embroidery*, Batsford, 1977

Sister Kathleen (Kathleen Snelus) 1903–

1932	Entered St Saviour's Priory, London
	No formal training in embroidery
	Made vestments for the Priory

1965	Until this date concerned chiefly with parish work
1955	Joined Beryl Dean's ecclesiastical classes at the Hammersmith College of Art and Building
	Learnt to appreciate modern design, but said that she was not a designer. She assisted Beryl Dean on some projects and carried out embroideries designed by others
Commissions designed by others	A lenten frontal for the High Altar, Gloucester Cathedral. Designed by L C Evetts
	A frontal for the restored Lady Chapel, Exeter Cathedral, designed by John Hayward
1965	A set of white vestments for Pope Paul VI, designed by Laurence King
1976–77	Helped on the St Paul's Cathedral Jubilee Cope
	A set of vestments and a very modern frontal, for a new church in Macclesfield designed by Peter Delaney; 'and other things around the country'

Margaret Kaye ARCA 1912–

1931–34	Training at Croydon School of Art – printed textiles. Board of Education, Industrial Design examination
1934–37	Royal College of Art – stained glass, fabric collage
Teaching 1937	Full-time lecturer in printed textiles, Birmingham College of Art
From World War Two until	Full-time lecturer, Guildford School of Art: lithography
1977	Freelance work Part-time lecturer, St Martins School of Art Part-time lecturer, Camberwell School of Art – lithography
1976	Visitor, West Sussex School of Art
1977	Retired from teaching
Collage Commissions	Include work purchased by education authorities, and by:
	The Victoria and Albert Museum
	The Festival of Britain
	The Contemporary Arts Society
	Murals for the Orient Line, for restaurants and private commissions
	Stained glass for private chapels; The Boltons, London; Chichester School; Formosa Rubey, Radnagé
	Restorations for the National Trust
Embroidery and collage commissions	Include ecclesiastical commissions for:
	Winchester Cathedral – frontals
	Marlborough College, Ghana (for the Queen)
	Eastbourne, Manchester, Southampton and others
	Two ballets designed, one with John Cranko for Sadlers' Wells; one for the Ballet Rambert, the Mercury Theatre
	Work purchased by the Victoria and Albert Museum

Nancy Kimmins (née White) NDD 1922–

1938	Training in Royal School of Needlework with Marguerite Randall
	During the War, nursed and medical laboratory technician
1947	Royal School of Needlework Teaching Diploma
1950	NDD at Bromley College of Art with Iris Hills – embroidery
Teaching 1950	Teaching for the ILEA, the Embroiderers' Guild and women's organisations
1950	Member of the Embroiderers' Guilds

Member of the Textile Studio, Beckenham; some teaching

Work sold to private and public bodies in Great Britain and overseas

Commissions Include ecclesiastical and ceremonial regalia

1975 Represented the Embroiderers' Guild at the Conservation Centre at Hampton Court Palace

1978 Participation in group commission for Winchester Cathedral with Barbara Siedlecka and Moyra McNeill

Marjorie Kostenz 1902–1979

1920 Training in Paris

1921 The Slade School of Fine Art – painting

1925 Married Mark Gertler, a painter

1952 Embroidery at Goldsmiths' School of Art, part time

Exhibitions At the Minories, Colchester

1972 Foyles Art Gallery

Exhibited in a number of other places in mixed shows

Work sold to schools, museums and private clients, including the Abbot Hall Gallery, Kendal and the Commonwealth Institute, London

Alison Liley (née Erridge) NDD 1929–

1948–50 Training at Ashton School of Art

1950–52 Bromley College of Art with Iris Hills – NDD in embroidery

1952 Scholarship – Norwegian Government

Teaching 1953–60 Colleges of art in Kent, Canterbury, Folkestone and Dover

1963–68 Loughborough College of Art

1967 Barry Summer School, adult education

1968–70 Head of the Textile/Fashion Department – Derby College of Art

1970 Moved to Western Ireland, partner in a small craft workshop to date

Exhibitions

1955 One-man show, Embroiderers' Guild

Exhibited with small group during 1953–60

Now exhibits with the workshop

Publications *The Craft of Embroidery*, Mills and Boon 1961

Embroidery, a Fresh Approach, Mills and Boon 1964

Many articles on crafts and educational subjects

Work in the collections of the Embroiderers' Guild, Gawthorpe Hall, and private clients

In 1962 Alison Liley was the first Chairman of the '62 Group

Moyra McNeill (née Somerville) NDD FSDC 1930–

1947–51 Training at Bromley College of Art – NDD in embroidery, hand and machine

Teaching 1952–70 Part time, Camberwell School of Arts and Crafts

Tonbridge Grammar School for Girls

Day schools/short courses – Embroiderers' Guild

Royal School of Needlework and Women's Institutes

1971 Part-time teacher at Beckenham Adult Education Centre; latterly in charge of the C & G classes

1974–77	Workshop tours in USA and
1978	Australia
Exhibitions	Two-man show – Crafts Centre, London
	The Embroiderers' Guild
	The Society of Designer Craftsmen
Commissions 1978	Joint commission with Barbara Siedlecka and Nancy Kimmins – five copes for Winchester Cathedral
	Work purchased by public and private collectors including:
	The Victoria and Albert Museum, London; Switzerland, Australia and the USA
Publications	*Blackwork Embroidery* (with Elizabeth Geddes), Mills and Boon, 1965
	Pulled Thread Work, Mills and Boon, 1971
	Quilting for To-day, Mills and Boon, 1975
	Articles published in magazines, including *Embroidery*, and in daily papers

Bridget Moss (née Knowles) ARCA 1913–

1931–34	Training at Maidstone School of Art – embroidery and calligraphy
1934	Industrial Design examination
1934–37	Royal College of Art – mural decoration
1937–40	Worked in advertising with Jenners of Edinburgh
1942–46	National Association of Girls' Clubs – art adviser in the Education Department
1946	Freelance book and educational magazine illustration
1974	Founder member of the Tunbridge Wells Branch of the Embroiders' Guild

Betty Myerscough (née Frazer) DA 1932–

1950–55	Training at Glasgow School of Art – embroidery and weaving
1955–59	Four years with J and P Coats
Teaching 1959–61	Full-time lecturer – Grays School of Art, Aberdeen
1961–63	Part time lecturer – Canterbury College of Art
1979 to date	Part-time – Chelsea School of Art
Exhibitions	With the Glasgow School of Art Embroidery Group
1975	One-man show at Ripley Art Centre, Bromley
1979 and 1980	The New Gallery, Hornsey Central Library, London
	Work in the collections of Glasgow Art Gallery, Manchester and London Education Authorities and purchased by private collectors in Great Britain, Norway, Sweden, Switzerland, Kuwait and the USA
Commissions	Aberdeen College of Education
	Secker and Warburg
	Scottish Hotel
	USA

Joan Nicholson ARCA MSIA 1924–

1941–44	Training at West Hartlepool College of Art – embroidery
1944–47	Royal College of Art
Teaching 1948	Lecturing and teaching adults and children – art and embroidery
1948–67	Part-time lecturer Farnham College of Art (West Surrey College of Art and Design)

1951–53 Regent Street Polytechnic part time – embroidery

Exhibitions Exhibition at the Design Centre to promote embroidery; led to election to the Society of Industrial Artists

Commissions The Needlework Development Scheme

The Festival of Britain

Designed the embroidered wall decorations for the bedroom of HM the Queen (now the Queen Mother) on the Royal Yacht Britannia; carried out by the Royal School of Needlework

Freelance designer working for William Briggs, J and P Coats and *Golden Hands*

Publications *Contemporary Embroidery Design*, Batsford, 1954

Simple Embroidery, Batsford 1973

Embroidery for Schools, Batsford, 1977

Checkweave Canvas Embroidery, J and P Coats, 1977

Margaret Nicholson 1913–

1928–33 Training at Sheffield College of Art – embroidery and dress design C & G bronze medal

1933–42 Worked in industry – dress design, with Brook of Northampton

Teaching 1932 Sheffield College of Art

1942 Part time, onwards

Chesterfield College of Art

West Riding of Yorkshire

Hammersmith College of Art and Building

Embroiderers' Guild

1960–78 Lecturer in hand embroidery, London College of Fashion

1978 Retired from full-time teaching

1978–80 Part time, London College of Fashion

Lecturer on many courses

Moderator, intermediate and advanced examinations in embroidery, C & G

1982 Member of Standing Advisory Committee, Associated Examining Board

Exhibitions Work exhibited in group shows

Commissions 1970 Banner for Mothers' Union, Coventry Cathedral

Altar frontal, church in Guernsey

Pulpit fall

Publications *Embroidery for Beginners*, Studio Vista, 1966

Articles in *Embroidery* magazine

Leaflet – National Federation of Women's Institute, on appliqué

Articles in *Creative Needlecraft*

Dorothea Nield 1917–

1933–36 Training at the Royal School of Needlework

1936–37 Training in Paris, also museum studies

1937–38 Experience in all departments of the Royal School of Needlework

Teaching 1938–39 Assistant teacher in the Training School, RSN

1939–45 War work

Attended Northwich College of Art – C & G in embroidery and art

1945–46 Assistant teacher in the Training School, RSN
1946–51 Freelance teacher and lecturer
1951–61 Head of Training School, RSN
1962–71 Adviser to the Embroiderers' Guild
Examiner for the Cambridge Institute of Education
On editorial board for *Embroidery* magazine
1972 Freelance teaching, lecturing, etc
Exhibitions Include London and New Zealand
Publications *Adventures in Patchwork*, Mills and Boon, 1975
Contributions to magazines, including *Embroidery*
Section on Lace – *Textile Crafts*, Pitman 1977

E Kay Norris NDD FSDC 1922–

Training at Bournville School of Arts and Crafts
C & G silver medal of the Institute
Merchant Taylor's Prize and James Pearsall and Company's prize
1951 Ministry of Education, Technical Teachers' Certificate, London
Bromley College of Art, part time
1957–59 Goldsmiths' School of Art, University of London – NDD, Special Level, embroidery
Teaching 1959–60 Part-time teaching posts, Bournville, Birmingham.
1960 to date In charge of embroidery at Chippenham Technical College, Wiltshire, part time Lectures and short courses for adult education
1959–63 Part-time assistant in Constance Howard's studio. Lectured and conducted short
Commissions
1976 Altar frontal for Marlborough College, Wiltshire
1978 Set of stoles for Devizes School, Wiltshire
1979 Chasuble for Marlborough College
1982 Altar frontal – St Martin's Hospital, Bath – for chapel, also a pulpit fall for the hospital
Exhibitions In group shows, in Great Britain and the USA
Work sold to education authorities and private clients

Mary Ozanne 1890–1976

Training at Royal School of Needlework
1935–74 Carried out work designed by other artists and architects. Among these were Stephen Dykes-Bower, Seeley and Padget, George Pace who designed for Llandaff Cathedral, and Lawrence Bond who worked for Lincoln Cathedral.

She was interested in technical perfection rather than in design, carrying out embroidery for copes for Canterbury and other places. She also carried out work for St Paul's, Lincoln, Durham, Hereford, Chester, Wells, Gloucester, and Exerter Cathedrals and Southall Minster. Some work was executed for ecclesiastical purposes in the USA

Pamela Pavitt (née Willard) NDD 1925–

1942–47 Training at Bromley College of Art – embroidery
1947–48 Institute of Education, London University

Teaching 1948–53 Willesden School of Art
1953–55 Hammersmith Day College
1955–57 Bromley College of Art
1952–57 Short courses conducted in Surrey, Kent, Carmarthen and for the London County Council
1968–81 Primary school teaching
1982 Textile Conservation Centre
Croydon Adult Education Centre
Publications Articles on machine embroidery for *Embroidery* magazine 1960–61
Commissions
1958 Pulpit fall – New College, London
1963 Pulpit fall – Trinity Congregational Church, Crawley
Member of Beckenham Textile Studio

Katherine Powell 1890–1977

Born with only one hand
1906 Queen Elizabeth Grammar School
Trained Hornsey School of Art, where embroidery was part of the general course
1908 C & G Examinations, ordinary level
1910 School of Art Prize for holiday work
1911 Two bronze medals for embroidery, National Competition, Board of Education
1919 Silver medal – Advanced level C & G examination
Examiner Grace Christie
During the First World War she painted numerals and letters on compasses for the Royal Flying Corps
Taught art and needlework in North London
Teaching 1920 Barry, South Wales
1927 Malvern Girls School, until her retirement in 1952
(Research by Joan Edwards, *Embroidery*, winter 1978)

Frances Richards ARCA 1901–

Training at Burslem School of Art
1924–27 Royal College of Art – mural decoration where she met Ceri Richards, the Welsh artist
Illustrated a number of books, obtaining some commissions when a student
Exhibitions One-man shows at the Redfern Gallery, London
1937+ Many group shows. Work is represented in galleries and museums, including the Tate Gallery, the Victoria and Albert Museum and the National Museum of Wales
1980 Retrospective exhibition
Publications *The Acts of the Apostles*, Cambridge University Press, 1930
The Book of Revelations, Faber and Faber, London; Scribner, New York; 1931
Drawings for *The Book of Lamentations*, Oxford University Press, 1969
Les Illuminations – ten lithographs and a title page to Rimbaud's work, Curzon Press, 1975

Christine Risley NDD MSIAD 1926–

1944–48 Training at Goldsmiths' School of Art, University of London, Goldsmiths' College – painting

1948–49 Goldsmiths' School of Art – ATD course

Teaching 1949–67 Part-time lecturer at St Martin's School of Art, London

1955–67 Part-time lecturer at Goldsmiths' School of Art

1967 to date Full-time lecturer and in 1975 senior lecturer at Goldsmiths' School of Art

1979 Principal lecturer, Goldsmiths' School of Art

Part-time visiting tutor at the Royal College of Art and other establishments, including lecturing at Bristol Polytechnic, Trent Polytechnic and the Embroiderers' Guild

1978 and 1980 Workshop – machine embroidery, Canada

Exhibitions

1950–69 Arts Council Travelling Exhibitions

Pictures for Schools, and other group shows

1973 Crafts '73, Victoria and Albert Museum, London, and other galleries in Great Britain and abroad

1981 London, Ontario, Canada

1983 Kyoto and Tokyo Fine Arts Museums

Works purchased by public and private collectors, including education authorities

Commissions (Commercial work)

1956 Advertisement for Yardley Cosmetics – full-page colour

1956 and 1958 Wallpaper designs – Palladio range

1959–60 Fabric designs, exhibited at Colour, Design and Style Centre, Manchester

1965 Machine embroidered ties

Appointments, awards, etc

1970 Elected as a member of the Society of Industrial Artists and Designers

1975 Appointed as External Assessor, Trent Polytechnic, for the textile course

1981 External Assessor, Ulster Polytechnic, for the BA Honours course in embroidery

1966 Invited to work at the Bernina Sewing Machine Factory, Steckbourne, Switzerland – one week

Publications *Machine Embroidery*, Studio Vista, 1961

Creative Embroidery, Studio Vista, 1969

Machine Embroidery – a complete guide, Studio Vista, 1973

Many articles for magazines

Embroidery in Easy Steps (editor), Studio Vista, 1976

*Machine Embroidery – a complete guide (*paperback edition*) 1981*

Pamela Anne Rooke NDD 1932–

1949–53 Training at Bromley College of Art – hand and machine embroidery

1953–54 University of London Institute of Education

1954 Art Teachers' Certificate (London)

Teaching 1954–59 Darlington College of Further Education, Darlington, County Durham

1960–61 Kenya High School for Girls, Nairobi, Kenya

1961–69 State House Road Girls' High School (formerly Delamere Girls' High School), Nairobi, Kenya

Both the Nairobi Schools mentioned are secondary schools where pupils are prepared for the Cambridge Overseas School Certificate examinations at both Ordinary and Advanced Levels. Embroidery was offered as one of the examination options.

Most of 1970 was spent in Stellenbosch in the Cape Province of South Africa

1971 to date	Trinity College, Carmarthen – Senior Lecturer specialising in embroidery
1977	A tutor for the West Wales Branch of the Embroiderers' Guild
Commissions	
1953	A green altar frontal for Bromley Parish Church
1953	Took part in an exhibition at Artists' House in London and sold a machine-embroidered panel entitled 'Crustacea'
1954	Canvas-work panel *Nursery Rhymes* reproduced in the *Saturday Book* (14th Issue)
1954–59	Embroidered works for the Needlework Development Scheme
1959	Banner for the Mothers' Union of St Hilda's Church, Darlington
1978	Designed and made a green chasuble and stole for use in the Parish Church of Llanstephan in memory of Mrs Amy Grace Reynolds
1982–	At present working on a pulpit fall for St Andrew's Church, Ferring-by-Sea, West Sussex

Pat Russell FSDC 1919–

	Training at Chelsea School of Art – writing and illumination
1960 to date	Machine collage for ecclesiastical vestments and furnishings carried out in Great Britain and Canada
	Also hangings and panels for interior decoration
Teaching	Courses on Calligraphy and lettering in Great Britain
1970s	Courses in Canada and the USA on ecclesiastical embroidery and design
	Fellow of the Society of Designer Craftsmen
1972	Member of the Art Workers' Guild
Exhibitions	Of ecclesiastical work and calligraphy in many galleries including the Victoria and Albert Museum, London; The Oxford Gallery; The Waterloo Gallery (Crafts Council) London 1982, and others including St Paul's Cathedral Crypt.
	Work purchased by public and private collectors including the Victoria and Albert Museum, Oxford City and County Museum, Reading Museum and abroad
Commissions	Many for cathedrals and churches in Great Britain, including: St Paul's Cathedral; Wells, Ely, Norwich, and Exeter Cathedrals; Pershore Abbey, Worcester; Shrewsbury School; St Mary's School, Wantage; Holy Trinity Church, Weymouth; Community Church, Leigham, Plymouth; St Matthew's Church, Wigmore, Kent; Wesley Memorial Church, Oxford; Kennington Methodist Chapel, London; The Tower of London, Chapel of St Peter ad Vincula; Liberal Jewish Synagogue, St John's Wood, London; Church of the Saviour, Waterloo, Ontario, Canada
Publications	*Lettering for Embroidery*, Batsford and Van Nostran Reinhold, 1971
	Articles in *Embroidery* magazine
1978	Consultant on colour and design for church embroideries
1980	Awarded a grant by the Crafts Advisory Committee for the pursuance of own work

Eirian Short NDD 1924–

	Training during the Second World War, served in the ATS
1946	Goldsmiths' School of Art, University of London, Goldsmiths' College – NDD in sculpture
Teaching	Part-time lecturer in the following schools:
1953–55	Gravesend School of Art

1954–68 Hornsey College of Art (now Middlesex Polytechnic)
1955–57 and 1969 Goldsmiths' School of Art
1969–70 Avery Hill College of Education, College of All Saints (both teacher training colleges in London)

Occasional visiting lecturer to Croydon School of Art, the Central School of Art and Crafts and Middlesex Polytechnic

Short courses for various authorities

Exhibitions
1951 on Pictures for Schools, English and Welsh shows
Mid-1960s to 70s Contemporary Hangings
From 1969 '62 Group
1969–75 Biannually with three other artists – 'Quad' Group
1982 Two-man show in Cardiff

Works purchased by the National Museum of Wales, Welsh Arts Council, various education authorities and other public and private clients

Commissions Ecclesiastical work, *Sunday Times*, John Lewis, J and P Coats and others
Publications *Embroidery and Fabric Collage*, Pitman, 1967

Introducing Macramé, Batsford, 1970

Introducing Quilting, Batsford, 1970

Quilting: technique and design, Batsford, 1974

Various articles in magazines, *Embroidery*, etc

Rachel K Shuttleworth 1886–1967

Attended art classes in Paris. She was interested in social welfare and organised needlework classes. Her collection began with visual aids. A friend of Mr and Mrs Lewis F Day

1914–18 Secretary of Civic Arts Association
1921 Founded the North West Branch of the Embroiderers' Guild
1949 Awarded the MBE
1951 Founded the Fellowship of Church Workers, to repair and care for embroideries. Classified the lace collection of the Embroiderers' Guild. Wrote articles and collected items for the 'craft house' she was aiming to found
1952 Gawthorpe Hall, Lancashire, was offered to the National Trust and she became its caretaker. Her collection was moved to the Hall and students began to use the now famous study centre. Gawthorpe Hall became a recognised centre for the study of lace and embroidery, administered by Lancashire County Council

Barbara Snook 1913–1977

Training at Brighton College of Art and Bromley College of Art

Teaching Various posts before obtaining a permanent post, Brighouse, Yorkshire
1944 Appointed Head of Art and Craft department, Chislehurst and Sidcup Grammar School for Girls. Specialised in teaching embroidery, for O and A level examinations
1949–50 Exchange teacher to the USA for one year
1973 Retired from teaching

Visited Ethiopia

1974 Kashmir, and after this visited Australia on a lecture tour for the Embroiderers' Guild

Publications by Batsford
Learning to Embroider, 1960
English Historical Embroidery, 1960
Learning to Sew, 1962
Embroidery Stitches, 1963
Creative Soft Toys, 1963
Puppets, 1965
Costumes for School Plays, 1965
Needlework for Juniors, 1966
Florentine Canvas Embroidery, 1967
Making Clowns, Witches and Dragons, 1967
Making Baby Clothes, 1968
Fancy Dress for Children, 1969
Scribble Stitchery, 1972
Making Masks, 1972
Making Birds, Beasts and Insects, 1974
The Zoo, 1975
Embroidery Designs from the Sea, 1977

Lilla Speir (née Hilda Norfolk) 1915–

Training by Constance Brown, her art teacher

1932–37 Chelsea School of Art, London – general course

Teaching 1937–43 West of England College of Art, Bristol

1944–49 Part-time at Beckenham and Croydon Schools of Art

1950–58 Part-time at Maidstone College of Art

1958–68 Full time at Manchester College of Art, starting the Dip AD course in embroidery

1968–76 Ulster Polytechnic, Belfast, full time, starting the BA Honours degree course in embroidery for the CNAA (Council for National Academic Awards)

1976 Retired to pursue her own work; moved to Scotland

1968–77 Examiner for embroidery. External examiner for the CNAA

Exhibitions Manchester College of Art

Arts Council Gallery, Belfast

Pictures for Schools

1978 One-person show, Gracefield Art Gallery, Dumfries

Guest craftswoman, Women Artists' Exhibition, Royal Scottish Academy, Edinburgh

1980 One-person exhibition, Broughton Gallery, Biggar, Lanarkshire. Quilts, small hangings

1981 In group exhibition, Philip Francis Gallery, Sheffield

1982 Studio exhibition. Past and present quilts. Corresponding with the Dumfries Festival

Marion Stewart DA 1931–

1949–53 Training at Glasgow School of Art, Diploma in Embroidery and weaving

1954 Post-Diploma scholarship. Visited European countries

1954–55 Jordanhill, College of Education – teachers' certificate

Teaching 1956–59 Lecturer at Grays School of Art, Aberdeen

1959 Duncan of Jordanstown College of Art, Dundee – senior lecturer in embroidery and in charge of women's crafts

1979 Assessor for CNAA, revalidation of embroidery, Glasgow School of Art

Member of Scottish Tourist Board Committee (Crafstman in Residence)

Exhibitions

1956 Founder member, Glasgow School of Art Embroidery Group

Group shows

Work purchased by public and private collectors, including the Royal Scottish Museum, Edinburgh

Commissions Manchester Education Committee

Cardiff College of Education

Earl Haig Collection
Work shown throughout Great Britain

Joyce Sturge (née Pybus) 1916–

1931 Training at Fine Art Department, Armstrong College, University of Durham (now King's College, University of Newcastle)

Teaching 1938 Secondary and day-continuation schools, training colleges for teachers and adult education

1947–78 Chief examiner in embroidery for O Level, University of London, 30 years, with breaks for other examining, University of Durham Schools Examinations Board and Associated Examining Board

Paintings and embroideries sold in Great Britain, Canada, the USA and Australia

Doris Taylor ARCA 1890–1978

1905 Training part-time at Oldham School of Art

1906 Manchester Municipal School of Art

1907 Full-time student at Manchester Municipal School of Art.
Studied stained glass, painting, leatherwork, embroidery, wood carving

1915 C & G Advanced embroidery

1916–19 Royal College of Art

Teaching 1919–21 Full-time lecturer, Hastings School of Art

1921–57 Head of Department in charge of dress and embroidery, Manchester Municipal School of Art

1950s Examiner for the Ministry of Education, Intermediate Examination in Art

1957 Retired from Manchester Regional College of Art (now Manchester Polytechnic)

Commissions Banners and other ecclesiastical embroideries:

Banner for The Young Australia League

Banner for the British Medical Association

Banner for the Mothers' Union

Banner for the Girls' Friendly Society

Private commissions

Ernest Thesiger CBE 1879–1961

Training at Slade School of Fine Art – painting
Also the Guildhall School of Music
He became a well-known actor

1914–18	Wounded and started a scheme to teach canvas embroidery to soldiers in hospital
1918–39	Experimented with various types of embroidery but preferred canvas work
1945	Vice patron, Embroiderers' Guild Interested in ecclesiastical work: Designed and worked two kneelers, Chelsea Old Church; wall hanging, Holy Trinity Church, Kensington Gore Restored eighteenth century chair seats, Templenewsam, Leeds. Made a large rug at the age of 81
Publications	*Adventures in Embroidery*, Studio Vista, 1941 revised 1947

Elizabeth Grace Thomson 1895–1981

	Training at Royal Academy School – painting
1920s	Croydon School of Art – embroidery and dress design Assisted Rebecca Crompton part-time in her classes and on courses
Teaching early 1930s	Became a full-time lecturer, Bromley School of Art
	Developed embroidery and dress design from a small to a large department
	Became Head of Fashion and Crafts, Bromley and Sidcup Schools of Art
1937	Responsible for Kent children's work – exhibition *Design in Education* promoted by the Council for Art and Industry
1939–46	Organised classes for Bromley School of Art
1946–52	Appointed His Majesty's Inspector of Women's Crafts – the first to be appointed
	Conducted a number of courses for the Ministry of Education, on fashion and embroidery
1952–61	Inspector of Women's Crafts in further and higher education for the London County Council
1961	Retired
Exhibitions 1932	Victoria and Albert Museum

June Tiley ARCA 1925–

1941–44	Training at Cardiff College of Art
1945–48	Royal College of Art – book illustration
1966	Sabbatical term Royal College of Art
Teaching 1948	Cardiff College of Art (later, Faculty of Design, South Glamorgan Institute of Higher Education)
	Fashion and embroidery
	Courses conducted for various summer and other schools, including, to date, the Barry Summer School
Exhibitions	With groups, including:
	The Embroiderers' Guild
	Society for Education Through Art (Pictures for Schools)
	'62 Group
	Founder member of '62 Group
Commissions	
1976	Royal National Eisteddfod of Wales
	Welsh Arts Council
	Burnley Building Society, Bangor
1978	Masquerade, touring exhibition, Welsh Arts Council
1978	Craft section National Eisteddfod
1978	Textiles – a broader definition – University of Wales, Aberystwyth

1963–78	Many collages and embroideries executed, among these:
1963	*Fantasy* panel
1966	*String and Glass Rods*
1973	Canvas work
1975	Hanging – needleweaving, wrapping and feathers
1976	Patchwork quilt – Celtic motif – Arts Council commission
	Work purchased by public and private collectors
1983	Lecturer at the World Crafts Council Conference, Shannon, Ireland

Margaret Treherne ARCA 1919–

	Training at Kingston-upon-Thames School of Art – dress design during Second World War
	Royal College of Art – stained glass, textiles; painting with Harry Thubron
Teaching 1950s	Part time, machine embroidery, College of the Garment Trades, Shoreditch, London (now part of the London College of Fashion)
	Hammersmith College of Art and Building
	St Martin's School of Art
	Goldsmiths' School of Art
Exhibitions	The Edinburgh Open Hundred
	Whitechapel Art Gallery
1959	Smithsonian Institute
	Pictures for Schools and others
1966	Represented Britain at the Commonwealth Art Treasures Exhibition, Burlington House
1975	The Tate Gallery and Morley Gallery, London, and the London Group
	One-man shows:
	Bear Lane Gallery, Oxford
	AIA Gallery, London
	Caldwell Gallery, Dublin
	Ogle Gallery, Eastbourne
	Regular exhibitions with Monika Kinley, London
Commissions	Ten windows for Chapel of Unity, Coventry Cathedral
	Parachute memorial, Manchester Airport
	Windows, Temple Emanuel, St Louis, Missouri, USA
	Banners flown at Tate Gallery, for 75th anniversary
	New Baptistry window, St Peter's Church, Nottingham
1977	Group of Banners, façade of Burlington House, Jubilee Exhibition at the Royal Academy of British Art 1953–77
1978	Dyed and draped fabric hangings – Brunel University, Middlesex
1979	One-man show, mixed media, including glass and textiles – Brunel University
	Works also in many places, stained glass and textiles, among these:
	Manchester Cathedral
	Liverpool Metropolitan Cathedral
	National Museum of Wales
	Victoria and Albert Museum
	Leicester Art Gallery
	Abbott Hall Gallery, Kendal

Stained glass and embroideries in Leicestershire Schools and other buildings and in public and private collections

Emmeline Williamina Thomson

Training at Burnley School of Art and Manchester School of Art

Teaching A few years at Nottingham County School of Art

1943 Appointed Art and Craft Adviser, North East Committee for Recreational Activities

1948 Art and Craft Adviser, Scottish Leadership Training Association

1949–63 Handicraft Supervisor, the Royal Highland and Agricultural Society of Scotland

1952 In charge of the Scottish Women's Rural Institute craft van

Isobel Watson NDD DA(Manchester) 1930–

1948–53 Training at Manchester Regional College of Art – printed textiles

1953 Art Teachers' Certificate

Teaching Full time at St Anne's School, Windermere

Part time at the Domestic and Trades College, Manchester (Hollins College)

St Catherine's Training College

Keswick School

Further Education classes in Cumbria

Member of Lake Artists Society and the Red Rose Guild of Designer Craftsmen

Work sold to Lancashire Education Committee and private collectors in Great Britain and abroad

Kathleen Whyte MBE DA 1907–

1934 Training at Grays School of Art, Aberdeen – DA embroidery

Teaching Art teacher in various schools in Aberdeen

Grays School of Art, evening class assistant – embroidery

1940 Organiser of crafts for youth clubs

1948 Senior Assistant in charge of embroidery and weaving, Glasgow School of Art

Exhibitions

1956 Organised exhibition of embroidery of former students of the embroidery department of Grays School of Art, which occur every two years in Glasgow from that date. Three tours sponsored by the Scottish Arts Council throughout Scotland; also shows in London, Edinburgh and Manchester

Societies Founder member, Scottish Crafts Centre

Ex-member of the Society of Scottish Artists

Member of the Scottish Society of Women Artists

Member of the Glasgow Society of Women Artists

Ex-member of the Council of the Embroiderers' Guild

Lectures 1967 Guest lecturer USA, 40th anniversary of the Needlework and Textile Guild of Chicago

1975 Lecture tour, Canada – Brantford, Calgary, Vancouver

Honours 1969 Awarded MBE

Publications *Design in Embroidery*, Batsford (London); Branford (USA); 1969; also a Dutch edition. New edition, Batsford, 1982

Commissions	Work in many Scottish churches
	Examples of work in the Victoria and Albert Museum; Royal Scottish Museum, Edinburgh; Scotch Whisky Association, London; National Gallery of Victoria, Australia; many private collections
1960s	Assessor for the Diploma in Art and Design
1974	Lecturer for the Scottish Arts Council
	Retired from the Glasgow School of Art

Rosamund Willis (Mrs Angus) ARCA 1903–1979

1921	Training at Cambridge School of Art. Embroidery with Constance Brown ARCA
1924–27	The Royal College of Art. Then with Heals for a short time
Teaching 1929–36	Lecturer, Armstrong College, Newcastle
1936–38	Principal, Luton College of Art
World War Two	Guide lecturer with the Arts Council, for which she organised exhibitions
Commissions	
1957–60	Four panels and a reredos, St Ninian's Church, Aberdeen
	A banner for St Mary's Church Great Shelford
1970s	Set of High Mass Vestments, designed by George Pace, St Olave's Church, York
	A panel depicting Brechin Castle for the Countess of Dalhousie
	Various exhibitions from the late twenties and local shows after 1960 in Aberdeen, Edinburgh, Harrogate and York

Evelyn Woodcock ARCA 1898–1978

	Training at Scarborough School of Art
1925–28	Royal College of Art – Diploma in Stained Glass
Teaching 1928 or 1929	Lecturer – Harrogate School of Art. Spent her whole teaching career there
1960	Retired from Harrogate School of Art
Commissions	Pictórial street map – Harrogate Corporation
	And other works

Bibliography

1939–63 *Embroidery* magazine

1947–52 Booklets published by the Ministry of Education on Art Examinations

1960–64 Booklet by the National Advisory Council on Art Education

1964 Booklet, Eton College Chapel Embroidery

1965 Embroideries from the Needlework Development Scheme, Royal Scottish Museum, Edinburgh

1966 Booklet 'The Hastings Embroidery'

1975 *In Vogue* – Georgina Howell – Allen Lane

1981 Leaflet, The Associated Examining Board

1979 Cultural Calendar of the Twentieth Century, by Edward Lucie Smith
Catalogues from exhibitions throughout the period 1940–63

Index

Figures in *italics* refer to illustration pages